Nietzsche's Animal Philosophy

John D. Caputo, *series editor*

PERSPECTIVES IN
CONTINENTAL
PHILOSOPHY

VANESSA LEMM

Nietzsche's Animal Philosophy

*Culture, Politics, and the Animality
of the Human Being*

FORDHAM UNIVERSITY PRESS
New York ■ 2009

Library of Congress Cataloging-in-Publication Data

Lemm, Vanessa.
    Nietzsche's animal philosophy : culture, politics, and the animality of the human being / Vanessa Lemm.
        p.   cm.
    Includes bibliographical references and index.
    ISBN 978-0-8232-3027-3 (cloth : alk. paper)—
    ISBN 978-0-8232-3028-0 (pbk. : alk. paper)
    1. Nietzsche, Friedrich Wilhelm, 1844–1900.   2. Philosophical anthropology.
3. Animals (Philosophy)   I. Title.
B3317.L433 2009
128—dc22

                                                                    2008047375

Printed in the United States of America
11 10 09   5 4 3 2 1
First edition

To Lou, Esteban, Alizé, and Miguel

Contents

	Acknowledgments	*xi*
	Abbreviations	*xiii*
	Introduction: The Animal in Nietzsche's Philosophy	*1*
1.	Culture and Civilization	*10*
2.	Politics and Promise	*30*
3.	Culture and Economy	*48*
4.	Giving and Forgiving	*61*
5.	Animality, Creativity, and Historicity	*86*
6.	Animality, Language, and Truth	*111*
	Conclusion: Biopolitics and the Question of Animal Life	*152*
	Notes	*157*
	Bibliography	*215*
	Index	*229*

Acknowledgments

Before all and most of all I am greatly indebted to my husband, colleague, and friend, Miguel Vatter, for his careful and timely reading of the various versions of the book manuscript in its entirety and for challenging me with his criticisms throughout the writing process. My special gratitude to Wendy Brown, Robert Gooding-Williams, Christoph Menke, and Samuel Weber for engaging one or more chapters as well as for their encouragement at various stages of this project. Two anonymous reviewers read the entire manuscript in draft, and their comments and suggestions for improvement were most valuable in the final revision of the manuscript.

Earlier versions of several parts of this book were generously engaged by audiences in a number of seminars, conferences, and workshops. I am especially thankful to the participants of the following three venues: The Political Theory Colloquium in the Political Science Department of Johann Wolfgang Goethe-Universität Frankfurt, directed by Rainer Forst, which critically engaged my approach to biopolitics through a treatment of the question of animal life in Nietzsche; the Nietzsche in New York Workshop in the Philosophy Department of Hunter College, City University of New York, held by Christa D. Acampora, which offered new perspectives on my reading of *On the Genealogy of Morals;* and the Nietzsche Research Center (Nietzsche Seminar Group) meeting in the Faculty of Philosophy of the University of Leiden, directed by Paul von Tongeren and Herman W. Siemens, which challenged the arguments laid out in Chapter 4.

I thank Helen Tartar, editorial director of Fordham University Press, for her advice and support during the publication of this book. I treasure having had the opportunity to work with her. Finally, I am grateful to my sweet children, Lou, Esteban, and Alizé, for their extraordinary patience and infinite generosity. I was most fortunate to have had their company while working on this project. This book is dedicated to them and to my husband.

Institutional support for this project came from the School of Political Science and the Institute of Humanities of the Universidad Diego Portales, Santiago de Chile. I was a recipient of a Fondecyt-Regular research project (Project No 1085238) that allowed me to finance the final stages of this project.

Permission to reprint material published elsewhere has been granted as follows: "Justice and Gift-Giving in *Thus Spoke Zarathustra*" in *Before Sunrise: Essays on Thus Spoke Zarathustra*, James Luchte, ed., London: Continuum International Publishers, 2008: 165–181, revised for a small portion of chapter 4. "Animality, Historicity and Creativity: A Reading of Friedrich Nietzsche's *Vom Nutzen und Nachtheil der Historie für das Leben*" in *Nietzsche-Studien* (36), 2007: 169–200, revised as chapter 5.

Abbreviations

References to Nietzsche's unpublished writings are standardized, whenever possible, to refer to the most accessible edition of Nietzsche's notebooks and publications, *Kritische Studienausgabe* (*KSA*), compiled under the general editorship of Giorgio Colli and Mazzino Montinari. References to the editions of letters, *Sämtliche Briefe: Kritische Studienausgabe,* are cited as *KSB*. In the cases in which the *KSA* are cited, references provide the volume number followed by the relevant fragment number and any relevant aphorism (e.g., *KSA* 10:12[1].37 refers to volume 10 fragment 12[1] aphorism 37). The following abbreviations are used for citations of Nietzsche's writings:

A	*The Antichrist*
AOM	*Assorted Opinions and Maxims* (*HH*, vol. II, part 1)
BGE	*Beyond Good and Evil*
BT	*The Birth of Tragedy*
CW	*The Case of Wagner*
D	*Daybreak* (alternately: *Dawn*)
DS	"David Strauss, the Writer and the Confessor" (*UM* I)
EH	*Ecce Homo* (sections abbreviated "Wise," "Clever," "Books," "Destiny"; abbreviations for titles discussed in "Books" are indicated instead of "Books" where relevant)
FEI	"On the Future of Our Educational Institutions" (*KSA* 1)
GM	*On the Genealogy of Morals*

GS	*The Gay Science*
GSt	"The Greek State" (*KSA* 1)
HC	"Homer's Contest" (alternately: "Homer on Competition") (*KSA* 1)
HH	*Human, All Too Human* (two volumes, I and II)
HL	"On the Use and Disadvantage of History for Life" (*UM* II)
KSA	*Kritische Studienausgabe*
KSB	*Sämtliche Briefe: Kritische Studienausgabe*
P	"The Philosopher. Reflections on the Struggle between Art and Knowledge"
PT	*Philosophy and Truth*
PTA	*Philosophy in the Tragic Age of the Greeks* (*KSA* 1)
PW	"On the Pathos of Truth" (*KSA* 1)
SE	"Schopenhauer as Educator" (*UM* III)
TI	*Twilight of the Idols* (sections abbreviated "Maxims," "Socrates," "Reason," "World," "Morality," "Errors," "Improvers," "Germans," "Skirmishes," "Ancients," "Hammer")
TL	"On Truth and Lies in an Extra-Moral Sense" (*KSA* 1)
UM	*Untimely Meditations* (alternately: *Untimely Considerations*) volumes I–IV
WP	*The Will to Power*
WS	*The Wanderer and His Shadow* (*HH*, vol. II, part 2)
Z	*Thus Spoke Zarathustra* (references to *Z* list the part number and the chapter title followed by the relevant section number when applicable)

Nietzsche's Animal Philosophy

Introduction

The Animal in Nietzsche's Philosophy

The theme of the animal was largely overlooked in twentieth-century Nietzsche scholarship and has only very recently started to attract attention in philosophy and the humanities.[1] This book aims to provide the first systematic treatment of the animal in Nietzsche's philosophy as a whole. I hope to show that the animal is neither a random theme nor a metaphorical device, but rather that it stands at the center of Nietzsche's renewal of the practice and meaning of philosophy itself.[2] *Nietzsche's Animal Philosophy* critically reexamines Nietzsche's views on culture and civilization, politics and morality, and history and truth based on the various perspectives manifest through a consideration of the human being as part of a continuum of animal life.

Throughout his writings Nietzsche speaks of the human being as an animal. What distinguishes the human animal from other animals is its culture. *Nietzsche's Animal Philosophy* pursues the dual questions of what it means for an animal to have culture and how animality engenders culture. In contrast to the Western traditions of humanism and Enlightenment, Nietzsche proposes to investigate culture not as a rational and moral phenomenon, but as a phenomenon of life. Viewed in this way, what makes culture interesting is that it is taken up by animality and not, as these traditions assume, because culture is the means through which humanity separates or emancipates itself from animality. In her groundbreaking book *Beasts of Modern Imagination*, Margot Norris calls this new approach to culture from the perspective of life "biocentric." She defines a "biocentric tradition" of thinkers, writers, and artists (including Nietzsche) who do not create *like* the animal or in imitation of the animal, but *as* the animal, with their animality speaking.[3]

This biocentric notion of culture in Nietzsche, as reconstructed in *Nietzsche's Animal Philosophy*, is different from previous materialist and spiritualist interpretations of his philosophy of culture, because it avoids the biologism of the first and the anthropomorphism of the second. An anthropocentric standpoint views culture as something disconnected from animal life: life is reduced to human self-interpretation and culture is the project of human self-creation.[4] A biologistic standpoint reduces culture to a means of preserving the biological life of the human species.[5] Although a biologistic approach takes into account the intimate relationship between human and animal life, it fails to provide an analysis of the meaning and significance of culture beyond the struggle for survival. Rejecting a biologistic interpretation of life, I consider Nietzsche's thesis to be that every organic cell has spirit.[6] In similar fashion, I reject an anthropocentric interpretation of life and consider Nietzsche's thesis to be that spirit is physiological.[7] The principles of Nietzsche's physiology, however, are not derived from the application of mechanical or chemical causality to inert matter. These principles can only be formulated through genealogies, which alone capture the spiritual historicity expressed in physiology.[8] Life is historical because matter is always already taken up in relation to memory and forgetfulness.

For Nietzsche, memory and forgetfulness are neither Kantian capacities of the mind nor Aristotelian potentials of substances, but rather they are equi-primordial forces of life. *Nietzsche's Animal Philosophy* investigates the relationship between life and culture through an analysis of his conception of memory and forgetfulness. Most commentators identify Nietzsche's notion of life with the will to power, and the will to power with memory.[9] Instead, I argue that the notion of the will to power reflects an antagonism between memory and forgetfulness and can be reformulated through this antagonism. I suggest that an analysis of this antagonism is the most direct way to access the relationship between life and culture and, more specifically, the relationship between animality and culture. Speaking schematically, one can say that forgetfulness in Nietzsche's discourse belongs to the animal, memory to the human, and promise to the overhuman. Since, in Nietzsche, these relationships are agonistic and not static, the animal, the human, and the overhuman are tied to each other and cannot be separated into distinct stages of evolution: "The human being is a rope, tied between the animal and the overhuman" (*Z*: 4 "Prologue").

Nietzsche affirms the continuity between the animal, the human, and the overhuman. He believes that human life is inseparable from the life of the animal and from the whole organic and inorganic world. He even claims to have discovered himself to be a being who continuously reflects a repetition and variation of the infinite poetic, logical, aesthetic, and affective becomings in the entire history of life (*GS* 54).[10] Nietzsche therefore rejects the view that human life constitutes an autonomous island within life. To the contrary, he holds that any form of life that is cut off from other forms of life declines because it is separated from that which generates its life. In keeping with this view, human life cannot bring itself forth by its strength alone, but lives entirely out of and against its relation to other forms of life.[11] Nietzsche's conception of life as a continuum breaks with the prevalent conception found in the Western traditions according to which the human being is the crown of evolution (*A* 14). His notion of life is, in this sense, comparable to Darwin's.[12] The perspective of continuity posits that human life does not play a central role in the totality of life, but is only a small and insignificant part of it. Nietzsche even speculates that nature uses human life as a means toward its own completion rather than the other way around (*AOM* 185).

The totality of life is an inherently historical process, which can be traced in the memory of each and every organic cell, down to the smallest entity (*KSA* 10:12[31]). From the perspective of organic memory, the becoming of one form of life is inextricably tied to that of all other forms of life.[13] Every form of life lives off the totality, just as the totality lives off every single form of life. The becoming of each organic cell is unique and singular in an absolute sense, but the uniqueness and singularity emerges from and against the totality of life. No organic cell is like any other organic cell. No animal or human being is like any other animal or human being. Nevertheless, in their singularity each cell or being reflects the totality of life, the past, present, and future of its becoming.

What distinguishes the organic memory of each and every cell is that it does not recall the history of the totality of life in an ideal continuity. Rather, the memory of organic life is constituted by a continuous movement of counterbecomings, an antagonism against forgetfulness, dissolving what has stabilized into a fixed identity.[14] The memory of organic life shows that the totality of life is not a stable and continuous striving of the whole toward the harmonious equilibrium of its parts.[15] Instead, the totality of life is constituted from an agonistic struggle that involves all forms of life for and against each other in a continuous pluralization of inherently singular forms of life.[16] Nietzsche holds that nature seeks the increasing pluralization of life, and he believes that this pluralization can be attained through culture as it emerges from an affirmation of the continuity that exists within the totality of animal, human, and other forms of life.[17]

In Chapter 1, "Culture and Civilization," I investigate the openness of human life to the horizon of becoming through an analysis of the competition between culture and civilization (*KSA* 13:16[73]; 16[10]). By means of this antagonism, Nietzsche puts forth a critique of civilization that does not imply a "return to nature" but is oriented toward a cultivation of animality. I define culture as cultivation and education and distinguish it from civilization, which I define as taming and breeding. The process of civilization, as Nietzsche conceives it, reflects a process of moral and rational improvement of the human being which does not cultivate animal life but "extirpates" and oppresses it (*TI* "Improvers" and "Morality"; *GM* II: 1–3). In contrast to civilization, the challenge of culture is to bring forth forms of life and thought which are not forms of power over animal life, but which are full of life, overflowing with life.[18] I argue that culture recovers this fullness of life in the dreams, illusions, and passions of the animal.

Nietzsche repeatedly speaks of the return of the human being to its animal beginning as a return to the dream life of the animal (*GS* 54; *HH* 13). A return to the animal beginning of human beings reveals that life is a dream and to be alive is, essentially, to be dreaming. Nietzsche's conception of life and culture breaks with the Western tradition of metaphysics which sees the rationality and sociability of the human being as marks of distinction with respect to other forms of life. For Nietzsche, the future of humanity crucially depends on the human being's ability to reconnect itself with the dream life of the animal, because only the latter can bring back to the human being the freedom and creativity of interpretation that it has lost in the process of its civilization and socialization. Nietzsche's approach is, in this sense, comparable to that of Freud, for they both not only contest the claim that rationality lies at the center of psychic life but also see in the dream-state the dissolution of civilization and consciousness, and, moreover, consider this dissolution to be crucial for the future enhancement of human life and culture.[19] For only if the human being recovers the freedom and creativity of dreams will it be able to keep on living, that is, dreaming, imagining, and inventing new forms of life to come.

In contrast to the traditional understanding of the overhuman in Nietzsche as the mythic embodiment of the self-sufficient individual (and of the autonomy of human culture), I argue that the overhuman is neither an expression of the human as a being independent from the rest of life or from the rest of its own species.[20] Rather, becoming overhuman is dependent upon one's openness to the animality of the human being. Animality is not overcome and sublimated, but resists in humans as much as in the overhuman. Indeed, one can understand what Nietzsche means by overhuman only as a function of such an animal resistance.[21] *Nietzsche's Animal Philosophy* examines the cultural and political significance of the resistance of the animal within the human. It argues that the resistance of the animal strives for an overcoming of domination toward freer forms of social and political life.

In Chapter 2, "Politics and Promise," I discuss the possibility of overcoming domination as it is articulated by the promise of the sovereign individual (*GM* II: 2). The promise of the sovereign individual has been traditionally understood as either antipolitical, with Nietzsche figuring as a precursor to totalitarian and authoritarian ideologies, or as nonpolitical, with Nietzsche figuring as a precursor to individual perfectionism. In contrast to these views, I argue that through the figure of the sovereign individual, Nietzsche puts forward an idea of freedom as responsibility that inherently concerns the political life of human animals. This interpretation of Nietzsche as a political thinker centers on the idea that the antagonism of human and animal life forces is the primary feature of human development: When humankind defines itself against its animality or denies its animality a productive role, forms of political life emerge based on domination and exploitation of humans by humans. Contrariwise, when humankind engages with its animality, it gives rise to forms of political life rooted in the sovereign individual's instinct of responsibility. This chapter seeks to show that responsibility, as Nietzsche conceives it, namely, as an instinct (*GM* II: 2), provides a way to understand the relationship between politics and animal life that moves beyond the political domination of life because it offers the animality of human beings a positive, creative role in the constitution of social and political forms of life. As such, the promise of the sovereign individual constitutes a political power that overcomes the practices which, since Foucault, we call biopolitical.[22]

In Chapter 3, "Culture and Economy," I further discuss the possibility of overcoming domination by differentiating between two different economical approaches to the animality of the human being which correspond to the contrasting ways of politicizing life in culture and in civilization. While the economy of civilization represents an exploitative approach to animality, whose aim is the self-preservation of the group at the cost of normalizing the individual, the economy of culture stands for a nonexploitative approach to animality directed toward the pluralization *'follow' — is not how Derrida understands this?*

of inherently singular forms of life. An analysis of these economies shows that culture cannot be attained through a politics of domination and exploitation.

According to Nietzsche, human life is the weakest and most fragile form of animal life. The vulnerability of the human animal is related to its relative inferiority and underdetermination with respect to other animals. Nietzsche claims that in order to overcome the dilemma of their relative weakness, humans have to "rob" the virtues of the other animals (*Z*: 22 "On Old and New Tablets"). They have to follow other animals and, in their own way, become more animal, more instinctive, more forgetful, and more natural.[23] In light of this idea, I suggest that the relationship between human life and culture must be understood in terms of a "becoming-animal" of the human being.[24] The becoming-animal of the human being is not a process of moral improvement or human self-perfection. On the contrary, its aim is the "magnification [*Vergrößerung*]" and "strengthening [*Verstärkung*]" of the human being (*KSA* 12:5[50]; 7[10]) attained through culture and its recovery of animality.

In Chapter 4, "Giving and Forgiving," I argue that Nietzsche's rejection of Christianity is motivated by an idea of justice which has its source in the practice of gift-giving. Nietzsche contrasts gift-giving with the Christian practice of forgiving: The latter fails to break the cycle of revenge while the form of giving found in Christian forgiveness does not enhance human life, but rather poisons it (*AOM* 224; *BGE* 168). The double failure Nietzsche detects in the Christian practice of forgiveness results from denying the animality of the human being a productive role in the constitution of forms of sociability. In particular, it ignores the value and significance of animal forgetfulness. In this chapter I argue that animal forgetfulness is indispensable not only to break the cycle of revenge but also to establish a relationship with others which is not based on utilitarian grounds and which respects both the freedom and the differences of the other. Because the forgetfulness of the animal is an essential component of Nietzsche's analysis of gift-giving, I suggest that the latter should be understood in the terms of an animal rather than a human virtue. The chapter concludes with a discussion of how Nietzsche's conception of justice as gift-giving opens to an alternative account of political friendship, which he contrasts with the Christian demand to love thy neighbor as thyself. In this chapter, I also discuss the similarities and dissimilarities I see between Nietzsche, Derrida, and Arendt on giving, forgiving, and friendship.

human — becomes

For Nietzsche, human life is not a given, a substance, or a nature, but rather something that becomes, something that, in the words of Ansell-Pearson, is "from the beginning of its formation and deformation implicated in an overhuman becoming."[25] The human being is, therefore, not an end in itself but an ongoing movement of becoming and self-overcoming. Nietzsche's narrative of human becoming is, above all, a narrative of human self-overcoming: "What is great in the human being is that it is a bridge and not an end: what can be loved in the human being is that it is an *overture* [*Übergang*] and a *going under* [*Untergang*]" (*Z*: 4 "Prologue"). The intimate relationship among the animal, the human, and the overhuman is peculiar because the continuity it affirms also brings about their simultaneous discontinuity. Nietzsche questions the commonly held belief that human life grows out of its animal past according to a linear conception of time as something from which it derives or as something from which it has successfully emancipated itself. Instead, animality features, in Nietzsche's thought, as an otherness, a reservoir of creative and regenerative forces of life that allows the human being to spring forward into the future.[26] For Nietzsche, the future emerges from the human's ability to overcome the self. In order to overcome itself, the human being needs to return to its animality (and animal forgetfulness). For this reason, the animal (forgetfulness) always stands at the beginning and at the rebeginning of culture. It is through the return to and of their animality that human beings are led toward their humanity because it is the animal which withholds the secret of how to bring forth a relationship with the past that disrupts and overturns the present in favor of future life to come. In this view, becoming overhuman depends on a return of and to animality as that force which irrupts its humanity, exceeds it and tears it apart, so as to make room for its future (overhuman) becoming.

Nietzsche's Animal Philosophy discusses the idea that animality (forgetfulness) enables the becoming human (memory) of the human being through a reading of "On the Use and Disadvantage of History for Life." Chapter 5, "Animality, Creativity, and Historicity," reevaluates the importance of animality and animal forgetfulness in Nietzsche's conception of history and historiography. I argue that the novelty of Nietzsche's history essay is contained in the thesis that animal forgetfulness is prior to and more primordial than human memory. Life is historical through and through because it is forgetful through and through. The perspective of animal forgetfulness reveals that memory is an artistic force (*Kunsttrieb*), and that historiography must therefore be understood as a work of art (*Kunstwerk*) rather than as science, concerned with interpretations rather than with the factual representation of the past. According to this new conception of historiography, a truly effective history is found in the works of the artist rather than in those of the historian, even if the latter is artistic and not scientific. In the period from 1886 to 1888, Nietzsche reedited all his books, adding new prefaces to his original editions. These prefaces reflect Nietzsche's rereading and rewriting of his own past. Chapter 5 ends with a discussion of Nietzsche's prefaces as examples of an artistic writing of history.

It is partly due to Nietzsche's privileging of the perspective of the artist over that of the scientist in his understanding of the project of philosophy that commentators have identified him as a relativist and as a denier of truth. In contrast to such views, Chapter 6, "Animality, Language, and Truth," argues that Nietzsche's critique of metaphysics aims at a renewal of the meaning of philosophy as the pursuit of truth. I maintain that, throughout his work, Nietzsche holds on to the controversial claim, put forth in his early essay "On Truth and Lies in an Extra-Moral Sense," that truth is a metaphor, and that, for that reason, a consideration of truth is inseparable from a consideration of language. He contends that because truth is a metaphor, it fails to capture life, and, moreover, that metaphors are rationalizations and abstractions that destroy life. From this perspective, philosophy, understood as a conceptual pursuit of truth, seems doomed before it even begins. Nietzsche finds a way out of this dilemma by distinguishing between metaphors (*Metapher*) and intuited metaphors (*Anschaungsmetapher*) (*TL*). Whereas the former make up an abstract world of regulating and imperative (linguistic) laws by means of abstract thinking, the latter make up an intuited world of first impressions by means of pictorial thinking. While abstract thinking, indeed, constitutes a threat to life, pictorial thinking engenders pictures that emerge from the immediacy of an encounter with life. These pictures have the power to render the truth of the underlying life experience without destroying it. Chapter 6 provides the argument that the philosophical pursuit of truth can only be redeemed when philosophy does not separate conceptual and abstract forms of thought from their ground in pictorial and imaginary forms of thought as they are expressed in intuited metaphors. Pictorial thinking is a form of thought Nietzsche associates with the animals. A renewal of the meaning of philosophy as a pursuit of truth, therefore, depends on the return to the animals' pictorial way of thinking. Consequently, animals in Nietzsche's philosophy are not simply metaphors or anthropomorphic projections that reinforce the traditional belief that animals are beings deprived of language. Rather, for Nietzsche, animal silence is the source of the metaphorical character of human animal *why silent?*

language. Indeed, human animal language is most properly directed at the silence that affords the communication between human animals.

Nietzsche rediscovers the centrality of animal life to the self-understanding of the human being, to its culture and its politics. I wish to conclude with some remarks on how this recovery of animality in Nietzsche's philosophy contributes to an understanding of what Foucault calls the "biological threshold of modernity."[27] I suggest that Nietzsche provides a new and productive way of understanding the relationship between animality and humanity by viewing it as developing a positive or affirmative sense of biopolitics.[28] I propose that affirmative biopolitics sees in the continuity between human and animal life a source of resistance to the project of dominating and controlling life-processes. Whereas the latter divides life into opposing forms of species life, the affirmative biopolitics I set out subverts such a division in place of cultivating inherently singular forms of animal life.

Culture and Civilization — *antagonism*

This chapter investigates the formations and transformations of human life and culture through a reevaluation of Nietzsche's discourse on culture and civilization. The key to this discourse is to understand culture and civilization as antagonists: *"Civilization and Culture: an antagonism"* (*KSA* 13:16[73]). In my view, the antagonism between culture and civilization has not been emphasized enough in discussions of Nietzsche's philosophy of culture. One reason for this is that commentators have interpreted the significance of the dualism of culture and civilization only within the context of its nationalistic use in the German academic and political debates of the nineteenth and early twentieth centuries, which discussed Germany's self-understanding as a *Kulturnation.* As a result of this debate, the notion of *Kultur* became discredited in the latter part of the twentieth century because of its appropriation by conservative and reactionary thinkers.[1] Another reason is that Nietzsche's notions of culture and civilization have often been collapsed into one another.[2] An analysis of their antagonism is crucial, however, because it is through such an analysis that Nietzsche puts forth a critique of civilization that does not imply a "return to nature" but, instead, predicts the eventual rule of culture over civilization.

My argument begins by showing that the antagonism between culture and civilization reflects an antagonism between human and animal life forces. In this antagonism, culture is defined as cultivation and is distinct from civilization, which is defined as taming and breeding. Whereas civilization distinguishes itself as the forgetting of the animal and of animal forgetfulness, culture distinguishes itself as the memory of the animal and of animal forgetfulness. The process of civilization aims at the moral and rational improvement of the human being. In contrast, the task of culture is primarily a critical one: Its function is to show that rationalization and moralization are techniques of domination directed against the animality of the human being. Culture, in its critical function, reveals that the "improvements" of civilization are "false overcomings."[3] The second task of culture is that of liberation: Its function is to overcome the domination of civilization. The challenge of culture is to bring forth not forms of life that are forms of power over life, but forms of life that are themselves full of life, overflowing with life. I argue that culture recovers this fullness of life in the dreams, illusions, and passions of the animal. The chapter ends with a discussion of Nietzsche's figure of the *Umgekehrte* (the subverted and subverting one) as an example of such a fullness of life. This chapter also discusses other figures in Nietzsche's work that reflect such a fullness of life, such as the overhuman and the genius of culture.

The Antagonism of Culture and Civilization

In Nietzsche's work, the formations and transformations of human animal life and culture are characterized in terms of the fundamental antagonism between culture and civilization (*KSA* 13:16[73]). A note written during the Spring–Summer of 1888 illustrates this idea:

> The highpoints of culture and civilization lie far apart: one should not be misled by the abyssal antagonism between culture and civilization. The great moments of culture have always been, morally speaking, times of corruption; and conversely the epochs of willed and forced animal taming ("civilization") of the human being have been times of intolerance of the spiritual and most bold natures. What civilization wants is something different from what culture wants: maybe the opposite [*etwas Umgekehrtes*]. (*KSA* 13:16[10])[4]

Nietzsche underlines the difference between culture and civilization as not only a difference in their opposing aims but also a difference in their highpoints. The highpoints of culture and of civilization alternate. In their continual competition only one of them may rule: When culture is at its height, it rules over civilization; conversely, when civilization is at its height, it rules over culture. Nietzsche conceives civilization as a moral and, therefore, as a forced and willed project. At its height, civilization manifests itself in the violence directed against the animality of the human being and, also, in its intolerance toward "the spiritual and most bold

Isn't the poss. of a son — punt to reflection: how would we ... ?!

natures." That civilization sees its enemy in animal as well as in spiritual and free natures reveals the intimate affinity Nietzsche sees between the freedom of the animal and the freedom of the spirit. In contrast to civilization, culture is explicitly immoral and corrupt. What defines culture is freedom from moralization, from the "willed and forced animal taming" of civilization, and from its intolerance toward "free spirits." When culture rules over civilization, what rules is the freedom of the animal and of the spirit.

The antagonism between culture and civilization is also reflected in the claim that "error has transformed animals into humans" and in the question that Nietzsche poses as to whether "truth is perhaps capable of returning humans into animals" (*HH* 519). In this antagonism, civilization represents the perspective of error that turns animals into humans, while culture represents the perspective of truth that turns humans back into animals. Whereas civilization claims that the truth of the human being consists of its moral and rational nature, culture shows that this truth is part of the set of errors that has turned animals into humans. From the perspective of civilization, what gives rise to error and illusion is the forgetfulness of the animal. Civilization understands itself as the process of improvement of the human being through the imposition of its truth as a corrective to its animal forgetfulness. Civilization corrects the human being's animal nature through the breeding of a specific kind of memory, a "memory of the will" (*Gedächtnis des Willens*) that remembers the truth of civilization and all its moral and rational norms and forgets all the rest (*GM* II: 1).[5] While civilization reflects the domination of the human animal through the imposition of another, supposedly morally superior, nature upon it, culture reflects the resistance to and the liberation from the oppressiveness of civilization.[6]

From the perspective of culture, the imposition of the truth (memory) of civilization on the human animal is itself based on error and illusion (*GS* 121). In contrast to the memory of civilization, culture brings forth a "counter-memory" that unveils the illusory character of the truth of civilization.[7] This counter-memory undoes the memory as well as the forgetfulness found in civilization. Under the rule of culture, the human animal forgets the moral and rational norms of civilization, and this animal forgetfulness, in turn, brings back to the human being the forgotten freedom of the animal and of the spirit. The liberation of the human animal through culture defines what Nietzsche calls cultivation in contrast to the taming and breeding that define civilizational practices. The practices of taming and breeding are primarily characterized by the desire to impose a form on human animal life. Instead, the cultural practice of cultivation

Foucault

reflects a desire to embrace life in all its forms: "Give me life and I will create a culture out of it for you" (*HL* 10). The practice of cultivation is, in this sense, a practice of hospitality, receiving and giving life. Rather than imposing one universal form on life, culture as cultivation is directed toward the pluralization of forms of life that are inherently singular and are irreducible to each other.

The imposition of memory on the precivilized animal functions as a corrective to its forgetfulness and irrationality. But, ultimately, this process of so-called improvement succeeds only because of forgetfulness— that is, because of the forgetting of the human being's animality. Despite the attempt by civilization to set itself apart from the forgetfulness of the precivilized animal, it reveals these very same features: forgetfulness, bad reasoning, error, and illusion. The memory of civilization cannot hide the "bestiality" of its forgetting of the animal. Nietzsche turns the prejudices of civilization against civilization itself and shows the alleged distance between civilization and animality to be a mere pretense. From the perspective of the animals, the illusion harbored by the human being that it is a moral and rational being does not make this animal any more moral, rational, or human, but only more prejudiced:

> *'Humanity'*.—We do not regard the animals as moral beings. But do you suppose the animals regard us as moral beings?—An animal which could speak said: "Humanity is a prejudice of which we animals at least are free." (*D* 333)

The task of culture is to free the human animal from the prejudices of civilization—that is, to lead the human animal beyond a moral and rational conception of its becoming toward the affirmation of life as inherently amoral, a-rational, and innocent. The innocence of life is an expression of its fullness: Life emerges and overflows, indifferent to the rationality and morality of its forms and, hence, powerful in its generosity and creativity (*WP* 1027).

Nietzsche's conception of human becoming and self-overcoming is incompatible with the optimism found in the project of civilization. More precisely, it conflicts with the belief that the human being's progressive emancipation from the animals will lead to greater freedom and autonomy. Nietzsche defines his own position as inherently pessimistic, claiming that true liberation can be achieved not through the overcoming of animality but rather through the overcoming of all-too-human forms of morality and of rationality as vehicles of civilization. Nietzsche confirms [*feststellen*] the human being's animality, and, in an attempt to restore their "animal common sense,"[8] he places humans back amid the other animals.

> We have learnt better. We have become more modest in every respect. We no longer trace the origin of the human being in the "spirit," in the "divinity," we have placed it back among the animals. We consider it the strongest animal because it is the most cunning: its spirituality is a consequence of this. On the other hand, we guard ourselves against a vanity which would like to find expression even here: the vanity that human being is the great secret objective of animal evolution. The human being is absolutely not the crown of creation: every creature stands beside him at the same stage of perfection. . . . And even in asserting that we assert too much: the human being is, relatively speaking, the most unsuccessful animal, the sickliest, the one most dangerously strayed from its instincts— with all that, to be sure, the most *interesting*! (*A* 14)

Nietzsche denies the modern belief in progress without advocating anything like a "return to nature" and dismisses the romantic longing for a return to a "higher" and more "human" origin as this belief is exemplified by Rousseau (*TI* "Skirmishes" 48). In contrast to the optimistic view that, at the beginning, one finds "good nature" (*D* 17), beauty, innocence, and harmony, Nietzsche holds the pessimistic view that every return to the beginning is a return to the cruel and the crude (*PTA* 1). These overly optimistic and naïve positions, one returning to the past and the other progressing toward the future, are symptomatic of weakness and of a denial of life. They reject life in favor of another, supposedly better life, projected either into the past or into the future. In opposition to this, pessimism reveals strength, health and ascending life, which result from embracing life here and now, affirming it in all its forms: human, animal, and other ("An Attempt at Self-Criticism" 2).[9]

The antagonism between culture and civilization is manifest in the agonistic "crossing" of Dionysus and Apollo in *The Birth of Tragedy*.[10] In this crossing, the Apollonian reflects the perspective of civilization, with its illusions of a rational and moral (also political) world order, and the Dionysian reflects the perspective of culture, seeing the world as an abyss with no orderly structure, no ultimate ground. The Dionysian vision of the world as chaotic, irrational, and purposeless triggers vertigo in those who contemplate this vision, which is disconcerting, unsettling, and terrifying. However, the destructive force that the Dionysian directs against the Apollonian order is not merely destructive, for it also gives rise to the creativity and freedom associated with culture. Depending on whether the

Dionysian or the Apollonian perspective of life prevails, the human being understands itself as either an artistic and creative or a rational and moral being and conceives of culture as either tragic and Dionysian (which is the sense I give to the term "culture") or scientific and Apollonian (which is the sense I give to the term "civilization").

The hegemony of one perspective over the other requires a form of forgetfulness. Under the rule of Apollonian illusion and dream, the human being forgets itself as animal and as creative. Under the rule of Dionysian frenzy (*Rausch*), the human animal forgets the moral and rational settings of Apollonian illusion: "The Individual, with all his limits and measures, became submerged here in the self-oblivion of the Dionysian condition and forgot the statutes of Apollo" (*BT* 4). Nietzsche privileges Dionysian forgetfulness because it is more fundamental than Apollonian forgetfulness, just as he privileges animal forgetfulness over the civilizational forgetfulness of the human being. Although Nietzsche praises the healing force of the Apollonian dream as it transfigures the unbearable vision of the world as an abyss, ultimately what reconciles humans with life, nature, and one another is the "magic of the Dionysian":

> Not only is the bond between human beings renewed by the magic of the Dionysian, but nature, alienated, inimical, or subjugated, celebrated once more her festival of reconciliation with her lost son, humankind. (*BT* 1)[11]

Under the impact of Dionysian magic, the human animal affirms and celebrates its animality as a source of life and culture. Only when surrounded by the Dionysian myth can the Apollonian dream preserve itself and be given a direction (*BT* 23).[12] The Dionysian (culture) leads the Apollonian (civilization) just as the animal leads the human being, giving the human being an aim: to produce the genius of culture, or what Nietzsche eventually calls the overhuman.

The affinity between the figure of the genius of culture in Nietzsche's early work and the figure of the overhuman in his later work is expressed, first, by their constituting the aim of culture and, second, by their achievement of this aim through an overcoming of the human: "[N]ot 'humankind' but overhuman is the goal!" (*WP* 1001). Examples from Nietzsche's early and late work confirm that, throughout his work, he holds on to the idea that it is the animal in the human which promises the further refinement of culture. In *Thus Spoke Zarathustra*, Nietzsche draws on the image of Zarathustra, who is led by the animals toward the overhuman—that is, toward the overcoming of the human (*Z*: 10 "Zarathustra's Prologue"). In accordance with this image, a citation from Nietzsche's early work suggests the same idea, namely that culture means, first, a following of the animal and, second, an overcoming of the human:

> If we speak of *humanity*, it is on the basic assumption that it should be that which *separates* the human being from nature and is its mark of distinction. But in reality there is no separation: "natural" characteristics and those called specifically "human" are grown together inextricably. The human being, in its highest, finest powers, is all nature and carries nature's uncanny dual character in itself. Those capacities of it that are terrible and are viewed as inhuman are perhaps, indeed, the fertile soil from which alone all humanity, in feelings, deeds and works, can grow forth. (*HC*)

Weighing the "human" against the "inhuman," Nietzsche asks whether priority should not be given to animality over humanity, as that is the aspect of the human being which provides the most favorable ground on which to foster greatness and virtue.[13] Nietzsche returns to the Greeks, the "models of all future cultured nations" and the heralds of agonistic competition, in order to gain further insight into the relationship between animality and culture (*HL* 10). The genius of Greek culture is contained in its knowledge of how to preserve and entertain a fruitful relationship with animality.[14] In the "cruelty" of the animal, the Greeks see not a lack of justice or morality but rather, a stimulant to agonistic competition and to the refinement of culture:

> Thus the Greeks, the most humane people of ancient time, have a trait of cruelty, of tiger-like pleasure in destruction, in them. . . . Without envy, jealousy and competitive ambition, the Hellenic state, like Hellenic man, deteriorates. (*HC*)

What Nietzsche finds remarkable is not only that humanity and animality lie side by side in the Greeks but, more important, that animality is a source of their humanity. The Greeks celebrate their animal instincts as inherently cultural forces, as carriers of life and artistic inspiration. Greek culture "teaches," first, that only those who follow the animal will attain a higher level of culture and, second, that only those who fully embrace life in all its forms—human, animal, and other—will be successful in bringing forth new, future promising forms of life and thought.

Still, for Nietzsche, one cannot, strictly speaking, "learn" from or be "led" by the animals, just as one cannot "learn" anything from the Greeks. Both are too futile, too fluid, too strange, too other:

> I received absolutely no strong impressions from the Greeks; and, not to mince words, they *cannot* be to us what the Romans are. One

Greece — culture
Rome — civil.

does not *learn* from the Greeks—their manner is too strange, it is also too fluid to produce an imperative, a "classical" effect. Who would have ever learned to write from a Greek! Who would have learnt it *without* the Romans! (*TI* "Ancients" 2)

living speech vs written laws !! ?

The difference between Greek and Roman culture reflects what I call the antagonism between culture and civilization. Whereas culture finds its exemplar in the Greeks, civilization finds it in the Romans. Nietzsche is interested in how the animals and the Greeks are inimitable.[15] Following their example means becoming an inimitable example of life and virtue.

The Forgetfulness of Civilization

Whereas culture is the memory of animality and the affirming and holding onto the human beings' continuity with the animals, civilization coincides with the forgetting of animality, the silencing of the animal within the human:

> *The forgetful.*—In the outbursts of passion, and in the fantasizing of dreams and insanity, the human being re-discovers its own and the humans' prehistory: *animality* with its savage grimaces; on these occasions its memory goes sufficiently far back, while its civilized condition evolves out of a forgetting of these primal experiences, that is to say out of a relaxation of its memory. The one who, as a forgetful one on a grand scale, is wholly unfamiliar with all this, *does not understand the humans,*—but it is to the advantage of all if here and there such forgetful ones appear as those who "do not understand the humans" and who are as it were begotten by divine seeds and born of reason. (*D* 312)

The forgetfulness of civilization displaces the memory of continuity between humans and animals. Under the rule of civilization, the human animal forgets what it was and what it is—an animal—in order to become what it is not yet—a moral and rational being. In this sense, the becoming rational and moral of the human animal depends on the gradual increase of the forgetting of the human beings' animality, or, as Nietzsche puts it, a "relaxation of its memory" (*D* 312). Civilization and forgetfulness belong together insofar as it is only because of the forgetfulness of the human being's animal beginning (animal origin) that it can come to understand itself as a moral and rational being, "begotten by divine seeds and born of reason" (ibid.). Furthermore, civilization and forgetfulness belong together insofar as continued forgetfulness is required to preserve the dominance of civilization.[16]

Nietzsche values the achievements of civilizational forgetting. Civilizational forgetfulness separates humans and animals and sets them against each other. It thus achieves a radical break with prior forms of human animal life, allowing the human animal to transform itself into something distinctly human and not animal. However, Nietzsche is also aware that civilization does not stand for the "smooth" forgetting of animality: It aggressively denies the animality of the human being and thereby destroys the "fertile soil" out of which humanity grows and keeps on growing:

> What in the competition against the animals brought about the humans their victory, at the same time brought about the difficult and dangerous sickness like development of the human being: the human being is the *not yet confirmed animal.* (*KSA* 11:25[428])[17]

Nietzsche warns that the denial of animality found in civilization provokes the degeneration of human life and culture. It leads to the inevitable decline (*Untergang*) of the rule of civilization.

The task of culture is to reconfirm the animality of the human being. Culture is in this sense a "return to nature" that cures the sickness of civilization by restoring a fruitful antagonism between human and animal life forces. What is important, for Nietzsche, is the preservation not of civilization (sickness) or of culture (health) as such but the preservation of the antagonism between civilization (sickness) and culture (health). Nietzsche acknowledges that it is the sickness of civilization which turns the human animal into an interesting and promising animal (*A* 14). This, however, is only because he believes that the sickening effect of civilization will eventually lead to the attainment of greater health under the rule of culture.

In Nietzsche's antagonistic account of the relationship between culture and civilization, the decline (*Untergang*) of civilization coincides with a transition (*Übergang*) to culture.[18] When Nietzsche praises the accomplishments of (the forgetfulness of) civilization (*D* 312), what he finds valuable is not what civilization brings forth by itself (if such a thing is possible), but what it brings forth in opposition to culture (nature). The danger of civilizational forgetting (denial) is, strictly speaking, not that it destroys that *out of* which it grows, but that *against* which it grows. Nietzsche wants to preserve the antagonism between human and animal forces because he believes that culture and civilization, just like human and animal life forces, cannot be viewed apart from each other. They are not autonomous and self-sufficient; rather, they are dependent upon each other. Another reason Nietzsche wants to preserve antagonism is that he sees, in the latter, a stimulant to the cultivation of a plurality of inherently singular forms of life. In "Homer's Contest," Nietzsche claims that once the Greeks had destroyed their enemy's independence, once they "made their superior strength felt," they destroyed the fruitful antagonism that was responsible for their culture's greatness. Accordingly, Nietzsche approves of certain doses of aggression against animality (nature) but rejects overdoses of civilizational aggression. The key is to maintain a fruitful conflict and tension between culture and civilization, animal and human life forces.

Morality as a False Overcoming — *story of the origin* *God–rational*

When civilization cuts off the human being from its animal beginning, this leaves a gap that civilization tries to fill with a narrative on the creation of the human being. In this narrative, the human being's origin is construed as a beginning (a substantial nature) that causally determines the future as that toward which history evolves (teleology). According to civilization's narrative of creation, the world constitutes a rational and moral order whose architecture is transparent to humans only when humans are conceived of as beings who are themselves inherently rational and moral, a reflection of their origin. In the Western tradition this narrative is intimately tied up with a religious and moral discourse, in particular with that of the Judeo-Christian doctrine:

> The presupposition that things are, at bottom, ordered so morally that human reason must be justified . . . is the after-effect of belief in God's veracity—God understood as the creator of things. (*WP* 471)

The discourses of civilization and Christianity are distinguished by their mutual interest in the moral improvement of the human being (*TI* "Improvers"). In this capacity, both discourses betray a hostility toward life: "For before the court of morality (especially Christian, which is to say unconditional, morality) life *must* constantly and inevitably be proved wrong because life is essentially something amoral" ("An Attempt at Self-Criticism" 5). This hostility toward life is reflected in the general belief that this life must be rejected in favor of another, better, improved life (*TI* "Anti-Nature" 1).[19] Furthermore, both discourses, insofar as they articulate a project of moral improvement, are discourses of domination. The desire to gain mastery over life is dominant in both the beliefs and practices of the Christian church (*TI* "Anti-Nature" 1, 2). The latter have not improved life, but rather weakened, sickened, and aggravated the human animal's condition:

hostile to life (amoral)

cf. grade

> To call the taming of an animal its "improvement" is in our ears almost a joke. Whoever knows what goes on in menageries is doubtful whether the beasts in them are "improved." They are weakened, they are made less harmful, they become *sickly* beasts through the depressive emotion of fear, through pain, through injuries, through hunger.—It is no different with the tamed human being whom the priest has "improved." (*TI* "Improvers" 2)

Christian morality reflects the hatred and resentment of the animal within the human that is found in the project of civilization. It stands for the erroneous and optimistic belief in the human being's superiority over the animals and all other forms of life. This stance leads not only to the belief that reason, language, and morality are the truly "superhuman" features of the human being but also to the belief that, in the name of God, one is justified in using and abusing animal life as a means toward the perfection of "higher" forms of human life. Nietzsche is particularly critical of this last trait of Christianity and compares favorably Eastern religions, which, despite an obsession with moral improvement, still respect and protect the animals as gifted (*WS* 57).

Nietzsche understands Christian morality as the process of turning the human animal against itself, that is, against its animality. Due to its overly aggressive denial of animality, however, this morality cannot succeed in generating the fruitful antagonism between human and animal life forces that can lead the human being beyond itself. Christian moralities' struggle against animality is the struggle of weak and declining life:

> *The over-animal.*—The beast in us wants to be lied to; morality is a necessary lie told so that it shall not tear us to pieces. Without the errors that repose in the assumptions of morality the human being would have remained animal. As it is, it has taken itself for something higher and imposed sterner laws upon itself. That is why it feels a hatred for the grades that have remained closer to animality: which is the explanation of the contempt formally felt for the slave as a non-human, as a thing. (*HH* 40)

The moral and civilized human being's claim that it has surpassed the animal does not, in the Nietzschean sense, reflect an instance of overcoming as the result of an agonistic encounter with the animals, but, on the contrary, signals the escape from open and honest competition. The attempt to rise above and beyond the animals, to become an over-animal, reveals a weakness and lack of courage. The over-animal is an animal that cannot afford to "confirm" its animality. It resembles the priestly type of *priestly man*

man that Nietzsche describes in *Twilight of the Idols*; he is too weak to confront his animal passions and instincts. The priestly man's weaknesses make him resent and hate animal passions so much that he cannot but exterminate them. Because he lacks the strength to live with and in opposition to these animal passions, castration and extirpation of his animality are his only options. The priestly man's attitude toward his animal instincts is revelatory of his general hostility toward life, for "to attack the passions at their root is to attack life at its root" (*TI* "Morality" 1). In the end, Christian morality does not improve the human being but, rather, bestializes the animal within the human:

result

> Morality is a menagerie; its premise, that iron bars are more useful than freedom, even for the captive; its other premise, that there are animal tamers who do not shrink from frightful means, who know how to handle red-hot iron. This horrific species, which accepts battle with the wild animal, calls itself "priest." (*KSA* 13:15[72])[20]

Morality = menagerie

Whereas violence has been traditionally attributed to the animal, Nietzsche attributes it to the human and, in particular, to the project of civilization and moralization. This reversal restores the so-called cruelty of the animal to its amoral innocence.

The prefix "over-" in the term "over-animal" designates the attempt to establish a hierarchical ordering of the human as superior to the animal. This superiority separates the human from the animal and thereby forecloses the possibility of an agonistic encounter. The over-animal exemplifies an animal whose feelings of "envy, jealousy, and competitive ambition" (*HC*) have been "exterminated." The meaning of the prefix "over-" in the term "over-animal" therefore is exactly the opposite of the meaning of the prefix "over-" in the terms "overhuman" and "overcoming," where "over" denotes the human's ability to overcome itself. While in the over-animal the prefix "over-" refers to a vertical relationship that establishes a hierarchy of the human ruling "over" the animal, in the overhuman the prefix "over-" refers to a horizontal relationship that establishes a "face-to-face" meeting of the animal and the human in which the animal and the human are recognized as equals. The horizontality of the overcoming of the human is expressed in the metaphor of the bridge and in the image of the wind (*Über-wind-ung*) blowing over the horizon. In the Nietzschean term "overhuman," the prefix "over-" is used neither to separate the human from the animal, nor to set one above the other, but to establish just enough distance (*Pathos der Distanz*) so as to open up the space for an agonistic encounter.

ÜM ~ 'noble soul' — horizontal vision

The figure of the overhuman, in contrast to the over-animal, is imbued with the courage to surround oneself with animals, for it is only in the eyes of the animals that one can detect whether one's will to power is rising or declining: "Must I look down on them today and fear them? And will the hour return when they look up at me in fear?" (*GS* 314). It is important to recognize the upward/downward perspective of the noble and powerful as distinct from the upward/downward perspective of the enslaved and weak. While the former is an expression of reverence and respect for the other, the latter is an expression of hierarchy and domination over others. In the noble and powerful, the respect and reverence for the other (including oneself) opens up a horizontal perspective, the perspective of agonistic struggle, par excellence (*BGE* 265).[21]

Nietzsche's vision of the antagonism between human and animal life forces in the self-overcoming (becoming overhuman) of the human being is in this sense continuous with his more general view that all forms of life are constituted by struggle. For Nietzsche, the organism reflects struggle as much as order (*KSA* 11:40[55]; 37[4]) and an organism is the "order of thousands of obedient forces" but of obedient forces that resist:

> Life would have to be defined as a continuous process of sizing up one's strength [*Kraftstellungen*], where the antagonists grow in unequal measure. Even in obedience a resistance [*Widerstreben*] subsists; one's power [*Eigenmacht*] is not given up. Similarly, in commanding there exists a concession that the absolute power of the rival is not defeated, not incorporated, not dissolved. "To obey" and "to command" are forms of competitive play [*Kampfspiel*]. (*KSA* 11:36[22])

Nietzsche's conception of order and of elevation should not be confused with the traditional understanding of hierarchy. Instead, his conception of order points to a relationship between forces where the commanding force does not oppress the obeying force and where the obeying force does not submit to the commanding force.[22] In the relationship between commanding and obeying forces, their respective differences are not given up, but persist and resist one another. The relationship between commanding and obeying forces in the overhuman animal is, therefore, not the site of domination, of one force setting itself above the other, but rather a rivalry between equal forces:[23]

> The highest human being would have the greatest plurality of instincts, and also in the greatest relative measure that can still be endured. Indeed: where the human plant shows itself strong, there we

find the instincts powerfully acting against each other. (*KSA* 11:27[59])

Whereas the so-called strength of the over-animal is reflected in its practice of extirpation and castration of animal passions, the strength of the overhuman is reflected in its ability to contain within itself an increasing degree of struggle between the greatest plurality of animal passions:

> The great human being is great because it opens up a space for the free play of its lusts: the great one is strong enough to make out of these animals [*Unthieren*] its domestic animals [*Haustiere*]. (*KSA* 13:16[7])

When Nietzsche here speaks of "domestic animals," he is not referring to the "type Christian" (*WP* 684) but to the animal as a friend, a companion, and a competitor.

The notion of the overhuman stands for an understanding of human life as something that becomes (*Werden*) rather than as something that is (*Sein*).²⁴ Being human means being in becoming (*ein Auf-dem-Weg sein*) and overcoming (*Übergang* and *Untergang*): "not an end but just a path, an episode, a bridge, a great promise" (*GM* II: 16). The possibility of the human self-overcoming (becoming overhuman) reflects the idea that the human being is not a function of what it is, moral or rational, but of what else it could become, if only it keeps overcoming itself. In other words, what is promising about the human being is the possibility of its infinite self-overcomings. Becoming overhuman, therefore, does not reflect an attempt to stabilize human life into some sort of ideal superhuman form but, rather, to provoke a counter-movement against that which stabilizes itself into a fixed identity and nature. It does not entail remaining identical to oneself, but altering oneself, becoming untruthful to oneself.²⁵ Nietzsche welcomes the return of the animal because he sees, in animality, a force that disrupts the human being's identity. It is a return that destabilizes what is in view of what shall be. Rather than reducing the future to one and only one all-too-human form of life, becoming overhuman points to a movement of excess and an extension of the human that leads it beyond its all-too-human form. It stands for a return of the animal in the human that opens up the possibility for the cultivation of a plurality of irreducibly singular forms of life.²⁶

The Memory of Culture

The memory of culture is the memory of the continuity of animal and human life forces (*D* 312), but this continuity does not collapse humans and animals into sameness and identity (*BT* 8).[27] Humans are animals, but they are unlike any other animal. From the perspective of culture, human animals are distinguished not only by their illusions of morality, rationality, and the use of the intellect as an instrument of truth (*TL*), but also by their ability to overcome these all-too-human illusions to become what Nietzsche calls overhuman.[28] The overcoming of the human depends on a return to the beginning, a return to animality and animal forgetfulness, but it does not call for a "return to nature" in the Rousseauian sense or for a fusion of the human animal with nature and the animals. Rather, the overcoming of the human depends on keeping alive the struggle against nature. This struggle for distance from the origin, to become unfaithful to it, is what Nietzsche defines as the liberating task of culture in *Untimely Considerations*: "Educate oneself, that is, by oneself against one's self, to a new habit and nature, out of an old first nature and habit" (*HL* 10). The aim of culture is to educate the human animal so as to "twist free" a "second nature," a "more natural nature" that betrays the features of its irreducible singularity. In *Nietzsche et la scène philosophique*, Sarah Kofman argues that nature does not precede culture and that nature is always already taken up by culture, because nature imposes itself as the task of culture to form and transform, to invent and reinvent nature.[29] But if nature is always already culture, then the nature contested by culture is not nature itself, but an interpretation of nature. What culture contests is a civilizational interpretation of (human animal) nature as moral and rational in favor of an interpretation of (human animal) nature as artistic and creative.

The question of whether culture is able to reverse the interpretations of civilization is inseparable from the question of whether truth has the capacity to turn humans back into animals (*HH* 519). Nietzsche associates this concept of truth with the figure of Circe, truth as seduction. This truth seduces the human being back to its origin, where it discovers (*sucht und versucht*) the illusion of its beginning. Nietzsche investigates the human being's beginning from the perspective of the animals. From that perspective, the very idea of such a thing as "the human being" seems dubious: "Human beings do not exist, for there was no first 'human being': thus infer the animals" (*KSA* 10:12[1].95). Analogously, he also rejects the idea of organic life having a beginning: "I do not see why the organic should be thought of as something that has an *origin* [*entstanden sein muss*]" (*KSA* 11:34[50]). Nietzsche questions the notion of a beginning that constitutes a given, stable, and unalterable origin that determines all future becoming. The truth about the beginning is not the truth of the origin, but a truth that dissolves the beginning.

Truth as Circe signifies that human life is not only deeply involved and dissolved in dream and illusion, but also that dreams and illusions are the only conditions under which life can strive and thrive.[30] Nietzsche gains this insight when he awakens within a dream to the consciousness that not only is life a dream, but also that dreams and illusions are essential to life, for to be alive means to dream and to fantasize (*GS* 54).[31] In a fragment from the *Nachlass,* Nietzsche defines the whole organic world as a "being with the habit of ordering in dreaming":

> The whole organic world is the weaving together of beings, each with their little imaginary world around themselves: their force, their lust, their habits are found in their experiences, projected as their *outside world.* The ability [*Fähigkeit*] for creation (formation, invention, imagination) is their fundamental capacity: of themselves, these beings have, of course, likewise only an erroneous, imaginary, simplified representation. "A being with the habit of ordering in dreaming"—that is a living being. Immense amounts of such habits have finally become so solid, that *species* live in accordance with these orders. Probably these habits are favorable to the conditions of their survival. (*KSA* 11:34[247])

It is interesting to note that, in Nietzsche, dreams and the imagination do not belong exclusively to the human, but are constitutive of the whole organic world.[32] Nietzsche identifies dreaming as the fundamental ability of all living beings in the sense that it not only preserves, but also enhances life (*BT* 1).[33] What defines the ability to dream is the ability to create. For a living being to be alive it must create, form, invent, and imagine. As dreaming beings, all living beings imagine, invent, and create for themselves a form of life and an imaginary outside world. As such, they are not only continuously dreaming but, more importantly, living in dreams of their own creation. Life is a dream that keeps on imagining and reimagining and creating and recreating itself through dreaming. But if life is a dream in which one comes to life through dreaming, then the consciousness Nietzsche awakens to must be understood as "just" another dream:

> Waking life does not have the *freedom* of interpretation possessed by the life of dreams, it is less inventive and unbridled—but do I have to add that when we are awake our drives likewise do nothing but interpret nervous stimuli and, according to their requirement, posit their "causes"? that there is no essential difference between waking and dreaming? that our moral judgments and evaluations too are fantasies based on a physiological process unknown to us, a kind of

> acquired language for designating certain nerve stimuli? that all our
> so-called consciousness is a more or less fantastic commentary on an
> unknown, perhaps unknowable, but felt text? (*D* 119)

Although Nietzsche holds that, strictly speaking, there is no difference
between waking and dreaming, he observes that it is while dreaming and
sleeping that the animal returns to the human being (*HH* 13).[34] That the
animal returns during dreaming and sleeping, rather than during waking
life, might be related to the greater "freedom of interpretation" that
Nietzsche attributes to the life of dreams. Waking life is, in this sense,
comparable to a state of civilization. While the freedom to affirm and
interpret oneself as an animal is possible within the life of dreams, this
possibility is foreclosed under the conditions of civilization. Civilization's
attempt to awaken and to enlighten the human being is, here, inseparable
from the attempt to keep the animal within the human being asleep. The
return of the animal to the human in dream life reveals that civilization's
efforts to tame the animal and frighten away the ghosts of the past are in
vain for, in the fragile states of dream and illusion, the animal returns.
The "savage grimaces" of the animal haunt the civilized human being (*D*
312).[35] Nietzsche's approach is comparable to that of Freud, for both see
in the dream-state the dissolution of the memory of civilization and of
consciousness.[36] Dreams are the space for the free expression of the
human being's forgotten animality.

Forgetfulness is one of the primary features of the human being's animality, for Nietzsche holds that dreaming is comparable to animal forgetfulness (*HH* 12).[37] Nietzsche views animal forgetfulness as the force that
brings back to the human being the creativity and freedom that enhances
its dream life. On these grounds, Nietzsche thinks that it is necessary for
the human being to affirm itself as an animal. In "On the Use and Disadvantage of History for Life," for example, Nietzsche places animal forgetfulness in contrast to human memory in order to show that the former is
necessary to the enhancement of life as a protection against an overdose
of civilization and consciousness (history). Nietzsche, however, simultaneously shows that forgetfulness, because it is a carrier of freedom and of
creativity, is the source of all noble and great actions (*HL* 1).[38]

What distinguishes the memory of culture from the forgetfulness of
civilization is that it remembers the dream life of the animal. Culture understood as a memory of the animal should not to be confused with a
voluntary act of bringing back the animal: it is an openness of the human
being to the possibility of a return of the animal.[39] The memory of culture
is not a means of mastery and domination over the past (and over life);

rather, it is the dream life of the animal, the animal's freedom and creativity, which erupts in memory beyond its control. Remembering is surprised by what exceeds the capacity to remember. Accordingly, culture does not understand memory as yet another capacity within the human being's conscious control, but sees in memory a form of attentiveness, a readiness to grasp the dream life of the animal when it comes forward to its encounter.

The figure of the genius of culture illustrates that the memory of culture is as much a return *to* the past as it is a return *of* the past. The genius of culture also encounters the dream life of the animal as much as it is being encountered by it:

> If anyone wanted to imagine a genius of culture, what would the latter be like? He would manipulate [*handhabt*] falsehood [*Lüge*], force [*Gewalt*], the most ruthless self-interest as his instruments [*Werkzeuge*] so skillfully he could only be called an evil, demonic being; but his objectives, which here and there shine through, would be great and good. He would be a centaur, half animal [*Tier*], half human [*Mensch*], and with angel's wings attached to his head in addition. (*HH* 241)

Nietzsche models the genius of culture after the figure of the Greek Centaur (Chiron), "half-animal, half-human," and the Roman figure of Genius, "with angel's wings attached to his head in addition" (*HH* 241). What distinguishes the virtue of the Centaur (Chiron) is his tactile sensibility. His hands (*chira*) master the art of grasping the occasion (*kairos*), the instant when animality comes forward through this encounter.[40] The tactile sensibility of the genius of culture is reflected in the terms Nietzsche uses to describe his skills: he uses "tools" (*Werkzeuge*) and "manipulates" (*handhabt*) his virtues. Whereas the Greek Centaur (Chiron) has the sensibility to grasp the singularity of the moment, the instant in time, Genius in the Romans has the ability to reveal the irreducible singularity of each individual. Genius unveils the inner, most intimate distinction of the individual self as the presence of something that does not belong to the self, something that comes to the self from another.[41] The term "genius" refers both to each individual's creative uniqueness and to something that comes to the individual and without which the individual's uniqueness could not become creative. A genius of culture, as Nietzsche imagines him or her, must therefore be like a Centaur (Chiron), that is, like someone who is able to grasp that which comes to the singular self, impregnating its singularity with life, turning that singularity into a source of life. What makes the self's irreducible singularity productive is the return of animality, the return of the freedom and creativity as they define the dream life of the animal.

From the perspective of civilization, the genius appears to be "an evil and demonic being," but from the perspective of culture his objectives are "great and good"(ibid.). The genius of culture contains a fullness of life that flows over to others and has a liberating and invigorating effect on them (*AOM* 407). The objectives of the genius are, therefore, not egoistic and narrow but "great and good." It is important to point out that the "objectives" of the genius are not intentional and explicit, but "here and there shine through" (*HH* 241). The genius of culture benefits others not as a matter of design or of will. She benefits others despite herself, giving to the other, unable to hold back (*TI* "Skirmishes" 44).[42] What is "good and great" in the genius of culture, what distinguishes her virtuosity and generosity, is not her morality, but her explicit immorality. In this respect, the genius of culture signifies an overcoming of the norms and values that define the rule of civilization.

The Subversions of Culture

The overcoming of civilization through culture is also expressed by the Nietzschean figure of the *Umgekehrten*. The *Umgekehrten* are those whose artistic and acrobatic twists and turns are inherently life-enhancing and life-affirming:

> We opposite human beings [*Umgekehrten*] having opened our eyes and conscience to the question where and how the plant "human being" has so far grown most vigorously to a height—we think that this has happened every time under the opposite [*umgekehrten*] conditions, that to this end the dangerousness of its situation must first grow to the point of enormity, its power of invention and simulation (its "spirit") had to develop under prolonged pressure and constraint into refinement and audacity, its life-will had to be enhanced into an unconditional power-will. We think that hardness, forcefulness, slavery, danger in the alley and in the heart, life in hiding, stoicism, the art of experiment and delivery of every kind, that everything evil, terrible, tyrannical in the human being, everything in the human being that is kin to beasts of prey and serpents, serves the enhancement of the species "human being" as much as its opposite [*Gegensatz*] does. (*BGE* 44)[43]

The task of the *Umgekehrten* is the *Umwertung aller Werte*, or the reversal of the whole hierarchy of civilizational evaluations. The *Umgekehrten*'s subversion of the values of civilization occurs through a becoming-animal of the human being, which indicates that the human being has again become strong enough to confirm its animality, its creative and artistic powers of life. The *Umgekehrten*'s subversion of the values of civilization has to be understood as a radical turn. Under suspicion are not simply some values, but all of them. It is impossible to overturn only one value. Rather, one must overturn the entire hierarchy of evaluations that define the project of civilization. Moreover, the *Umgekehrten*'s twists and turns do not simply proclaim a good where the discourse of civilization proclaims an evil, or proclaim an evil where civilization proclaims a good. Instead, the *Umgekehrten* twists free the idea of values from the dualism proper to a moral discourse of civilization, which sees either good or evil in everything; a metaphysical discourse, which sees either error or truth in everything; and a discourse of human nature, which sees either the animal or the human in everything. In place of the logic of the excluded third, the *Umgekehrten* counters with a logic of the inclusive "and . . . and." *Umkehrung* involves the opposite poles of dualistic evaluations for and against each other, so as to show that good and evil, error and truth, human and animal are inseparable parts of a continuum of life, human, animal, and other.

Nietzsche legitimately questions whether such free and subverting spirits still exist (*GS* 347).[44] He turns to the past for encouragement, seeking the company of the geniuses of culture: Goethe, Schopenhauer, and all those who promise that the animal cannot be finally tamed and bred, just as forgetfulness and life cannot be finally mastered (*D* 126). Their examples show that the animality of the human being resists the mnemotechnics of civilization and exceeds the rational and moral grid of civilizational evaluations.[45] The animal's ability to resist in the past promises its return in the future. The thought of the animal's return is an encouraging thought because it promises to bring forth lighter and freer forms of life. It is this effect that Nietzsche tries to achieve through his own narrative of natural history:

> *How natural history should be narrated.*—Natural history as the history of the war of the spiritual-moral forces against fear, imaginings, inertia, superstition, foolishness, and their victory over them, ought to be narrated in such a way that everyone who hears it is irresistibly inspired to strive after spiritual and bodily health and vigor, to the glad feeling of being the heir and continuator of the human, and to an ever nobler desire for new undertakings. (*AOM* 184)

2

Politics and Promise

For Nietzsche, the possibility of human self-overcoming is represented by the promise of the overhuman. In this chapter, I investigate the idea of this promise through a reevaluation of Nietzsche's distinction between promise as an artifact of civilization (the memory of the will [*Gedächtnis des Willens*]) and promise as an artifact of culture (the promise of the sovereign individual) (*GM* II: 1, 2). The promise of the overhuman has been traditionally understood to be either antipolitical or nonpolitical. While, in an antipolitical interpretation, Nietzsche figures as a precursor to totalitarian and authoritarian ideologies, in a nonpolitical interpretation, he figures as a moral perfectionist who can be assimilated to liberal democracy.[1] In this chapter I argue that, from the perspective of Nietzsche's animal philosophy, the promise of the overhuman embraces an idea of freedom as responsibility, which inherently concerns the political life of human animals.

What distinguishes Nietzsche as a political thinker is that he believes politics should be studied from the perspective of life, and not, as the Western tradition of political thought largely assumes, as a means to protect human life against the animality of the human being.[2] This assumption is exemplified by Hobbes, who maintains that the human being is a wolf to other human beings and, therefore, social and political organization should be thought of as a mechanism to control the animality of the human being.[3] My reading of Nietzsche as a political thinker centers on the claim that the antagonism between human and animal life forces is the principal feature of human development. When the human being either defines itself against its animality and animal forgetfulness or denies them a productive role, cultural and political life assume forms that hinge on domination and exploitation of humans by humans. The breeding of the memory of the will (*Gedächtnis des Willens*) as an attempt to transcend or extirpate animality is an example of one of these forms of domination. Contrariwise, when the human being engages with its animality, it gives rise to forms of cultural and political life that are rooted in individual self-responsibility.[4]

Individual self-responsibility is centered on an experience of freedom, which is inherently antagonistic in the sense that it stands for a continuous resistance to the institutionalization of freedom.[5] Nietzsche does not object to the need for political institutions (and for the breeding of the memory of the will). On the contrary, he welcomes strong institutions but believes they require a counterforce that calls into question the fact that they were founded on domination and exploitation. This chapter argues that Nietzsche addresses the question of how to counteract a politics of cruelty, based on animal taming and breeding, through his conception of the promise of the sovereign individual. The promise of the sovereign individual is a counterpromise to the memory of the will, which protects the freedom and plurality of human life through the practice of what could be called an agonistic politics of responsibility. What distinguishes the latter, however, is not antagonism toward animality and forgetfulness. Rather, the very promise of the sovereign individual betrays the features of animality and animal forgetfulness indicating that, in the promise of the sovereign individual, the animality of the human being has become creative and productive.

The Promise of Civilization

Generally speaking, Nietzsche considers forgetfulness and memory to be two different forces of life. Whereas forgetfulness is an articulation of singularity as something that cannot be shared, memory is an articulation of universality as something that can only be shared. While forgetfulness gives rise to an equality rooted in difference, that is, in the radical otherness of singulars, memory gives rise to an equality rooted in identity, that is, in the radical sameness of universals. Memory and forgetfulness are involved in an agonistic struggle against one other. In this struggle, memory dissolves singularity into a universal form while forgetfulness disrupts universality in the name of the cultivation of singularity. In *On the Genealogy of Morals*, this antagonism takes the form of a conflict between the memory of the will as an artifact of civilization and the promise of the sovereign individual as an artifact of culture. What distinguishes the memory of the will is that it overcomes singularity in favor of establishing a uniform, stable, and fixed identity that is characteristic of a type of animal that lives in groups (herds). What distinguishes the promise of the sovereign individual is that it disrupts universal identity in favor of ennobling elevation, which is characteristic of a singular and forgetful animal that stands on its own.

In *On the Genealogy of Morals*, Nietzsche claims that forgetfulness in the human animal reveals strength and health. It is memory, he argues, that is symptomatic of weakness and need:

> And precisely this necessarily forgetful animal, in whom forgetting is a strength, representing a form of *robust* health, has bred for itself a counter-device, memory, with the help of which forgetfulness can be suspended in certain cases,—namely in those cases where a promise is to be made: consequently, it is by no means merely a passive inability to be rid of an impression once it has made its impact, nor is it just indigestion caused by giving your word on some occasion and finding you cannot cope, instead it is an active not-*wanting*-to-let-go, a will to keep on wanting what has been, on some occasion, willed, a real *memory of the will* [*Gedächtnis des Willens*]. (*GM* II: 1)

According to Nietzsche's genealogical discourse, the human animal could not maintain the great health of the singular and forgetful animal. In order to survive, it had to transform itself into a herd animal—an inherently social and group-oriented being. The rise of social and political forms of life coincides with the rise of civilization. The project of civilization is to secure and preserve human life in response to a need, namely, the need to overcome the relative weakness and inferiority of the human animal with respect to its environment.[6] Although Nietzsche seems to privilege the solitary and forgetful animal over the herd animal, he acknowledges that the process of civilization responds to a need and, therefore, not only is this political institution necessary for the preservation of life, but its accomplishments are also praiseworthy.

Civilization accomplishes the transformation of human animal life into an explicitly social and political form of life through the institution of a *Gedächtnis des Willens,* or a memory of the will on the forgetfulness of the human animal.[7] The *Gedächtnis des Willens* is a promise that civilization employs as a means of domination in order to provide a solution to the question of how societies are kept together. That is, it explains how human animals can be made to dedicate themselves, willingly, to the welfare of society and the state.[8] Society is instituted and preserved through the manipulation of its members such that every member of society commits and submits (promises) itself "freely" to the norms and rules of civilized life.[9] The making of the memory of the will is an inherently violent and cruel process:

> "How do you give a memory to the animal? How do you impress something on this partly dull, partly idiotic, inattentive mind, this personification of forgetfulness, so that it will stick?" . . . This age-old question was not resolved with gentle solutions and methods, as can be imagined; perhaps there is nothing more terrible and strange in the human prehistory than its *technique of mnemonics.* . . . The human being was eventually able to retain five or six "I-don't-want-to's" in its memory in connection with which a *promise* had been made, in order to enjoy the advantages of society—and there you are! With the aid of this sort of memory, people finally came to "reason"!—Ah, reason, solemnity, mastering of emotions, this really dismal thing called reflection, all these privileges and splendors humans have: what a price had to be paid for them! How much blood and horror lies at the basis of all "good things"! (*GM* II: 3)

Nietzsche dismisses the assertion that society and the state are founded on a social contract made among human beings who voluntarily and peacefully agree to submit themselves to a set of common rules. In line with Machiavelli, Nietzsche argues, throughout his work, that society and the state always begin with violence and bloodshed in an illegitimate act of injustice.[10] Violence and injustice define not only the founding moment but also the continuous process of civilization and socialization. If the individual commits itself to the herd, it is not because it wants to, but because it has been and is continuously *made* to want to. As such, the institution and execution of political power always contain an inevitable kernel of violence and injustice. Nietzsche does not object to violence as such, for he sees in violence an indispensable means of politics. He is, however, critical of the hypocrisy of a politics that tries to obscure the violence it employs in order to protect the stability and continuity of its rule. Rather than making responsible use of violent means, such a politics degenerates into moral dogmatism, political terror, and irresponsibility (*BGE* 44, 62).[11]

One important aspect of the memory of the will is forgetfulness, namely, the forgetting of the violence of foundation as well as the violence that the members of society are subject to in the ongoing process of their civilization and socialization.[12] This forgetfulness is achieved through a form of historical narration and memory that veils and obscures the violence of civilization and its beginning. Society's narration of its own history is inherently ideological and false, but it is nonetheless life-enhancing because it holds the members of a civilized society together and, thereby, secures and preserves their form of life.[13] The forgetfulness of the memory of the will (civilization) should not, as I pointed out in the previous chapter, be confused with the kind of animal forgetfulness that characterizes the memory of culture. What distinguishes the violence of the foundation of society and the state is that it is committed against the singular and forgetful animal. Examples from Nietzsche's early and late work confirm that what defines the politics of civilization is a "continued cruelty to animals" (*SE* 6). Because the animal resists the continued process of its civilization and socialization, "[s]truggling 'civilization' (taming) needs every kind of irons and torture to maintain itself against terribleness and beast-of-prey natures" (*WP* 871).

The most effective way to secure the rule of civilization is through the taming and breeding of an animal that thrives in society (in the herd) but would perish on its own. Such an animal would be docile, tame, predictable, reliable, submissive, and obedient—entirely devoted to the good of society. The aim of taming and breeding an animal devoted to the good of society reveals the intimate link between the project of civilization and that of moral improvement.[14] From the perspectives of civilization and moral improvement, the animal that stands on its own manifests a potential threat to the fabric of the group because, by definition, it undermines the norms accepted and exemplified by the herd animal.[15] The animal that can stand on its own is the antithesis of the "good human being":

> The "good human being" in every stage of civilization, the one who is at the same time useful and innocuous: a kind of middle point, the expression of something that for common sense is not to be feared but that *nevertheless* should not be despised. (*KSA* 13:16[8])

Insofar as the animal resists the "leveling" process of herd-formation, that is, of socialization, moralization, and humanization, it is the declared enemy of civilization:

> In the fight against *great* human beings lies much reason. These beings are dangerous, accidents, exceptions. Storms, strong enough to question what is patiently-built and -grounded. Human beings who pose question-marks to solidified beliefs. Not only to disarm such explosives, but, if somehow possible, to *prevent* their emergence and

multiplication: this is what the instinct of all civilized societies dictates. (*KSA* 13:16[9])

The memory of the will is a means of preventing the emergence of "great human beings" who live by their forgetful animal natures. It is a means directed against the exceptional animal in order to make it sick, to bring it down to the norm.[16] The memory of the will is designed to fabricate an identity and keep the human being identical to itself, that is, tied to an identity forced onto the individual through processes of civilization and socialization. Turning the human animal into something identical and generally identifiable is a way to gain mastery over life and over the future.[17] The animal that opposes itself to the herd identity of the leveled group is criminalized and marginalized[18]:

> The criminal-type is the type of the strong human being under unfavorable conditions, a strong human being made sick. What he lacks is the wilderness, a certain freer and more perilous nature and form of existence in which all that is attack and defense and the instincts of the strong human being *comes into its own*. Its *virtues* have been excommunicated by society; the liveliest drives within it forthwith blend with the depressive emotions, with suspicion, fear, dishonor. But this is almost the *recipe* for physiological degeneration. (*TI* "Skirmishes" 45)[19]

The criminalization and marginalization of the singular and forgetful animal is mainly achieved through a moral discourse which asserts that singularity is revelatory of egoism and forgetfulness is revelatory of irresponsibility. Both are declared evils that need to be "extirpated" in the name of altruism and love for one's neighbor (*TI* "Morality").[20]

From the perspective of the exceptional animal, the memory of the will is antithetical to (virtuous) animal nature. Conversely, from the perspective of civilization, the memory of the will, that is, the "voluntary" agreement to submit oneself to the moral and political norms of civilization reflects an achievement of the highest form of freedom and responsibility.[21] The opposition between these two perspectives, that is, civilization understood as an imposition of moral and rational norms as absolute guidelines for life, and culture understood as a liberating cultivation of animal life, is, as I show in Chapter 1, not static but dynamic. The disciplining of the human animal calls for an inevitable countermovement, an inevitable counterculture (*WP* 866).[22] Despite itself, the process of civilization provokes the return of the singular and forgetful animal, which revolutionizes, disrupts, explodes, and overthrows the rule of civilization (*TI* "Skirmishes" 44).[23] Nietzsche repeatedly emphasizes the value of civilization (and of the memory of the will) not only insofar as it preserves human life by taming and breeding inherently obedient herd animals but also insofar as it provokes the resistance of those animals that stand out as exceptions. Nietzsche warns, however, that the taming and breeding of obedient herd animals may lead to an overly strong hatred of the exceptional animal. When opposition turns into hatred, when the exceptional animal is marginalized for the "benefit" of the herd and when the latter no longer encounters the resistance of the former, the rule of civilization has destroyed a potentially fruitful antagonism with culture. As a result, civilization ends up producing inherently irresponsible and dangerous animals, that is, overbred herd animals, animals that are too obedient and too tame, animals whose promises cannot be trusted.[24]

The Promise of Culture

In *On the Genealogy of Morals*, Nietzsche asserts that the cultivation of an animal that can make promises is the highest task because it provides an answer to the question of how humans can live freely together with others within the confinements of social and political structures:

> To breed an animal *which is able to make promises*—is that not precisely the paradoxical task which nature has set itself with regard to human beings? Is it not the real problem *of human beings*? (*GM* II: 1)

This task is "paradoxical" because it calls on the human animal to reverse its animal nature. The human animal, a forgetful animal, has to become the opposite—a reliable animal. The challenge is to engender a form of memory that recognizes in animal forgetfulness a force necessary to the enhancement of future life. From the perspective of someone who (like Nietzsche) "can fully appreciate the countervailing force, forgetfulness," the memory of the will, only solves the problem of bringing forth an animal that can make promises "to a large degree" (*GM* II: 1). It provides a solution to the question of how societies can be kept together—how forgetful and solitary animals can be made to dedicate themselves willingly to the welfare of society and the state. However, since it fails to valorize animal forgetfulness, the memory of the will is not entitled to the privilege of making promises. The institution of the memory of the will, moreover, fails to solve the problem of freedom. It attempts to do so with socialization and civilization, but both are inherently violent techniques of domination directed against the human being's animality and singularity (individual genius). Therefore, for Nietzsche, the question remains how to bring forth forms of memory and promise-making, which, despite being directed against the forgetfulness of the animal, see in this forgetfulness a force necessary to the constitution of social and political forms of life.[25]

This problem cannot be solved through politics and civilization alone. It also requires culture.[26] From the perspective of culture, the crucial question of the promise is how to counteract the violence and domination that are involved in making the memory of the will at the moment of the foundation of political power and in the stabilization of political power. Furthermore, from the perspective of culture, the problem of the promise is not the violence of the animal, for it considers the animal to be inherently innocent,[27] but the human violence directed against animals or, more precisely, directed against their own animality and animal forgetfulness: "For the human being is the cruelest animal" and "The human being is the cruelest animal against itself" (*Z*: 2 "The Convalescent"). The question, therefore, is how to make a promise without relying on the violence and injustice committed against the human beings' animal life. Nietzsche addresses this question in his interpretation of the power to promise in the sovereign individual. This latter type of animal overcomes a politics of violence and domination through the cultivation of individual self-responsibility, which is, itself, rooted in the animality and animal forgetfulness of the human being.

The sovereign individual is "an autonomous, supra-ethical individual," who deserves "the privilege to make promises" because it "has freed itself from the morality of customs" (*GM* II: 2). The overcoming of the "morality of customs" depends on a return to animal forgetfulness as that force which allows the sovereign individual to twist free from and forget the moral and political norms of civilization (memory of the will) in the name of its "own standard of value" (*GM* II: 2). But, in the sovereign individual, animal forgetfulness is not only indispensable to self-overcoming—it also contributes to the liberating transformation of given social and political forms of life. In Nietzsche's narrative, the human being overcomes the domination and exploitation associated with the animal taming and breeding of civilization when its promises betray the features of animality and animal forgetfulness, that is, when freedom as responsibility has become animal and unconscious, when it has become the "dominant instinct" of the human being (*GM* II: 2). Knowing not only how to remember (like humans) but also how to forget (like animals) is the reason why the sovereign individual's promises can be trusted and can become the source of forms of sociability that are free from domination and exploitation:[28]

The proud realization of the extraordinary privilege of *responsibility*, the awareness of this rare freedom and power over himself and his destiny, has penetrated him to the depth and become an instinct, his dominant instinct. (*GM* II: 2)

The sovereign individual's instinct of responsibility should not be confused with its willpower. What makes for sovereignty is not the fact that the individual is free and could have acted otherwise, but that it is subject to the necessity of responsibility and, hence, could not have acted otherwise. In light of this, Nietzsche contests the Christian ideal of moral responsibility according to which human action results from the individual's free will (*TI* "Errors" 7). Genuine responsibility occurs when views (needs), such as the Christian belief in free will, have been overcome. Responsibility in the sovereign individual is promising because it is amoral rather than moral; unconscious rather than conscious; instinctive rather than reflected; necessary rather than free; a form of forgetfulness rather than a form of memory.

Nietzsche identifies the instinct of responsibility with the sovereign individual's conscience. Conscience is not rooted in the memory of the will, but in probity brought forth against the rule of civilization.[29] Conscience as the dominant instinct of responsibility is of greater political value than the memory of the will because it stands for a commitment to continuous self-overcoming[30] that is inseparable from a commitment to the continuous resistance to and overcoming of social and political forms of life that are based on the domination and exploitation of animal life. Responsibility in the sovereign individual is promising because it reclaims freedom and responsibility for the singular and forgetful animal against the institutionalization of freedom and responsibility found in civilization. What distinguishes the political value of the promise of the sovereign individual is not institutionalization. For Nietzsche, the promise is inherently counter-institutional. Its function is to submit the established authority of the memory of the will and its moral and political standards to a continuous and radical critique. It is by means of critical questioning that Nietzsche hopes to increase the human animal's sovereignty and power.

As I interpret Nietzsche, it is a mistake to think that the promise constitutes a "faculty," a self-sufficient power that is cut off from life. It should be understood neither as a faculty in the Kantian sense nor as a self-sufficient organ. Instead, the promise is a force of life that has to be investigated from the perspective of life. The latter reveals that the promise is not a form of memory but, on the contrary, that every promise reflects an antagonistic involvement of memory for and against forgetfulness. Every promise is, in this sense, not simply a form of memory turned toward the past, but also a form of forgetfulness turned toward the future. Accordingly, one can distinguish between two kinds of promises. On the one hand, there are those promises that indicate a prevalence of memory over forgetfulness. These are promises made in the name of the past. They are, like the memory of the will, a means of stabilizing and securing the continuity of past, present, and future against the uncertainties of the future. On the other hand, there are those promises, exemplified by the promises of the sovereign individual, that indicate a prevalence of forgetfulness over memory. These are promises made in the name of the future. They are a means not only to break with the past but also to revolutionize the present in light of future life to come. Against the dangers inherent in a politics where the past dominates the future, this promise welcomes the return of animal forgetfulness as a means of disrupting the identities among past, present, and future in the name of the free and spontaneous generation of life. Both kinds of promises, the one that stabilizes and secures the rule of the group and the one that revolutionizes it, are of equal value to social and political life. Depending on whether life needs to be preserved or whether life needs to be renewed, either the first or the second kind of promise will protect the freedom and plurality within society.

Furthermore, from the perspective of life, a promise made in an attempt to master the future, to make life more predictable and less susceptible to contingency, reveals weakness and the need for the illusion of a stable and secure world, where things in the future always already reflect how they are in the present. In contrast, a promise made in an attempt to revolutionize the present in the name of the future requires that one give up the will to control life-processes and expose oneself to their radical contingency. For Nietzsche, only such a promise reveals genuine sovereignty because it betrays the strength and courage required to overcome the need to gain mastery over life and over the future. Consequently, since the latter kind of promise is one that stands under the rule of animal forgetfulness, it is forgetfulness rather than memory, animality rather than humanity, which accounts for the sovereignty of the human action.

Sovereignty Beyond Domination

Nietzsche's critique of civilization is directed at the transformation of human animal life into a totality under which all individuals are subsumed and in which all individuals relate to each other in accordance with what Lévinas calls the Same.[31] The promise of the sovereign individual constitutes a point of rupture with this kind of totality insofar as it sees in every human individual a unique miracle (*Wunder*), that is, an animal that deserves admiration precisely because of its irreducible singularity (*SE* 1). The promise of the sovereign individual gives rise to forms of sociability that cannot be inscribed within a frame of reciprocal and symmetrical relationships, but must be understood as an articulation of the uniqueness and incommensurability of each and every individual. This is the only way in which the promise of the sovereign individual can enhance freedom and plurality against the totalizing powers of politics.

In contrast with the notion that sovereignty in Nietzsche designates an empowerment of the self over others, I argue that sovereignty is an empowerment of the self that results from overcoming the need to dominate others.[32] Sovereignty arises from a self-overcoming that leads the self beyond itself, toward the other and toward a free commitment to the other. It overcomes civilization and leads to forms of sociability that are based on unlimited self-responsibility.[33] Responsibility in the sovereign individual is the privilege of giving and promising oneself to another and seeing in this gift the greatest extension of one's power. Freedom without responsibility and responsibility without freedom are meaningless artifacts of civilization which elevate neither the individual nor the group. Instead, the promise of the sovereign individual constitutes a gain for all because freedom as responsibility extends the limits of the self toward the other.

In the sovereign individual, freedom as responsibility is like a gift-giving virtue, a prodigal, wasteful, and dissipating force constituted by the self's (animal) forgetting of itself (*Z* "The Gift-Giving Virtue"). Freedom as responsibility is a going-under toward the other: "I love the one whose soul is overfull so that it forgets itself and all things are in it: thus all things spell its going under (*Z*: 3 "Prologue"). The sovereign individual's self-forgetfulness is an overflowing of the self that reminds us of the tragic hero's going-under (*Untergang*) as the going-over (*Übergang*) to something that exceeds the hero's self:

> The heroic human being despises his happiness and his unhappiness, his virtues and vices, and in general the measuring of things by the standard of himself; . . . His strength lies in forgetting himself. . . . (*SE* 4, see also *BT* 21)

Both the tragic hero and the sovereign individual betray the traces of animal forgetfulness, characterizing it as that force which disrupts a 1 economy of survival (the memory of the will) and harkens toward an economy of giving beyond calculation (the promise of the sovereign individual).[34] In both figures, power signifies a diversifying and pluralizing augmentation of life beyond the need for self-preservation.[35] The pluralization of life achieved in the promise of the sovereign individual and in heroic action is of great importance to Nietzsche not only because it reflects a free relationship to the other but also because it has a liberating effect on the other. The promise of the sovereign individual as well as heroic action reflect self-overcomings (pluralization of the self), which, in turn, stimulate the self-overcoming of the other (pluralization of the other). It is due to the freedom that relates the sovereign individual to the other that forms of sociability based on the promise of the sovereign individual can be compared to those initiated by the gift-giving of the genius of culture:

> Of what account is genius if it does not communicate to the one who contemplates and reveres it such freedom and elevation of feeling that one no longer has need of genius!—*Rendering themselves superfluous* [*sich überflüssig machen*]—that is the glory of the great. (*AOM* 407; see also *TI* "Skirmishes" 44)[36]

In this account, freedom is not something that belongs to the human animal or exists in its relationship with itself but, more importantly, is something one experiences in one's relationship with the other as something arising from the other. This is why the high point of freedom in Nietzsche is always a going-under of the self before the other rather than a rising of the self above the other.

An Agonistic Politics of Responsibility

Nietzsche's notion of freedom as responsibility does not reflect a concern for the "individual" or "its freedom," and hence should not be confused with a modern understanding of individual freedom as the highest aim of society and the state (*WP* 687). Rather, the promise of the sovereign individual reflects a preoccupation with the cultivation of freedom as responsibility that overcomes the kind of individualism that devalues the political, on the one hand, and that overcomes the kind of politics that devalues individual freedom and responsibility, on the other. This is not to say that Nietzsche objects to the need for political institutions as such. On the contrary, he favors strong institutions, but believes that they require a counterforce that is strong enough to continuously overcome them. The promise of the sovereign individual is a counterpromise to the memory of the will, which protects the freedom of the singular individual through the practice of an agonistic politics of responsibility. Responsibility is agonistic because it promotes a continuous resistance to the institutionalization of freedom. Freedom is anarchical: it is neither what one has by virtue of an instituted right nor what one is given by virtue of a mutual agreement. Instead, it is always only what one fights for, what one conquers:

> The free human being is a *warrior*.—How is freedom measured, in individuals as in nations? By the resistance [*Widerstand*] which has to be overcome, by the effort it costs to stay *aloft*. One would have to seek the highest type of free human being where the greatest resistance is constantly being overcome: five steps from tyranny, near the threshold of the danger of servitude. (*TI* "Skirmishes" 38)[37]

It is in this agonistic struggle that Nietzsche finds the true guarantee of freedom and responsibility. From the perspective of culture, strong political institutions are desirable insofar as they constitute a power against which the individual can prove its freedom. Nietzsche, for example, emphasizes the will to authority, tradition, and solidarity as they define Roman politics as particularly life-enhancing, not because they encourage self-responsibility but, on the contrary, because they are directed against the will to self-responsibility (*TI* "Skirmishes" 39).[38] In opposition to those who argue for a weak state in the name of individual freedom, Nietzsche holds that freedom in the individual does not develop in isolation, but in competition against an institution, whether in the form of a state, church, or university.[39] Freedom is neither the possession of a singular individual nor of an institution. Instead, the freest institutions are those that are engaged for and against the will to self-responsibility while the freest individuals are those who are invested in the fight for freedom against institutions. In this antagonism between the individual and the institution (the state), the aim is not to win over the opponent or to center rule either on the freedom of the individual or on the power of the state, but to preserve their rivalry. After all, it is essentially the struggle for and against rule that generates freedom and responsibility.[40]

The idea that freedom can only be preserved through a struggle against rule is one of the main insights Nietzsche finds lacking in modern political ideologies, whether socialist, nationalist, or liberal.[41] Nietzsche is particularly critical of ideologies that aim to overcome the distance between the rulers and the ruled. He believes that once the differences between rulers and ruled are abolished, the possibility of attaining genuine freedom is similarly abolished. What is crucial in this distinction is not an affirmation of power over others but, on the contrary, an affirmation of difference as a precondition for conflict and struggle. Nietzsche believes a fruitful antagonism is threatened in a society of equal rights, where equality names the universal identity of all rather than universal respect being owed to each and every individual on the basis of their differences. While equality based on the recognition of universality (civilization) forecloses the possibility of struggle and, hence, of freedom as responsibility, equality based on the recognition of difference (culture) generates freedom as responsibility.[42] It is also important to note that the distinction between the rulers and the ruled is inherently contingent and, therefore, always contestable and reversible. Those who are subject to rule today are always already those who may potentially rule tomorrow.[43] As a consequence, the struggle of culture against the rule of civilization in the name of freedom as responsibility has to be understood not only in terms of an open-ended struggle but also in terms of a struggle directed toward the future. Insofar as the promise of the sovereign individual is a promise that opens up the future, it is essentially a promise of freedom as responsibility to come.

The Posthumous in Sartre and Nietzsche

In Nietzsche, the promise of freedom as responsibility affects the present posthumously. It is a counterpromise that reverses the flow of time because it anticipates the future in order to turn it against the present.[44] The coincidence of the future and the present in the present is a noncoincidence, a disjunction, an interruption between the present and the future within the present itself. The return of the anticipated future opens an abyss within the present because the present returns to itself from the future it anticipates, a future experienced in the present that cannot yet be lived in the present.[45] The return of the anticipated future problematizes and complicates the present. Nietzsche calls this effect of the promise its posthumous effect and claims that it is the posthumous afterlife of one's vision of the future that has the greatest effect on the present:

> Posthumous human beings—like me, for instance—are not so well understood as timely ones, but they are *listened to* better. More precisely: we are never understood—and *hence* our authority . . . . (*TI* "Maxims" 15)

Furthermore, Nietzsche holds that "the significant human being gradually learns that *insofar as he produces an effect* he is a *phantom* in the heads of others" (*Effect a phantom, not reality* [*Der Wirkende ein Phantom, keine Wirklichkeit*], *AOM* 330). In other words, what impacts the other is the human being's becoming other (animal), his or her becoming a ghost, a specter, a phantom.[46] For a solitary person like Nietzsche, the knowledge that one's posthumous afterlife, one's life as a ghost in the head of others, which will affect others, is a true consolation:

The hermit [*Einsiedler*] speaks again. . . . But there are other ways and tricks for "wandering amongst," for "associating with," people: for instance, as a ghost . . . . The latter is the trick of *posthumous* people par excellence. ("And what were you thinking?" one of them said impatiently; "Would we wish to endure this estrangement, coldness, and sepulchral silence enveloping us, the entire subterranean, hidden, mute, undiscovered loneliness that we call life but might as well be called death unless we knew what will *become* of us and that it is only after death that we come into *our* life and become alive—oh, very much alive, we posthumous ones!") (*GS* 365).

Interestingly, throughout his work, Sartre also thematizes the intimate connection he sees between the promise of freedom as responsibility and the posthumous afterlife. The posthumous afterlife of the promise in Nietzsche is comparable to the posthumous afterlife of the writer's commitment to his or her age in Sartre. In Sartre, the posthumous effect of writing (*littérature engagée*) is exemplified by the myth of the Marathon Messenger:

It was said that the courier of Marathon had died an hour before reaching Athens. He had died and was still running; he was running dead, announced the Greek victory dead. This is a fine myth; it shows that the dead still act for a little while as if they were living. For a little while, a year, ten years, perhaps fifty years; at any rate, a *finite* period; and then they are buried a second time. This is the measure we propose to the writer: as long as his books arouse anger, discomfort, shame, hatred, love, even if he is no more than a shade, he will live. Afterwards, the deluge. We stand for an ethics and art of the finite. ("Writing for One's Age," 245)

For Sartre, the myth of the Marathon Messenger is valuable because it illustrates the meaning of responsibility.[47] When addressing the myth of the Marathon Messenger directly to the writer, Sartre does not seek to console him or her, like the "posthumous being" in Nietzsche's imaginary dialogue (*GS* 365). Instead, he wants to encourage the writer to take responsibility for his or her age. According to Sartre, for a writer, embracing responsibility is to write for his or her age: "not to reflect it passively" but "to want to maintain it or to change it, thus to go beyond it towards the future" ("Writing for One's Age," 243). What is crucial in the writer's investment [*engagement*] of him- or herself in the present age is that it be an investment for the benefit of the future. Responsibility for Sartre, as for Nietzsche, is, above all, responsibility for the future.

The similarities between the two thinkers on this topic do not end here. The temporality of responsibility in Sartre is comparable to the temporality of the promise in Nietzsche. For both authors, responsibility concerns a return of the future to the present. In Sartre's work, the future projection of the self is the "basis" to which one needs to "go back to" in order to interpret the meaning of the present (ibid., 243). For both authors, it is the (spectral) return of the future that gives meaning to the present. In other words, the present is meaningful only in light of its (possible) projection into the future. This is why, according to Sartre, "one cannot be a human being or become a writer without tracing a horizon line beyond oneself" (ibid.). The human being, by virtue of projecting itself beyond itself, must be conceived of as the center of the unexpected and the unforeseeable, or, in Nietzschean terms, as the miraculous (*SE* 1). However, what distinguishes Sartre's conception of responsibility is that it is a projection toward the future that overcomes the present. Both in Sartre and in Nietzsche it is through the overcoming, the going beyond oneself (and one's age), that one's anticipation of the future becomes effective. A promise of responsibility that does not result in the overcoming of the present is like an empty promise that does not hold what it promises. It is a promise that does not carry future life.

The overcoming of the present, the liberation of the present, further depends on a posthumous return of one's projection into the future. Responsibility as the double movement of a projection into and a return from the future requires the self to become spectral. In Sartre's terms, it requires a becoming other of the self (*se faire autre, se deliverer*), what I have been referring to as a becoming-animal of the self in Nietzsche. It is in the return of the other, the other that one has become in the investment of one's self in one's age, that one spectralizes the present and thereby effects the overcoming of the present. Derrida notes that if responsibility is understood as a relationship to the other as other, those to whom the "good news" is addressed have to be, in turn, spectral addressees (*des destinataires aussi spectreux*) or posthumous beings that are not yet alive, not yet born.[48] The relationship between the writer and those to whom she addresses her message becomes a spectralized relationship among posthumous phantoms in a virtual space. Following Derrida, one could say that Nietzsche's books are comparable to virtual spaces: They are written with the author's awareness of their posthumous effect and are addressed to future readers.

According to Sartre, the posthumous return of the future is reflected in the death of the Marathon Messenger. The death of the messenger does not imply the absolute loss of the message, because the message is transmitted even after death. The message stays alive through the survival of the event to come, namely, the victory of Greece, the liberation of Athens. The returning dead, the radically other, becomes the mediator of freedom, the carrier of future life. Moreover, the death of the Marathon Messenger expresses the idea that responsibility entails taking on risks, including the risk of death, which is the *"gage"* (stake) of the writers' *engagement*, or what responsibility for their age costs them. For both Sartre and Nietzsche, risk-taking is indispensable because the human condition obliges us to choose in ignorance: "it is ignorance which makes morality possible" ("Writing for One's Age," 242). "If we gambled on a sure thing," Sartre claims, "the risk would disappear; and with the risk, the courage, and the fear, the waiting, the final joy and the effort; we would be listless gods, but certainly not human beings" (ibid.). Responsibility cannot be attained through mastery and control over life, but rather rests on an affirmation of human finitude as the site of human greatness, that is, of the individual's will to self-responsibility and the courage to take risks.[49] The latter are expressed in the image of the Marathon Messenger's crossing of an unknown space, a space that contains routes but no destinations. His enterprise requires irrational perspicacity and the instinct of a blind person.[50] The writer who adopts the "measure" of the Marathon Messenger's courage must have qualities similar to those of Nietzsche's spiritual nomad who willingly exposes his life and thought to the outside, to that which comes toward the self from an other.[51] For both authors, freedom and responsibility are associated with instinct and intuition, rather than with reason and rationality. The figure of the sovereign individual in Nietzsche and that of the writer in Sartre resemble beings "without heads." They are like André Masson's Acéphale, guided entirely by their "guts": "I love him who has a free spirit and a free heart: thus his head is only the entrails of his heart, but his heart drives him to go under" (Z: 5 "Prologue").[52] Finally, the myth of the Marathon Messenger illustrates the idea that responsibility as a projection and an opening up of the future requires being ahead of, aside, and apart from one's age. It requires, in Nietzschean terms, that one be "untimely." The untimeliness of responsibility is yet another expression for responsibility as the becoming other (*se faire autre*) or the spectral, the becoming of a ghost or shadow of the self. After all, only a posthumous being who returns from the future as a ghost anticipates that which cannot be anticipated.

Nietzsche's vision of the future is that of the becoming overhuman of the human animal. The promise of this becoming has its greatest impact (*Wirkung*) as a spectator of and on the present. Only if announced by a returning ghost, like Nietzsche himself, does the vision of the becoming overhuman of the human being have an effect. The overhuman and the promise of its (be-)coming does not describe a reality or a given, but is always only an anticipation of the future that spectralizes the present, which puts the present in a critical light, thereby furthering the overcoming of the present in order to produce a "better" future. The promise of the overhuman in Nietzsche, his vision of the becoming overhuman of the human being, is effective because it is virtual, "*ein Wirken*" (an effect), and not "*eine Wirklichkeit*" (a reality) (*AOM* 330).[53]

3

Culture and Economy

One of Nietzsche's narratives about becoming overhuman takes the form of a vision of a "higher aristocracy" of the future (*WP* 866; 898). This vision has frequently been interpreted as if Nietzsche were offering a political program that pursues the implementation of "higher culture" by means of authoritarian politics of domination and exploitation.[1] The view that a politics of domination and exploitation is a means to achieve "higher culture" presupposes that politics, as an "inferior" means of culture, can be identified with culture. From this perspective, culture and politics both pursue the same aim—an ennobling elevation of the human being—and both seek to attain this aim by the same means: authority, hierarchy, and slavery. But, by falsely identifying culture and politics in Nietzsche's thought, this interpretation fails to recognize the crucial difference between culture and civilization that I emphasize throughout this book: Namely that politics not only is an "inferior" means of culture but also that it cannot adequately address the matters of culture (*KSA* 13:19[11]).[2]

I hold that the distinction between culture and civilization in Nietzsche is more fundamental than the distinction between culture and politics. The distinction between culture and civilization shows that there are two different, antagonistic ways in which human animal life can be politicized. On the one hand, there is the politics of civilization, and on the other, there is the politics of culture.[3] Whereas the politics of civilization institutes forms of social and political organization that require the disciplining and domestication of the animality of the human being, the politics of culture provides a reconceptualization of the relationship between life and politics that emancipates life from being the object of political domination. The objective of the politics of civilization is to produce a normalized society through the practice of domination and exploitation. In contrast, the objective of the politics of culture is to cultivate an aristocratic society through the revival of an antagonistic conception of public action (inspired by the Greek city-state and the city-state of the Renaissance) which fosters individual self-responsibility.[4] These two ways of politicizing life presuppose what could be called two different economies of life. In this chapter, I argue that the economy of civilization requires an exploitative relationship with animality, where the objective is to draw maximal utility from the human animal. The economy of civilization aims to preserve the group through an accumulation of resources, despite the fact that the cost is the enslavement of the individual. In contrast, the economy of culture seeks to overcome this form of enslavement. The economy of culture requires an expenditure of the community for the sake of individual plurality. The expenditures of culture are directed toward establishing forms of social and political life that are based on a free relationship to the other, which is beyond calculation.

My argument is based on an examination of Nietzsche's controversial claim that the realization of higher culture "needs slavery in some sense or other" (*BGE* 257). In order to understand the relationship between culture and slavery, I begin by distinguishing among the various uses of the term "slavery" found in Nietzsche's work. Nietzsche uses the term, first of all, to define a condition of human life. Human life is enslaving insofar as it is not self-sufficient, but subject to the necessities of life, such as self-preservation. In a second sense, the term "slavery" describes the character of human life as it unfolds in society. As I showed in the previous chapter, the human animal could not maintain the health of the singular and forgetful animal, and was drawn to seek the company of others in order to survive. Life in society with others is experienced as enslaving precisely because it is a reminder of the human animal's lack of self-sufficiency. Insofar as the project of civilization is aimed at solving the problem of necessity, slavery constitutes an aspect of civilization. On the contrary, culture takes up the problem of slavery in civilization with the aim of overcoming it and moving toward forms of sociability that are experienced as free, as a luxury rather than as an obligation or a need. Subsequently, I provide an analysis of Nietzsche's notion of an economy of life through a reading of examples from his early, middle, and late works.

These examples further support my claim that the rule of "higher culture" is incompatible with a politics of domination and exploitation.

Slavery in Some Sense or Other

When Nietzsche contemplates "the necessity for a new slavery," a "new type of enslavement" (*GS* 377) to further the cultivation of the human animal, he insists that the latter concerns the "entire animal 'human being'" (*BGE* 188).[5] This "new type of enslavement" conducive to the becoming of "higher culture" should not be confused with the enslavement of a majority for the sake of a minority. Nietzsche does not suggest that some should be subject to domination and exploitation for the benefit of others. Rather, he concludes that what is necessary for the elevation of the human animal is for the "entire animal 'human being'" to be subject to the moral discipline of civilization. The moral discipline of civilization, here, consists of an "enslavement of the individual," but this enslavement is for the sake of the preservation of the individual insofar as it is a "means for ensuring the duration of something beyond individuals" (*WP* 730). Nietzsche insists that a higher type of human being is possible "only through the subjection of the lower" (*WP* 660). I suggest that, in this citation, "higher" and "lower" refer to different stages in the development of human life. Whereas "lower" designates the process of civilization, "higher" designates the process of cultivation. The question is whether the "lower" (civilization) can become a means for the elevation of the "higher" (culture). In other words, the question of culture is "how could one sacrifice the development [*Entwicklung*] of the human kind to help a higher kind [*Art*] than the human being to come into existence?" (*WP* 859; *KSA* 12:7[6]), or, how can the long history of "moral improvement" in the human being become a means of cultivating a higher, freer type of human animal? Nietzsche's answer to this question is clear: Only insofar as civilization (moral discipline) calls for a countermovement that leads to its own overcoming does it become meaningful to culture, that is, to the cultivation of a higher type of human being (*KSA* 12:5[98]).

Before culture takes up this question, slavery is already a reality that inherently defines the process of human civilization and socialization. Nietzsche understands this process to be one of increasing enslavement insofar as the bonds of society (and of the state) are experienced by an animal which is forgetful and solitary as restrictions on its freedom.[6] As long as human beings live in civilized societies, they are subject to some sort of slavery because slavery defines life in society irrespective of whether that society has a liberal, socialist, or nationalist political orientation.

Nietzsche is particularly critical of the hypocrisy of socialists who promise the impossible: a "free society" (*GS* 356), a society free from slavery. He also distances himself from their faith in "the community as their *savior*" (*BGE* 202). Against socialists (and Christians), Nietzsche holds that by virtue of having become human in and through socialization, one no longer has the option of living in a society that is not enslaving.[7] But, if slavery is inherent to life in society, then the question becomes: In what sense does "higher culture" need "slavery in some form or other" (*BGE* 257)?

Besides the form of slavery inherent to civilization and socialization, Nietzsche contends that slavery defines human life at an even deeper, existential level. Human life is not self-sufficient but stands in need of protection and preservation. The latter need is particularly acute when life is threatened by "unfavorable circumstance," or, to use economic terms, when the will to power is short on reserves (*BGE* 262). The problem of necessity is the problem of civilization par excellence insofar as civilization is continuously struggling against the always latent threat of a state of necessity (*Notzustand*): "[H]uman beings are together there [the commonwealth] who are dependent on themselves and want their type to prevail, most often because they *have* to prevail or run the terrible risk of being exterminated" (*BGE* 262). The project of civilization addresses this problem by taking economical measures: "The will to accumulate power is special to the phenomenon of life, to nourishment, procreation, inheritance" and inherently belongs to "society, state, custom, authority" (*WP* 688). But since, for Nietzsche, "every living thing does everything it can not to preserve itself but to become more" (*WP* 688), when the human animal is subject to the need for self-preservation, it experiences this need as a restriction of its will to power. From the perspective of life as will to power, the need for self-preservation is enslaving.[8] To live only seeking self-preservation or, in economic terms, only seeking to get out of the red, is the most demeaning form of life because it is the most slavish, the least free form of life. Nietzsche regrets that this "is however what we all do for the greater part of our lives" (*SE* 5). Although human life "for the greater part" is defined by slavery, by working in order to make up a deficit, the question remains whether life as slavery (as debt) can be overcome—not indefinitely, because that is impossible, but at least temporarily. The historical moments when culture rules suggest that such an overcoming of slavery (debt) is possible. When culture is at its height and it rules, freedom from slavery is attained, if not indefinitely, then at least for a limited time (*BGE* 262).

In "Schopenhauer as Educator," Nietzsche claims that "higher culture" can only be attained on the basis of transcending "the struggle for existence," that is, life as self-preservation (*SE* 5). Throughout the text, he associates the "struggle for existence" with animal life and the attaining of a "higher culture" with a "truly human" form of life (*SE* 5). The conjunction of animality and self-preservation on the one hand, and of true humanity and culture on the other, has led many commentators to assume that culture in Nietzsche must denote an overcoming of animality.[9] In contrast, I argue that this reference to animality is a specific reference to the animality of the civilized human being, that is, to an animal that is inherently defined by its struggle for self-preservation. This "barbaric" kind of animality found in civilization has to be overcome in order to attain culture, but this overcoming depends on a return of animality understood as a force overfull with life, which carries the human being beyond its need for self-preservation. In my view, the animality of the civilized human being in "Schopenhauer as Educator" has strong affinities with what Nietzsche later refers to as "all-too-human." Therefore, as discussed in Chapter 1, culture must be understood as an overcoming of the all-too-human rather than an overcoming of the animal.

Throughout his work, Nietzsche uses images of fragmentation and completion to describe both the formations and transformation of human animal life in general and of the higher (overhuman) type in particular.[10] In my view, the image of the human being as a fragment concerns the question of whether slavery (incompleteness), as something that inherently belongs to human life, can be overcome (completed).[11] In his early work, Nietzsche defines culture as the conviction that:

> almost everywhere we encounter nature pressing towards the human being and again and again failing to achieve it, yet everywhere succeeding in producing the most marvelous beginnings, individual traits and forms: so that the human beings we live among resemble a field over which is scattered the most precious fragments of sculpture where everything calls to us: come, assist, complete, bring together what belongs together, we have an immeasurable longing to become whole. (*SE* 6)

The same idea persists in a text from his later work:

> Most human beings represent pieces and fragments [*Einzelheiten*] of the human being: one has to add them up for a complete human being to appear. Entire ages and people can be fragmentary [*Bruchstückhaftes*] in this sense. It is perhaps part of the economy of the

human development [*Entwicklung*] that the human being should develop piece by piece. (*WP* 881; *KSA* 12:10[111])

According to Nietzsche, the fragmentation and incompleteness that characterize human life are completed, become whole, through the appearance of "great human beings," that is, through the appearance of higher (over-human) natures:

> I teach: that there are higher and lower human beings and that a single human being can under certain circumstances justify the existence of whole millennia—that is, a full, rich, great, whole human being in relation to countless, incomplete, fragmentary human beings. (*WP* 997)

These exceptional human animals are miraculous (*Wundertiere*) (*BGE* 269) because, through them, one can see how far human life has developed: They are "milestone human beings who indicate how far humanity has advanced so far" (*WP* 881).

Some commentators argue that incompleteness in Nietzsche defines the form of life of the majority; that the incompleteness of the many is the price that must be paid for the completeness of the few, select, noble human beings. I hold the view that while incompletion inherently belongs to civilization, completion belongs to culture. Under the rule of civilization, the full realization of human animal life is impossible. Its development needs to remain fragmentary and incomplete in order to secure not only the preservation of human animal life as such but also that of any given social or political form. Incompleteness must, in this sense, be understood as the aim of every society:

> A division of labor among the affects within society: so individuals and classes produce an incomplete, but for that reason a more useful kind of soul to what extent certain affects have remained almost rudimentary *in every type within society.* (*WP* 719)

Incompleteness, like slavery, defines society in general and is not a specific feature of an aristocratic society. On the contrary, an aristocratic society, as Nietzsche imagines it, is the kind of society that wishes to overcome the incompleteness produced by socialization and civilization and promote greatness conceived as a "range [*Umfänglichkeit*] and multiplicity [*Vielfältigkeit*] in the human beings' wholeness [*Ganzheit*] in manifoldness [*Vielen*]" (*BGE* 212).

In the end, however, this appearance (*Erscheinen*) of wholeness and completeness is only an illusion (*Schein*). The becoming of human animal life, in general, and the becoming of the higher (overhuman) type, in particular, knows neither beginning nor end. It is not a teleological assembling of incomplete fragments directed at an endpoint that is achieved when the whole appears to be complete. On the contrary, the becoming of a higher (overhuman) type, like the becoming of human animal life, is an open-ended assembling of fragments that cannot be completed, that cannot become whole.[12] From the perspective of life and becoming, culture is never an actual becoming whole, but always only an "immeasurable longing to become whole" (*SE* 6). Culture sees in this longing for wholeness a desire that should not be consumed, for it stimulates the further self-overcoming of the human. Consequently it seems that, in the end, human animal life, whether under the rule of civilization or under the rule of culture, cannot be completed or become whole. Rather, it must always remain fragmentary and incomplete. Nevertheless, there remains one significant difference between the incompleteness of culture and that of civilization. While civilization sees, in the incompleteness of the human being, reductions and lowerings that are of instrumental value to the preservation of the group, culture sees, in the incompleteness of the human being, the production of "the most marvelous beginnings" and the "most precious fragments," which are signs of its inherent plurality (*Vielartigkeit*) (*SE* 6).

The Economy of Life

Examples from Nietzsche's different phases as an author show that he formulates the question of how to overcome slavery in economic terms. In "Schopenhauer as Educator," this question takes the form of a narrative on the economy of nature.[13] Nietzsche claims that nature is inherently prodigal and extravagant, not economical and calculating: "Nature is a bad economist: its expenditure is much larger than the income it procures; all its wealth notwithstanding, it is bound sooner or later to ruin itself" (*SE* 7). Nature's problem is that it would like to be generous and charitable, for "nature wants always to be of universal utility" (*SE* 7), but it does not know how to employ its forces economically so as to produce the best and most suitable means and instruments for the welfare of everyone and everything.[14] In other words, nature would like to be egalitarian, but it is not. Its incapacity to provide equally for all is what causes its suffering and melancholy (*SE* 7). Nietzsche believes that the only way to redeem nature and make up for its "weakness" is to further the pluralization of singularity through culture.

Culture aims at the cultivation of the genius and, therefore, privileges the singular individual over the group. What characterizes the genius of culture, as discussed before, is that she spends and wastes herself. The genius of culture gives herself over to all when nature fails to be generous and charitable to all. The overall goal of culture is:

> to acquire power [*Macht*] so as to aid the evolution of the *physis* and to be for a while the corrector of its follies [*Thorheiten*] and ineptitudes [*Ungeschicklichkeiten*]. At first only for yourself, to be sure; but through yourself in the end for everyone [*Alle*]. (*SE* 3)

Nietzsche detects this strategy in nature itself, in particular, in the life of plants and animals. Nature, according to this view, is indifferent to the individual and always strives only for the health, life, and future of the whole. Nature only brings forth its highest examples in order to redeem itself for being incapable of giving equally to all. The bringing forth of its highest examples is a means of overcoming its own economic limitations so as to carry all of nature beyond itself (*SE* 6). Nietzsche suggests adopting this strategy and investing in the cultivation of singularity as a means of overcoming the inequality found in nature.

In *Beyond Good and Evil*, Nietzsche elaborates on this economic problem by distinguishing between an economy of civilization, oriented toward conservation, and an economy of culture, oriented toward free expenditure.[15] According to this distinction, civilization is a means used by nature to impose a stricter economy on itself. Civilization reduces expenditures, narrows perspectives, and limits horizons:

> Consider any morality with this in mind: what there is in it of "nature" teaches hatred of the *laissez aller*, of any all-too-great freedom, and implants the need for limited horizons and the nearest tasks— teaching the *narrowing of our perspective*, and thus in a certain sense stupidity as a condition of life and growth. (*BGE* 188)

Nietzsche sees, in this self-imposed narrowing, a valuable aspect of the economy of civilization and wants to redeem this stupidity as a form of animal intelligence necessary to the enhancement of life.[16] The stupidity of civilization reveals civilization as still part of animal life. It reflects the need for what Nietzsche calls a horizon in "On the Use and Disadvantage of History for Life." Only within a horizon can the human animal focus on one aim, one direction, and one belief. The economy of civilization, therefore, stands not only for a moment of reduced creativity and limited pluralization of forms of life but also for a moment of accumulation of life forces that is a precondition for the free expenditures of culture.

In the late *Nachlass*, becoming overhuman is identified with the free expenditure of culture that rests on and lives off civilization. The latter is understood as the "transformation of the human being into a machine":

> As the consumption of the human being and of the human beings becomes more and more economical and the "machinery" of interests and services is integrated ever more intricately, a counter-movement is inevitable: I designate this as the secretion of a luxury surplus of the human being: it aims to bring to light a stronger species, a higher type that arises and preserves itself under different conditions than those of the average human being. My concept, my metaphor for this type is, as one knows, the word "overhuman." (*WP* 866)

Nietzsche accepts the exploitation of the human animal by the economy of civilization only on the condition that the latter is counteracted by culture, that is, by the aim to overcome exploitation toward free expenditure. He is critical, however, of political mass ideologies, whether socialist, liberal, or nationalist, because these ideologies appear to be instituting an exploitation that pursues no higher aim beyond itself (*WP* 866).[17] Mass political ideologies lack the insight that the further enhancement of life is inherently dependent on culture: "Our society of today only *represents* culture, the cultured human being is lacking" (*WP* 883). Lack of (a politics of) culture and economic optimism are symptoms of declining life characteristic of modern mass political ideologies.[18] The latter exemplify the risk that the economy of civilization may lead to increasing expenditures of everybody, amounting to a "collective loss."[19] Despite their optimistic outlook and promise to bring about "the greatest happiness of the greatest number," mass egalitarian ideologies make the human individual weak, sick, and unfit for freedom. Civilization's repressive and restrictive techniques are meaningful and praiseworthy only insofar as the economy of self-preservation is not understood as an end in itself, but always only as a means to accede to what Bataille calls the "insubordinate function of free expenditure."[20] In contrast, what distinguishes the economy of culture is that it opens up a free relationship to the other that is not dominated by utilitarian considerations. As I argued in the previous chapter, this freedom is essentially characterized as a freedom to lose. It reflects the constitution of a positive property of loss from which nobility, honor, and rank may arise in an order that gives expenditure beyond utility its significant value and meaning. Nietzsche refers to this order as that of the "higher aristocracy" of the future (*WP* 866).

Perhaps surprising to some readers, Nietzsche contends that the democratic movement of the nineteenth century provides a suitable ground for such a future "higher aristocracy."[21] He believes that the democratic movement will lead, despite itself,[22] toward a higher and nobler type of human animal:

> But while the democratization of Europe leads to the production [*Erzeugung*] of a type that is prepared for *slavery* in the subtlest sense, in single, exceptional cases the *strong* human being will have to turn out stronger, richer than perhaps ever before. . . . (*BGE* 242)

The democratization and homogenization of Europe should not be obstructed, but hastened (*WP* 898), precisely because it provides the best conditions for the ennobling pluralization of singularities.[23] The reason is that Nietzsche sees in the democratic movement not an overcoming of slavery ultimately, because a political event cannot solve an "existential problem" (*SE* 4), but a "new and sublime development of slavery" (*WP* 954).

He further sees in the democratic movement the "heir of the Christian movement," that is, the continuation of civilization, moralization, and humanization by means of domination and exploitation (*BGE* 202). His views on the democratic movement echo his praise for and critique of the project of civilization. The democratic movement is a movement of civilization and, in this sense, also betrays all the features of its politics of cruelty. Even though the means of civilization in the age of democratization have become more refined and more subtle, this does not mean that the overall techniques of civilization in this age have become less cruel. On the contrary, slavery, in the age of democratization, is a "piece of barbarism" compared, for example, with slavery in the Greek polis (*WP* 758). After all, the only thing that has been refined is the subtlety with which modern mass societies (based on utilitarian morality) draw maximum utility from human animal life. Mass political ideologies and their political economies transform the human animal into a machine (*WP* 866). They equip the human animal with the "virtues" of a machine: uniformity, regularity, and efficiency in view of maximal exploitation (*WP* 888; *TI* "Skirmishes" 37). What Nietzsche is primarily concerned with is whether the development of a maximal economy of use in mass societies can build up enough tension to provoke a countermovement that will overtake this "new type of enslavement" and lead to the cultivation of a higher and freer type of human animal. I suggest that aphorism 262 in *Beyond Good and Evil* provides an answer to this question.

The Rule (*Herrschaft*) of Higher Culture

In aphorism 262 of *Beyond Good and Evil*, Nietzsche claims that the rule of "higher culture" succeeds when the circumstances are favorable or, economically speaking, when there is no power deficiency. When the economy of civilization has accumulated enough wealth, the need for self-preservation ceases to dominate the forms of production and sociability. Then:

> At one stroke the bond and constraint [*Zwang*] of the old discipline [*Zucht*] are torn: it no longer seems necessary, a condition of existence—if it persisted, it would only be a form of *luxury*, an archaizing *taste*. (*BGE* 262)

When the "old discipline" is no longer needed to preserve life, when life has overcome need, then life is no longer experienced as slavery and debt, but as surplus, luxury, and overflowing (*Überfluss*).

The surplus of power and wealth that enhances the development of culture directly affects the way in which life is being politicized. Under the rule of civilization, "education" is essentially conceived as "the means of ruining the exceptions for the good of the rule," and "higher education" is essentially conceived as "the means of directing taste against the exceptions for the good of the mediocre" (*WP* 933). But, under the rule of culture, education becomes "a hothouse of the luxury cultivation of the exception, the experiment, of danger, of the nuance" (*WP* 933). The luxury cultivation of culture can no longer be contained by "the bonds and constraint [*Zwang*] of the old discipline [*Zucht*]" and exceed them as the infinite pluralization and variation of human animal life. That "higher culture" lives beyond morality explains why Nietzsche believes that "the greatest moments of culture have always been, morally speaking, times of corruption" (*KSA* 13:16[10]).

Furthermore, the luxury cultivation of culture manifests itself as the opening up of a public space (*Schauplatz*) within which the human individual can dare again to become visible as animal and as forgetful, as singular and as unique:

> Suddenly appears on the scene [*Schauplatz*] in the greatest abundance and magnificence; the singular individual [*Einzelne*] dares to be singular [*einzeln*] and different [*sich abzuheben*]. (*BGE* 262)

This public space of culture is modeled after the agora, the marketplace of the Greek polis, where people meet to compete and challenge each other to accrue greater virtue.[24] The politics of culture opens up a public space that is not within the state's reach. This is why Nietzsche contends that "all great times of culture were politically impoverished times" (*KSA* 13:19[11]; see also *TI* "Germans" 4).

The emphasis on the suddenness and the unforeseeable change of luck associated with culture's rule indicates that the rule of civilization should not be misunderstood as a conscious and calculated saving up of reserves in preparation for a better future. Instead, culture exists beyond mastery and control, despite the fact that Nietzsche himself, at times, seems to call for exactly the opposite, namely, a conscious provocation and manipulation of favorable circumstances.[25] The becoming of culture is a matter of luck and "lucky circumstances" (*Glücksfälle*) (*BGE* 262), even if one has "five hundred hands" to "tyrannize the moment" (*BGE* 274).

Nietzsche describes culture's rule as a dangerous and uncanny "turning point of history" (*Wendepunkt der Geschichte*):

> We behold beside one another, and often mutually involved and entangled, a splendid, manifold, junglelike growth and upward striving, a kind of *tropical* tempo in the competition to grow, and a tremendous ruin and self-ruination, as the savage egoisms that have turned, almost exploded, against one another wrestle "for sun and light" and can no longer derive any limit, restraint, or consideration from their previous morality. It was this morality itself that dammed up such enormous strength and bent the bow in such a threatening manner; now it is "outlived" [*überlebt*]. The dangerous and uncanny point has been reached where the greater, more manifold, more comprehensive life *lives beyond* the old morality; the "individual" appears, obliged [*genöthigt*] to give itself its own laws and to develop its own arts and wiles for self-preservation, self-elevation, self-redemption. (*BGE* 262)

What distinguishes the rule of culture is the dangerous and uncanny entanglement of what otherwise appears to be separate and incompatible, namely, the joining of growth and ruin, life and death, sublimity and monstrosity, gain and loss, surplus and deficit. All of these distinctions are momentarily blurred and one sees everything turning into its opposite, or, rather, one sees everything metamorphosing into something else. At the turning point of history, life cannot preserve itself and, even if it could, it could not do so for long. It is always already turned toward its death. The freedom achieved through culture manifests itself as gain and surplus, but because it also manifests itself as unlimited expenditure, every gain or surplus is always already wasted or spent. It is a freedom that is always already too fragile to maintain itself. The freedom of culture is uncanny and dangerous because the liberation it achieves is everywhere evident, yet it is so fleeting that it vanishes before it can be stabilized into a form of life.

As a consequence, the high point of culture can only be a turning point and must be short-lived for economic reasons.[26] The decline of culture is unavoidable: it is as sudden as the rise of culture, but not as unpredictable. Once the culture's surplus of power and wealth is exhausted, a "new morality" and "discipline," a new economy of self-preservation, is needed. When the "old morality" has been outlived, when the singular and forgetful individual is "obliged [*genöthigt*] to give itself its own laws and to develop its own arts and wiles for self-preservation, self-elevation and self-redemption" (*BGE* 274), it cannot maintain itself for very long, no longer than a lifetime, for everything beyond an individual's lifetime requires civilization, socialization, and humanization (*WP* 730). As soon as the singular and forgetful one has spent its excess of life and power, it is confronted with a new state of necessity and stands in need of a new calculating and self-preserving economy.

Ultimately, however, the rule of culture is sure to be short-lived because culture, like civilization, is not self-sufficient. Culture and civilization depend upon each other for their preservation and elevation. Culture does not stand on its own, but stands on the "old morality": "It was this morality itself that dammed up such enormous strength and bent the bow in such a threatening manner" (*BGE* 274). Once the ties of the "old morality" are broken, once culture stands alone, the expenditures of the animals' freedom and creativity will soon be exhausted. What is then needed is a new beginning, a new saving up of strength and power. But this new rule of civilization to come draws its life from the rule of culture that preceded it, just as much as the rule of culture draws its life from the old rule of civilization that preceded it.[27] In other words, just as culture depends and stands on a prior disciplining and exploiting of the animal through civilization, so civilization depends and stands on the prior liberation and elevation of the animal through culture. Although culture and civilization are mutually dependent upon the agonistic relationship they have with one another, Nietzsche assigns priority to culture over civilization. Culture is the source of the meaning and significance of civilization: culture gives the economy of civilization an aim. Only culture has the power to break open the economic cycle of civilization: culture overcomes a form of production defined by exploitation and domination.

4

Giving and Forgiving

Nietzsche's opposition to Christian morality is commonly thought to be an aspect of his immorality or nihilism. In this chapter, I argue that Nietzsche rejects Christianity in favor of a positive morality that has its source in the practice of gift-giving. Gift-giving is of great importance to Nietzsche—especially in *Thus Spoke Zarathustra*—for its ability to promote freedom and justice. Not only does gift-giving liberate both the one who gives and the one who receives, but it is also a way to do them justice. In this sense, the virtue of gift-giving belongs to a positive conception of morality that is political, revealing an aspect of gift-giving that has not been sufficiently taken into account by recent commentaries on *Thus Spoke Zarathustra*. By "political," I mean a conception of justice that gives priority to the relationship with the other. Nietzsche's vision of justice, like Rawls's, rejects utilitarian conceptions on the grounds that they reduce the other to a permutation of the self.[1] What distinguishes Nietzsche's anti-utilitarian conception of justice from other critiques of utilitarianism is that it does not base the relationship to the other on the notion of a social contract in which the self and the other have a reciprocal relationship, such that the terms for the relationship that the self offers to the other must be terms that the other can envisage offering back to the self. For Nietzsche, justice is structured by gift-giving, where the relationship between the self and the other is not symmetrical.[2] In such an asymmetrical relationship, what the self gives to the other and the other to the self stand as acknowledgments of the distance and difference between the self and the other. There is also a second sense in which Nietzsche's virtue of gift-giving is political. Namely, insofar as it revives the Greek conception of political friendship, *philia politiké*, it can be understood as a bond between equals who stimulate each other to develop their own virtue. Greek political friendship preserves the other's freedom through distance, while continually challenging the other to enhance that freedom through struggle and competition (*agon*). According to Nietzsche, these political friendships constituted by gift-giving stand in opposition to the Christian idea of fellowship or companionship based on the love for one's neighbor.

The practice of gift-giving contrasts sharply with the Christian practice of forgiveness. Nietzsche provides two primary reasons for contesting the latter. First, Christian forgiveness fails to break the cycle of revenge. It does not redeem the past, but rather stirs up feelings of resentment, hatred, and revenge. Second, Christian forgiveness does not enhance human animal life, but poisons it (*AOM* 224; *BGE* 168).[3] In contrast, Nietzsche only approves of those practices of forgiveness that are fueled by gift-giving and that redeem the past. The overcoming of revenge is crucial to the possibility of a positive notion of forgiveness insofar as Nietzsche sees, in the desire for revenge, an obstacle to the development of forms of sociability that are based on gift-giving. I argue that the double failure Nietzsche detects in the Christian practice of forgiveness results from denying the human being's animality a productive role in the constitution of sociability. In particular, Christian forgiveness ignores the value and significance of what Nietzsche refers to as the forgetfulness of the animal. Animal forgetfulness is not only indispensable to breaking the cycle of revenge, but also to establishing a relationship with the other that is based on gift-giving. Because the forgetfulness of the animal is an essential component of Nietzsche's analysis of forgiveness as gift-giving, I contend that the gift-giving virtue should be understood as an animal rather than a human virtue.[4] Likewise, friendship, as Nietzsche conceives it in opposition to Christian love for one's neighbor, has its source in the antagonism between human and animal life forces. The idea that the animal (the other) challenges the development of greater freedom and virtue is best illustrated by the friendship between Zarathustra and his animals.

In current ethical reflection, Derrida's recent work on forgiveness and friendship bears the strongest affinity with Nietzsche's critique of Christian morality.[5] In my discussion of Nietzschean morality, I will point out the similarities I see between Nietzsche and Derrida on giving, forgiving, and friendship.[6] Arendt is the other major contemporary thinker who has thought about political justice and political friendship by offering an original synthesis of Nietzschean motives and Judeo-Christian forgiveness. I, therefore, contrast Nietzsche's and Derrida's conceptions of forgiveness with Arendt's conception of forgiveness as an alternative to judgment and punishment.[7] I begin with Nietzsche's general critique of the Christian practice of forgiveness and proceed to a discussion of the relationship among forgiveness, redemption, and revenge. The chapter ends with a reading of the gift-giving virtue in *Thus Spoke Zarathustra,* understood as political friendship and an alternative to Christian neighborly love, which gives rise to freedom and justice.

Nietzsche's Critique of Forgiveness

Recognizing that no political community will be possible until the cycle of revenge is broken, the Christian practice of forgiveness seeks to break this cycle by redeeming both the individual and the community, thereby helping them cope with a past plagued by guilt and discord. It promises that a wrong can be undone by being first regretted and then forgiven. When a demand for forgiveness is answered with forgiveness, those who committed a trespass in the past are supposedly reconciled with both themselves and others. In this account, the possibility of forgiveness, reconciliation, and redemption depends upon institutions such as the Christian church and, more recently, the modern state, which claims the power to reconcile and to redeem by granting forgiveness. According to both Nietzsche's and Derrida's critiques of Christian forgiveness, the modern state does not redeem the individual and the community, but only encourages their dependence on institutions that claim for themselves the power to administer forgiveness. Both authors suspect that behind this claim to power lies the desire to dominate and control individual and communal life.

Nietzsche criticizes Christian forgiveness as an economic transaction constituted by the attribution of guilt and moral responsibility on the one hand, and as the restitution of justice through judgment and punishment on the other (*GM* I, II; *TI* "Errors" 7). In so doing, the practice of forgiveness establishes an inequality between the one who forgives and the one who is forgiven. It presupposes a moral superiority that authorizes the one who forgives to judge and evaluate the one who asks for forgiveness in order to determine whether the latter can, in fact, be granted forgiveness. But, when forgiveness reflects a claim to power as well as a practice of judgment and punishment, it increases the individual's and the community's debt to the past and widens the (economic, moral, and political) gap that exists between those who forgive and those who need to be forgiven. Accordingly, it fails to achieve redemption and reconciliation. Derrida agrees with Nietzsche on this point. He claims that "what makes the

'I forgive you' sometimes unbearable or odious, even obscure" is that "it is often addressed from the top downward."[8] As a consequence, Derrida argues that forgiveness should not be "the correlate to a judgment and the counter-part of a possible punishment."[9]

Nietzsche questions whether we are able to forgive at all, given that no one has the right to judge or to punish:

> How can one forgive them at all, if they know not what they do! One has nothing whatever *to* forgive.—But does a human being ever know completely what it does? And if this must always remain at least *questionable*, then human beings never do have anything to forgive one another and pardoning is to the most rational human being a thing impossible. Finally: *if* the ill-doers really did know what they did—we would have a right to *forgive* them only if we had a right to accuse and to punish them. But this we do not have. (*WS* 68)

From Nietzsche's point of view, the Christian doctrine of forgiveness is irrational in the sense that it holds people responsible for their actions even if they are unaware of them or their consequences. If it is "at least questionable" whether anyone ever fully knows what he or she is doing, then it stands to reason that no one needs to be forgiven. Furthermore, even if a person knows what they are doing and even if they have committed some kind of transgression, no one has the right to forgive because no one has the right to judge or to punish the other: "No one is accountable for his deeds, no one for his nature: to judge is the same thing as to be unjust. This also applies when the individual judges himself" (*HH* 39).

Although Arendt, in agreement with Nietzsche, argues that the consequences of human actions are unpredictable and lie outside of the human agent's conscious control, she bases her notion of forgiveness on the idea that humans are responsible for the consequences of their actions. Arendt identifies "Jesus of Nazareth" as "the discoverer of the role of forgiveness in the realm of human affairs."[10] In agreement with the Christian doctrine, she claims that humans need to be forgiven because "they do not know what they do":

> The possible redemption from the predicament of irreversibility—of being unable to undo what one has done though one did not, and could not, have known what one was doing—is the faculty of forgiveness.[11]

Forgiveness and punishment have something in common insofar as "men are unable to forgive what they cannot punish and are unable to punish what has turned out to be unforgivable."[12]

In contrast with Arendt's position, Nietzsche argues that when forgiveness is based on judgment and punishment, it generates injustice rather than justice:

> The error lies not only in the feeling "I am accountable [*verantwortlich*]," but equally in that antithesis "I am not, but somebody has to be."—This is, in fact, not true: the philosopher thus has to say, as Christ did, "judge not!" and the ultimate distinction between philosophical heads and the others would be that the former desire *to be just* [*gerecht*], the others *to be a judge*. (*AOM* 33)

While Arendt sees, in the figure of Jesus, the discoverer of forgiveness, understood as the correlate of judgment and punishment, Nietzsche sees the figure of Jesus as an example of the kind of forgiveness that "bears not only all punishments but also all guilt": [13]

> I do not like your cold justice; and out of the eyes of your judges there always looks the executioner and his cold steel. Tell me, where is that justice which is love with open eyes? Would that you might invent for me the love that bears not only all punishments but also all guilt! Would you might invent for me the justice that acquits everyone, except him who judges! (*Z* "On the Adder's Bite")

Nietzsche rejects justice as punishment and judgment because it degrades and belittles, unless a punishment "is not also a right and an honor for the transgressor" (*Z* "On the Adder's Bite"), that is, something that elevates and distinguishes both the one who punishes and the one who is punished. Ultimately, however, it is best to refrain from judgment and punishment altogether because "it is nobler to declare oneself wrong than to insist on being right—especially when one is right. Only one must be rich enough for that" (*Z* "On the Adder's Bite").[14] Nietzsche warns against those "in whom the impulse to punish is powerful," and against those "who speak of their justice," for they are those who "lack more than honey" because they have nothing to give (*Z* "On the Tarantulas"). Their quest for justice is a pursuit for revenge, for "when they say 'I am just [*gerecht*],' it always sounds like 'I am revenged [*gerächt*]!' With their virtue they want to scratch out the eyes of their enemies, and they exalt [*erheben*] themselves only to humble others [*erniedrigen*]" (*Z* "On the Virtuous"). In the end, the problem with the Christian practice of forgiveness is that, since it fails to be giving, it can never truly forgive. Nietzsche claims to "despise those who do not know how to forgive," perhaps because they are those who do not know how to give (*KSA* 10:15[2]).

The Christian practice of forgiveness presupposes the doctrine of "free will" (*TI* "Errors" 7). According to this doctrine, humans are always already in the wrong and guilty because they act freely and in accordance with their will. According to Nietzsche, the doctrine of free will "has been invented essentially for the purpose of punishment, that is, of *finding guilty*" (*TI* "Errors" 7). Its ultimate purpose is to satisfy its authors' "desire to create for themselves a *right* to ordain punishment—or their desire to create for God a right to do so . . ." (*TI* "Errors" 7). Offering an alternative to the Christian doctrine of "free will" and its corresponding practice of judgment and punishment, Nietzsche puts forward the idea of the innocence of becoming, according to which "[n]o deed can be undone by being regretted, no more than by being 'forgiven' or 'atoned for,' for this would require being a theologian who believes in a power that annuls guilt" (*WP* 235). Instead, "we immoralists prefer not to believe in 'guilt' " (*WP* 235) but in the idea that "everything is innocence":

> The complete unaccountability [*Unverantwortlichkeit*] of the human being for its actions and its being is the bitterest draught the man of knowledge [*Erkennende*] has to swallow if he has been accustomed to seeing in accountability [*Verantwortlichkeit*] and duty the patent [*Adelsbrief*] of his humanity [*Menschenthums*]. . . . As he loves a fine work of art but does not praise it since it can do nothing for itself, as he stands before the plants, so must he stand before the actions of the human being and before his own. . . . Everything is necessity—thus says the new knowledge: and this knowledge itself is necessity. Everything is innocence: and knowledge is the path to insight into this innocence. (*HH* 107)[15]

Humans are like animals and plants: they lack the freedom to act at will. In his account, actions should not be thought of as willed or as conscious (*TI* "Errors" 7). Nietzsche insists that it is only because "the human being *regards* itself as free, not because it is free, that it feels remorse and pangs of conscience" (*HH* 39):

> The evil acts at which we are now most indignant rest on the error that he who perpetrates them against us possesses free will, that is to say, that he could have *chosen* not to cause us this harm. It is this belief in choice that engenders hatred, revengefulness, deceitfulness, all the degrading our imagination undergoes, while we are far less censorious towards an animal because we regard it as unaccountable. (*HH* 99)

The point of Nietzsche's critique is that the Christian doctrine of "free will" and its corresponding idea of moral responsibility fail to generate genuine responsibility because they deny the innocence inherent to plant, animal, and human life. The human being recovers its animal innocence when it recognizes in an "action compelled (*zwingt*) by the instinct of life" and carried out with "joy [*Lust*]" the "right [*rechte*] action [*Tat*]" (*A* 11).[16]

The idea of the innocence of becoming is inseparable from the idea that "nothing exists apart from the whole" and that therefore "the fatality of . . . [human] nature cannot be disentangled from the fatality of all that which has been and will be" (*TI* "Errors" 7). The fact that everything belongs to the whole means that there exists nothing that can judge, measure, compare, and condemn parts of the whole, for that would be to judge, measure, and condemn the whole (*TI* "Errors" 7). This is impossible, for it would require adopting a perspective commensurate with "God's point of view," which is outside and above the whole. One of Nietzsche's main objections to Christian morality and its practice of forgiveness is that it presupposes the existence of a moral standard (God) outside and above life, from which to evaluate life. Yet every perspective on life, including a moral one, is always also a perspective of life, that is, a perspective that is part of life, not outside and above it.

The insight that every perspective is a perspective of life is important precisely because it restores the innocence of becoming and, with it, the innocence of the human animal, that is, the fact that no one can any longer be made accountable (*TI* "Errors" 7). It shows, first, that the "problem of the value of life" is an inaccessible problem (*TI* "Errors" 7); and, second, that "even that *anti-nature morality* which conceives God as the contrary concept to and condemnation of life is only a value judgment on the part of life" (*TI* "Morality" 5). The question is no longer whether an act is "good or evil" since, from the perspective of life, "every action is of identical value at root" (*WP* 235). Instead, the question is whether an act enhances, augments, and diversifies life or, conversely, whether it declines, debilitates, and condemns life (*TI* "Morality" 5). For Nietzsche, the problem with the practice of forgiveness is to find out whether it is a gift-giving practice that augments life, or whether it is a gift-giving practice that poisons (*Gift*) and, ultimately, destroys life. Nietzsche's analysis of forgiveness, redemption, and revenge suggests that the Christian practice of forgiveness fails to be genuinely giving or, in other words, its gifts are poisonous presents that stir feelings of hatred, resentment, and revenge.

The Redeeming Power of Animal Forgetfulness

In *On the Genealogy of Morals,* Nietzsche argues that the foundation and preservation of institutions such as the Christian church and the modern state coincide with the breeding of a particular kind of animal, namely, a social and civilized animal that is inherently reliable, predictable, and devoted to the good of society (*GM* II). Furthermore, he maintains, as I show in Chapter 2, that this breeding process is an inherently violent one directed against the animality of the human being and, in particular, against its animal forgetfulness (*GM* II: 1). According to Nietzsche's genealogical discourse, the transformation of the human animal into a social and civilized being was achieved through the imposition of what he calls the memory of the will (*Gedächtnis des Willens*) on the forgetfulness of the animal. This memory is of such great value to the above-mentioned institutions because it functions as a means of mastery and control over the life of the individual and the community. Interestingly, the memory underlying the practice of Christian forgiveness, as Nietzsche critically depicts it, reflects the same features as the memory of the will, suggesting that Christian forgiveness is, like the former, a means to control and manipulate human animal life. In order to counteract the memory of the will, it is necessary to reevaluate the role played by animal forgetfulness in the constitution of forms of sociability (*GM* II: 1). As I argued in Chapter 2, the promise of the sovereign individual constitutes a counterforce to the memory of the will, precisely because this capacity results from the successful recovery of animal forgetfulness. Similarly, Nietzsche argues that there is a direct relationship between the overcoming of revenge and the recovery of animal forgetfulness (*GM* I: 10). The distinction between slave and noble morality and their different perspectives on the past illustrates this idea.

Nietzsche defines slave morality as a moral perspective on past suffering that ignores the ways in which human animals need forgetfulness and, consequently, generates resentment and desire for revenge on the past (*GM* I: 10). In contrast, noble morality reflects what could perhaps be called an artistic perspective on past suffering that is defined by the power of forgetfulness. The noble person, as Nietzsche genealogically reconstructs it, is "incapable of taking its enemy, its accidents, even its own misdeeds seriously for very long" (*GM* I: 10). Such an attitude

> is the sign of rounded natures with a superabundance of power which is flexible, formative, healing and can make one forget (a good example from the modern world is Mirabeau, who had no recall for the insults and slights directed at him and who could not forgive, simply because he—forgot). (*GM* I: 10)

Those who have recovered the forgetfulness of the animal are those who do not dwell on the past. They feel no resentment for the past because they are powerful enough to form and transform past suffering into future life (*HL* 6). In *Thus Spoke Zarathustra*, Nietzsche establishes a similar connection between forgetfulness and the overcoming of revenge, commenting that "[g]reat indebtedness does not make grateful but vengeful; and if a little charity [*Wohltat*] is not forgotten, it turns into a gnawing worm" (*Z* "On the Pitying").[17]

The inability of the slave type to forget prevents this morality from coming to terms with the past and its "it was":

> 'It was'—that is the name of the will's gnashing of teeth and most secret melancholy [*Trübsal*]. Powerless [*Ohnmächtig*] against what has been done, he is an angry spectator of all that is past. . . . This, indeed this alone, is what *revenge* is: the will's ill will [*Widerwille*] against time and its "it was." (*Z* "On Redemption")

As such, Christian forgiveness achieves the opposite of what it promises: instead of redeeming the past and opening it up to the possibility of a new beginning, forgiveness stirs feelings of resentment and hatred for the past. Rather than releasing the past into the flow of becoming and augmenting the past by carrying it into the future, forgiveness reaffirms the "it was" and prevents its transformation into "thus shall it be" (*WP* 593; see also *Z* "On Redemption"; *Z*: 3 "Of Old and New Tablets").

For Nietzsche, such transformation requires not only memory but also forgetfulness. Forgiveness redeems the past, overcomes revenge, and generates a new beginning only when it is constituted by a form of memory that is actively forgetful, instead of opposed to forgetting.[18] Nietzsche ascribes great importance to animal forgetfulness because he sees in the latter a force that has the power to subvert a moral perspective on the past that considers the past necessary, stable, and fixed. Animal forgetfulness makes it possible to see the past as contingent, fluid, and reversible. Transforming the "it was" into "thus shall it be" redeems the past by turning past contingencies into future necessities: instead of having the past impose itself on the future with necessity, the future imposes itself on the past with necessity. From the perspective of the freedom of re-beginning, necessity does not lie in the past, but always only in the future: "All 'it was' is a fragment, a riddle, a dreadful accident—until the creative will [*schaffende Wille*] says to it, 'But thus I willed it'" (*Z* "On Redemption").[19] From this perspective, how one sees one's present crucially affects the very meaning of one's past, and since the future is yet to come, neither the significance nor the meaning of the past is settled. The narrative that relates the past to the present, and the present to the future, is always alterable, and it is precisely because the meaning and the direction of the past can be altered that the past can be redeemed.

Like Nietzsche, Arendt also argues that forgiveness has the power to break the cycle of revenge because it reflects an act of memory that initiates a new beginning. She holds that revenge always acts in the form of reacting to an original trespass. It is an automatic, calculable reaction to transgression, and therefore it stands in direct opposition to the idea that humans are the origin of unexpected action and, thus, inherently free. In contrast to revenge, forgiveness can never be predicted. It is a thing that "arrives, that surprises, like a revolution, the ordinary course of history, politics and the law."[20] It acts anew, unexpected and unconditioned by the act that provoked it. This is why, for Arendt, forgiveness, unlike any other reaction, retains something of the original character of action. It is not imposed on action from the outside, but is itself an articulation of natality.[21]

Some commentators argue that since the capacities Arendt ascribes to forgiveness are similar to those Nietzsche ascribes to forgetfulness, forgiveness in Arendt should be understood as a form of forgetfulness.[22] Contrary to this view, I hold that forgiveness in Arendt is a faculty of the human mind that reflects a capacity for memory and thus cannot be understood in terms of Nietzschean animal forgetfulness. For Arendt, forgiveness is an articulation of natality because forgiveness is a form of memory that, like the promise, has the capacity to bring the human agent to the past from which it began and from which it can begin again. What distinguishes the promise from forgiveness is that, while the promise is a form of memory that seeks control over the future, forgiveness is a form of memory that seeks control over the past.[23] Arendt privileges the backward glance over the forward glance, the "it was" over the "thus shall it be" and memory over forgetfulness because, in her view, the past is necessary and, in its necessity, reassuring. The backward glance gives the human being the feeling of having at least some control over the contingency of time, rather than being completely exposed to it. In contrast, she sees in the forward glance a threatening perspective that confronts the human being with its impotence, its incapacity to foresee and to control the contingencies of time. On this point, Arendt's and Nietzsche's positions seem to be irreconcilable. While Arendt privileges the past over the future, her overall concern is with the problem of how to secure the past against the future. Nietzsche, on the other hand, privileges the future over the past. His overall concern is with the problem of how to secure the future against a past that obstructs its future enhancement.

Derrida

Derrida, like Nietzsche, argues that giving and forgiving involve both memory and forgetfulness. For him, there is a sense in which forgiveness is incompatible with forgetfulness, precisely because what is erased, repressed, and forgotten can never lead to forgiveness. A past trespass can only be forgiven if it remains unforgotten, inscribed within memory. But because there can be no gift without forgetfulness, there is another sense in which forgiveness is incompatible with memory:

> For there to be gift, not only must the donor or the donee not perceive or receive the gift as such, have no consciousness of it, no memory, no recognition; he or she must also forget it right away, "à l'instant," and moreover this forgetting must be so radical that it exceeds even the psychoanalytical category of forgetting. . . . So we are speaking here of an absolute forgetting—a forgetting that also absolves, that unbinds absolutely and infinitely more, therefore than excuse, forgiveness or acquittal.[24]

Derrida argues that a gift without ambivalence, a gift that is not a poisonous present but a good, is possible only "in a time without time." The event of the gift must happen in such a way that the forgetting forgets itself. At the same time, however, this forgetfulness, without being something present, presentable, determinable, sensible, or meaningful, is not nothing either. For Derrida, the question is how can one want to forget, how can one want not to keep. I suggest that Nietzsche's analysis of the gift-giving virtue in *Thus Spoke Zarathustra* offers an answer to this question.[25]

Forgiveness and Political Friendship

Before addressing the question of how it is possible to desire to forget and to desire not to keep, it needs to be emphasized that the kind of forgetfulness that is at stake in giving and forgiving should not be confused with what both Nietzsche and Derrida reject as civilizational forgetfulness. When forgiveness is instrumentalized, when it becomes a means to a higher (moral or political) end, such as the preservation of an individual's "good conscience" or the unity of the nation-state, then what we are dealing with is not genuine forgiveness but "simulacra, the automatic ritual, hypocrisy, calculation and mimicry."[26] The main issue in Nietzsche's and Derrida's critiques of forgiveness concerns the question of how to counteract civilizational forgetfulness by bringing back an idea of forgiveness that is "a gracious gift, without exchange, and without condition"[27] and, *print* therefore, constitutes a return to the past that truly generates a new beginning. This requires, in Derrida's terms, taking forgiveness "beyond the juridical-political instance," "beyond the nation state,"[28] or, in Nietzsche's terms, "beyond good and evil."

Interestingly, both authors locate this "beyond" in a relationship that engages two singular individuals. This move signifies neither a retreat to the private sphere nor a reduction of the problem of forgiveness to a moral or ethical one. On the contrary, any relationship that engages two singularities designates a *philia politiké*, or a political friendship whose political significance derives from the fact that it may be the only kind of relationship that generates freedom and justice. In Nietzsche, forgiveness is possible only between friends, that is, between equals[29] who have overcome the need to judge and evaluate each other:

> And if a friend does you evil [*Übles*], then say: "I forgive you what you did to me; but that you have done it to *yourself*—how could I forgive that?" Thus speaks all great love: it overcomes even forgiveness and pity. (*Z* "On the Pitying")

What distinguishes forgiveness between friends is that they respect each other's singularity, but they do so at a distance. A friend knows that there can be no such thing as equal retribution, for "what you do nobody can do to you in return" (*Z*: 4 "On Old and New Tablets"). There is nothing more foreign to friendship than the desire to confess and to be confidential. Opposed to the need to enter into language as a realm of common and rational measures, the preferred manner of communication between friends is nonverbal and silent: "*Silentium.*—One should not talk about one's friends: otherwise one will talk away the feeling of friendship" (*AOM* 252).[30] Silence protects the irreducible singularity of the friend and preserves the other's essential secret: "It is difficult to live with people because it is difficult to be silent" (*Z* "On the Pitying"). After all, speech has the power to ruin, corrupt, degrade, and belittle the greatness Nietzsche attributes to friendship. Language not only constitutes a danger to friendship but also does not lend itself to giving and forgiving insofar as they are essentially silent and solitary acts: "Oh, the loneliness [*Einsamkeit*] of all givers [*Schenkenden*]! Oh, the taciturnity [*Schweigsamkeit*] of all who shine!" (*Z* "The Night Song").

Like Nietzsche, Derrida holds that "forgiveness must engage two singularities" and that this is why "the anonymous body of the State or of a public institution cannot forgive."[31] Furthermore, he holds that forgiveness calls for a kind of personal interaction that cannot be mediated by language.[32] Friendship, giving, and forgiving, can only be exercised "in a sort of counter-culture of knowing how to keep silent."[33] Insofar as both Nietzsche and Derrida take friendship, giving, and forgiving outside of conceptual language, their ideas of forgiveness stand in direct conflict with those of Hegel, who argues that confession and forgiveness reflect the ethical urge for the individual to enter into language, to manifest itself within and through language understood as a rational measure held in common with others.[34]

It is worth noting that Hannah Arendt also understands forgiveness as "an eminently personal (though not necessarily individual or private) affair in which *what* was done is forgiven for the sake of *who* did it."[35] According to her, forgiveness arises from respect understood as a *philia politiké*:

> [A] kind of "friendship" without intimacy and without closeness; it is a regard for the person from the distance which the space of the world puts between us, and this regard is independent of qualities which we may admire or of achievements which we may highly esteem.[36]

Despite this broad agreement among Arendt, Nietzsche, and Derrida, for Arendt, friendship and the world it institutes is a human (maybe all-too-human) world. Nietzsche's and Derrida's accounts of friendship are, by contrast, explicitly antihumanistic insofar as both authors hold that friendship occurs only through an encounter with the other's (animal) otherness. Friendship opens up a world to the human, but that does not mean that it is constituted by the human or that it belongs to the human.

For Nietzsche and Derrida, the question of whether forgiveness must be limited to a relationship between friends leads directly to the question of whether it must be limited to humans, that is, to animals who speak. Derrida asks whether one should refuse the experience of forgiveness to those who do not speak. Or, to the contrary, should one see in silence the proper element of forgiveness?[37] Furthermore, the question of the relationship between language and forgiveness touches directly on the question of the animal and human properties of forgiveness. Contrary to the prejudice found in the Judeo-Christian tradition of forgiveness, Derrida upholds the "undeniable possibility and necessity" that there is a type of forgiveness that is not verbal and not human:[38] rather, Derrida refers to a silent, animal forgiveness that manifests all the features of what he defines as pure and unconditional forgiveness and what Nietzsche defines as the highest virtue: "the gift-giving virtue" (*Z*: 1 "On the Gift-Giving Virtue").[39]

The gift-giving virtue, like all noble virtues (*GM* I: 10), arises from an affirmation of the animality of the human being. It is distinguished by the fact that it encourages friendship between humans and animals, opening an arena of competition that enhances the development of greater freedom and justice. The figure of Zarathustra illustrates the idea that gift-giving is possible only on the basis of a friendship between humans and animals. Throughout *Thus Spoke Zarathustra,* Nietzsche not only refers to Zarathustra's gifts as honey, but also notes that Zarathustra receives this honey from his animal friends who have gathered it for him so that he can offer it to his hosts, strangers and friends alike.[40] Furthermore, Zarathustra's example suggests that he can become a giver of gifts only by having the courage to enter into an agonistic competition with the animals, affirming them as enemy-friends worthy of respect and, hence, as adversaries who induce his own virtue to grow stronger as a result of this rivalry:

> But courage and adventure and pleasure in the uncertain, in the un-dared—*courage* seems to be the human beings' whole prehistory. He envied the wildest, most courageous animals and robbed all their virtues: only thus did he become human. This *courage*, finally refined, spiritualized, spiritual, this human courage with the eagles' wings and serpents' wisdom—*that*, it seems to me, is today called— *Zarathustra!* (*Z* "On Science")

Zarathustra's gift-giving virtue exemplifies that the courage to surround oneself with animals is essential to the development of virtue and, in particular, to that of the gift-giving virtue.

In *Thus Spoke Zarathustra,* Nietzsche uses gold (both the metal and the color) as a metaphor to describe the gift-giving virtue.[41] Gold serves as "an image of the highest virtue" because it is, like the gift-giving virtue, "uncommon [*ungemein*] and useless [*unnützlich*] and gleaming [*leuchtend*] and gentle [*mild*] in its splendor" (*Z*: 1 "On the Gift-Giving Virtue"). In what follows, I discuss Nietzsche's conception of justice in relation to the four main characteristics that gold shares with the gift-giving virtue. The intimate relationship between gift-giving and justice in Nietzsche is reflected by his use of the expression "*rechtschaffendes Gastgeschenk*" (*Z* "The Welcome"), that is, a gift that creates justice, *schafft Recht*; a gift that hosts, accommodates, and receives the other justly. The term "*rechtschaffendes Gastgeschenk*" expresses the idea that justice is a gift-giving virtue and, conversely, that gift-giving is justice. From this perspective, justice presupposes not only that one has something to give but also that one desires not to keep it. It conflicts with a strictly economic idea of distributive justice, which, according to Derrida, transforms the gift into an "exchangist, even contractual circulation."[42]

The Gift-Giving Virtue and Singularity

The gift-giving virtue reflects a relationship between the self and the other in which justice signifies reverence and respect for the singularity of the self and the other. The gift-giving virtue is uncommon (*ungemein*) because it is inherently unique, exceptional, and incomparable. It reflects the individual's irreducible singularity and distinctiveness. The gift-giving virtue shares this feature with virtue in general: "your virtue is yourself and not something foreign" (*Z* "On the Virtuous"). Virtue must be one's "*own* invention," one's "*own* most personal defense and necessity," for "in any other sense it is merely a danger" (*A* 11). This is why Nietzsche believes that:

> One should defend virtue against the preachers of virtue: They are its worst enemies. For they teach virtue as an ideal for *everyone*; they take from virtue the charm of rareness, inimitability, exceptionality and unaverageness—its aristocratic magic. (*WP* 317)

The gift-giving virtue stands out and alone, over and above all measures. Since it exceeds all measures, it "permits no one to judge it, because it is always virtue for itself" (*WP* 317). The gift-giving virtue is uncommon not only because it cannot be measured but also because it does not measure;[43] it not only withdraws itself from judgment but also does not judge. The gift-giving virtue does not provide a moral standard against which one can measure and compare other virtues and moral practices. Virtue "does not communicate itself" (*WP* 317). Virtue cannot be shared in the way that, for example, a moral standard can be shared with others. As such, the uncommonness of the gift-giving virtue signifies its incommunicability and the fact that it cannot be named.[44]

The gift-giving virtue is, furthermore, a carrier of justice insofar as it is inherently antiutilitarian.[45] This is why:

> Virtue has all the instincts of the average human being against it: it is unprofitable, imprudent, it isolates; it is related to passion and not very accessible to reason; it spoils the character, the head, the mind—according to the standards of the mediocre human being; it rouses to enmity toward order, toward the lies that are concealed in every order, institution, actuality—it is the worst of vices, if one judges it by its harmful effect upon others. (*WP* 317)

From the perspective of the average human being, the gift-giving virtue is unprofitable. It neither fulfills a particular function or purpose nor satisfies a particular interest or need. Nietzsche insists, through the words of Zarathustra, that "there is no reward and paymaster" for virtue "[a]nd verily, I do not even teach that virtue is its own reward" (*Z* "On the Virtuous"). The virtuous and noble, as Nietzsche imagines them, know that "whatever has a price has little value" (*Z*: 12 "On Old and New Tablets"), or, conversely, that "the value of a thing sometimes lies not in what one attains with it, but in what one pays for it—what it *costs* us" (*TI* "Skirmishes" 38). The virtuous and noble receive life as a gift and understand their own life as a response (-ibility) and a giving back to life:

> This is the manner of the noble souls: they do not want to have anything for nothing; least of all, life. Whoever is of the mob wants to live for nothing; we others, however, to whom life gave itself, we always think about what we might best give in return. And verily, that is a noble speech which says, "What life promises us, we ourselves want to keep to life." (*Z*: 5 "On Old and New Tablets")[46]

In their view, returning to life what one has received from life exceeds a calculation of costs and benefits. The noble and virtuous do not give back because they feel guilty or obliged by a debt. Rather, they give back for no reason, innocently, as it were.[47] They do not know how to keep themselves, but always only how to offer and spend themselves.

For Nietzsche, the uselessness of the gift-giving virtue takes justice beyond any utilitarian calculus (*HH* 48). It reflects an overfullness of life, an overflowing, wasteful, and dissipating force that gives gratuitously, free from the expectation of receiving material or spiritual compensation in the future:

> I love him whose soul squanders [*verschwendet*] itself, who wants no thanks and returns none [*nicht zurückgiebt*]: for he always gives away [*schenkt*)] and does not preserve [*bewahren*] himself. (*Z*: 4 "Prologue")[48]

The gift-giving virtue disrupts economies of self-conservation in order to give without calculation of costs or benefits. The genius "in work and deed" shows that the act of gift-giving is careless and imprudent:

> The instinct of self-preservation is as it were suspended; the overwhelming [*übergewaltige*] pressure of the energies [*Kräfte*] which emanate [*ausströmmenden*] from him forbid [*verbietet*] him any such care [*Obhut*] and prudence [*Vorsicht*]. (*TI* "Skirmishes" 44)

Nietzsche contrasts those who possess the gift-giving virtue with those whose virtue makes them small and in whom virtue is the carrier of injustice, for they practice virtue only in order to profit, in order to receive greater benefits in return. When, for example, the latter praise, they pretend to be giving back, when in truth they want more gifts (*Z*: 1 "On Virtue That Makes Small"; see also *KSA* 12:9[79]).

The Gift-Giving Virtue and Other-Directedness   *"Live like the Sun"*

The gift-giving virtue turns the self toward the other and outside of itself, where it is "gleaming" (*leuchtend*) like the sun. The gift-giving virtue establishes a relationship between the self and the other in which justice is not a function of mutual self-preservation but a function of the expenditure of the self in which the self simultaneously asserts itself and "goes-under" before the other. In his prologue, Zarathustra praises the "golden sun," the "great star," for having shown him that to give means to "go under [*untergehen*]" and "to carry everywhere the reflection of your light" like the sun carries everywhere the reflection of its light (*Z*: 1 "Prologue"). Zarathustra loves those who live like the sun, that is, those "who do not know how to live, except by going under [*welche sich nicht bewahren wollen*], for they [*Untergehenden*] are those who cross over" (*Z*: 4 "Prologue").[49] Gift-giving shares this aspect with virtue in general because "virtue is the will to go under" (*Z*: 4 "Prologue").

Like the movement of light, the movement of gift-giving overflows from its source and moves toward the other, spreading itself evenly everywhere without drawing distinctions among people or places. The metaphor of gleaming light indicates that gift-giving de-centers the individual self in order to open it up to a relationship with the other that is free from social, political, or moral classifications. As such, gift-giving is a love that knows no distinctions, that is excessive and all inclusive, unlike the Christian "love of the One" in which Nietzsche sees "a barbarism; for it is exercised at the expense [*auf Kosten*] of all others" (*BGE* 67). Gift-giving love overcomes the Christian "love of the One." It is a love "beyond good and evil" (*BGE* 153).

The difference between Christian love and gift-giving love is paramount in the conversation between Zarathustra and the saint (*Z*: 2 "Prologue"). When the saint asks Zarathustra why he is descending from his mountain, Zarathustra replies: "I love the human being" (*Z*: 2 "Prologue"). The saint recalls that it was love for the human being that led him into solitude. For the saint, love for the human being is a thing of the past; in solitude he has found love for God. At this point in the conversation Zarathustra realizes that while the saint was driven away from the human beings out of love, he is drawn toward the human beings by the gift-giving virtue, and so he quickly adds: "Did I speak of love? I bring the human beings a gift" (Z: 2 "Prologue").[50] Furthermore, while the saint's love for God separates him from the human beings and confirms that he does not need the human beings anymore (Z: 2 "Prologue"), the love of gift-giving has provoked a different change (*Verwandlung*) in Zarathustra (Z: 1, 2 "Prologue"). It has led him to overcome the belief that an individual can be self-sufficient. Zarathustra no longer believes that the self-sufficiency of the solitary one stands higher than friendship (GS 61).[51] The gift-giving virtue leads Zarathustra out of solitude and toward the other, toward the affirmation of his need for entering into a gift-giving relationship with others. However, this affirmation of need should not be misunderstood: when Zarathustra exclaims that he needs hands outstretched to receive his gift, the need at stake should not be confused with the neediness of those who are too poor to give or of those who give alms. Zarathustra confirms that he gives no alms: "[f]or that I am not poor enough" (Z: 2 "Prologue"). In contrast, Zarathustra sees his poverty reflected in the fact that he cannot not give: "This is my poverty that my hands never rest from giving" (Z "The Night Song").

In praising the sun, Zarathustra calls it an "over-rich star" (Z: 1 "Prologue"), indicating that gift-giving occurs always only through an abundance, a surplus, and an exuberance (*Überfluß*) of the self. Zarathustra exemplifies this idea when he compares himself to "a bee that has gathered too much honey" and that needs "hands outstretched to receive it" (Z: 1 "Prologue").[52] Zarathustra has reached saturation (*Überdruss*); he has accumulated so many riches that these riches aspire to be distributed and given out. His suffering from saturation reflects the impatience of the one who wants to give, that is, to destroy the boundaries that are too tight to contain his riches.

The idea of gift-giving as an overflowing (*überfliessen*) and going-under (*untergehen*) of the self signifies not only that gift-giving cannot be understood as an exchange of objects or as an exchange between subjects but also that justice cannot be given a contractual basis. After all, what flows over to the other is something that resists reduction to the status of a subject or object.[53] Gift-giving cannot be understood as an exchange of objects because, to give, essentially, means to give who one is rather than what one possesses. Zarathustra sees this desire to give who one is reflected in his disciples:

Verily, I found you out, my disciples: you strive, as I do, for the gift-giving virtue. . . . This is your thirst: to become sacrifices and gifts yourself; and this is why you thirst to pile up all the riches in your soul. (*Z:* 1 "On the Gift-Giving Virtue")[54]

Gift-giving presupposes a readiness to sacrifice one's life, "to live on and live no longer" for the sake of virtue (*Z:* 4 "Prologue"; see also, in comparison, *TI* "Skirmishes" 38). In *Assorted Opinions and Maxims*, Nietzsche already wonders whether every act, moral or immoral, is not self-sacrifice simply by virtue of the fact that every act presupposes an involvement of the self:

Do you think that the mark of the moral action is sacrifice?— But reflect whether sacrifice is not present in *every* action that is done with deliberation [*Überlegung*], in the worst as in the best. (*AOM* 34)

Although Nietzsche repeatedly speaks of the gift as a sacrifice (*Z:* 4 "Prologue"; *Z:* 1 "On the Gift-Giving Virtue"), it is important to note that he distinguishes his idea from the Christian understanding of the morally good act as an act of self-sacrifice.

In "The Honey Sacrifice," Zarathustra confesses that his speaking of sacrifices is mere "cunning" (*List*): "Why sacrifice? I squander what is given to me, I—squander it with a thousand hands; how could I call that sacrificing?" (*Z* "The Honey Sacrifice"). The crucial difference between squandering and sacrifice in the Christian sense is that while the former is constituted by egoism, the latter is constituted by selflessness.[55] Whereas the squanderer is full of him- or herself and therefore rich in gifts, the one who sacrifices him- or herself is selfless and thus has nothing to give. Nietzsche regrets:

that everything great in the human being has been interpreted as selflessness, as self-sacrifice for the sake of something else, someone else, that even in the man of knowledge, even in the artist, depersonalization has been presented as the cause of the greatest knowledge and ability. (*WP* 296)

Rejecting the idea that "what makes an act good is that it is unselfish" (*Z* "On the Virtuous"), Zarathustra teaches his disciples to let "your self be in your deed as the mother is in her child—let that be *your* word concerning virtue" (ibid.). What hides behind the idea of "selflessness" as exemplified in the Christian notion of love for one's neighbor is a lack of self, an impoverished self: "You flee to your neighbor from yourself and you want to make a virtue out of it: but I see through your 'selflessness' " (*Z* "On Love of the Neighbor"). Their love of the neighbor is nothing but an attempt to compensate for their own interior emptiness. In contrast, it is not the selflessness (*selbstlos*) of an act, but its fullness of self that distinguishes it as virtuous. Zarathustra praises the selfishness of his disciples, their insatiable striving for "treasures and gems," their forcing "all things to and into themselves" as "whole and holy," for he believes this egoism to be inseparable from their insatiable desire "in wanting to give" (*Z*: 1 "On the Gift-Giving Virtue"). What distinguishes the egoism of the squanderer is that it results in an excessive overflowing and explosion of the self that de-centers and destroys the self in order to enrich the other (*TI* "Skirmishes" 44).

Nietzsche compares the overflowing of the self in the act of squandering to the natural movement of a river that overflows its banks. Both movements are "involuntary [*unfreiwillig*]"; they cannot be traced back to an intentional subject, a conscious decision, or a willful act. Throughout his work, he describes the absence of an intention, a consciousness or a reason at the source of gift-giving, in terms of the forgetfulness of the animal. In the prologue, Zarathustra confirms the intimate relationship between giving and forgetfulness: "I love the one whose soul is overfull so that he forgets himself, and all things are in him: thus all things spell his going under" (*Z*: 4 "Prologue"). In agreement with Nietzsche, Derrida insists that the gift can take place "only along with the excessive forgetting or the forgetful excess."[56] The direct involvement of gift-giving with forgetfulness suggests that what "acts" or is active in gift-giving is the forgetfulness of the animal. Accordingly, gift-giving for Nietzsche, and perhaps also for Derrida, should be understood as an animal rather than a human virtue. The possibility of gift-giving depends on something other and more than itself: on the recovery of animal otherness as an overfull force of life that allows the individual to enter into a gift-giving relationship with others.

The Gift-Giving Virtue and Distance

Finally, the gift-giving virtue is a relationship between the self and the other in which justice is liberating for both because it is nonpossessive. Gift-giving constitutes a flowing over of the self to the other, which is free from the desire to dominate and possess the other. The image of gold expresses this idea because, like gift-giving, it is "gentle [*mild*] in its splendor" (*Z*: 1 "On the Gift-Giving Virtue"). Whereas justice is usually thought to be what keeps people bound together, justice, as Nietzsche understands it, is what establishes the distance that protects the self from being appropriated by the other's claim for unity. Gift-giving is gentle (*mild*) for it is practiced with the awareness that it always stands in danger of losing the "shame" (*Z* "The Night Song") needed to preserve a "distancing relationship on the basis of which there is something to honor in virtue" (*WP* 317). As such, gift-giving protects both the one who gives and the one who receives from being made small by virtue (*Z*: 1–3 "On Virtue That Makes Small"). The giver of gifts approaches the other always only at a distance and with reverence (*Ehrfurcht*) for the other's inaccessible distinctiveness and irreducible singularity. Gift-giving, therefore, not an exchange based on reciprocity and symmetry or comparison and mutual sharing because this exchange seeks to keep the other in the relationship. Instead, for Nietzsche, gift-giving is the basis of a just relationship with the other precisely because it constitutes an inherently nonunitary relationship to the other.

Nietzsche warns not to give in to proximity and identification, to the fusion or the permutation of you and me but, instead, to keep distance between the self and the other, for he sees, in the proximity of the neighbor, a ruse of property and appropriation. Such a desire for ownership and unity hides behind the Platonic idea of justice as a "giving to each his own." Nietzsche replies to Plato with a pun: "But how could I think of being just through and through? How can I give each his own? Let this be sufficient for me: I give each my own" (*Z* "On the Adder's Bite"). According to Nietzsche, the desire for ownership also hides behind "the things people call love":

> Our love for our neighbor—is it not a craving for new *property*? . . . When we see someone suffering, we like to use this opportunity to take possession of him; that is for example what those who become his benefactors and those who have compassion for him do, and they call the lust for new possessions in them "love"; and their delight is like that aroused by the prospect of a new conquest. (*GS* 14)

Contrary to the Christian notion of love for one's neighbor (*Nächstenliebe*), Nietzsche upholds the love that relates friends, for the latter overcomes the "greedy desire of two people for each other" and moves toward a "new desire and greed, a shared higher thirst of an ideal above them," namely, that of friendship (*GS* 14). In *Thus Spoke Zarathustra*, Nietzsche returns to this idea by prescribing friendship, "flight from the neighbor and love of the farthest [*Fernsten-Liebe*]," as an antidote to love for one's neighbor (*Z* "On Love of the Neighbor").

In Nietzsche, a "distancing relationship" between the one who gives and the one who receives takes the form of a friendship, understood as an agonistic competition between opponents who challenge each other to greater virtue.[57] In the agonistic confrontation between friends, winning is not central. The adversaries are not to be destroyed, but affirmed. Their fight is not undertaken in the spirit of mistrust, but reveals the aggression shown to a rival of whom one is proud and whom one loves and respects:

> The heroic consists in doing a great thing . . . without feeling oneself to be in competition *with* others *before* others. The hero always bears the wilderness [*Einöde*] and the sacred, inviolable borderline [*unbetretbaren Grenzbezirk*] within him wherever he goes. (*WS* 337)[58]

Friendship is a relationship that does not make singularities common to each other. What friends have in common is what distinguishes them. What they share is what cannot be shared. Friendship stands for the love of the other, where love does not lead to the fusion and confusion of me with you.[59] Friendship protects the plurality of the friends by affirming that the respective ways of two singularities are irreducibly distinct.[60] Friends are against each other, which literally means to be at the same time the closest (*gegen*) and the furthest apart (*gegen*) from each other. Friendship overcomes difference and distance while, at the same time, preserving it. Accordingly, what reveals the friends' affinity and relatedness to each other is not the way they approach each other, but the way they part from each other (*AOM* 251):[61]

> Humanity in friendship and mastery [*Meisterschaft*].—"If you are going towards the morning I shall draw towards evening"—to feel thus is a high sign of humanity in closer association [*Verkehre*] with others: in the absence of this feeling every friendship, every discipleship and pupilage, becomes sooner or later a piece of hypocrisy. (*AOM* 231)

Zarathustra's departure from his disciples also exemplifies this idea (*Z*: 3 "On the Gift-Giving Virtue"). What distinguishes friends is that they do not subordinate themselves to any authority, but mutually share and offer to each other their freedom. Among friends, the ruling principle is not that of the reciprocity of charity, but that of the absolute probity of its members without hidden thoughts and interests. What binds friends to each other is a gift-giving that stimulates the friends' self-overcoming.

This is why the gift-giving virtue is, like all virtues, before all "delight in war and victory" (*TI* "Skirmishes" 38) and, as such, presupposes suffering, struggle, and a striving for power:

Not contentment [*Zufriedenheit*], but more power [*Macht*]; *not* peace at all, but war; *not* virtue, but proficiency [*Tüchtigkeit*] (virtue in the Renaissance style, *virtù*, virtue free of moralic acid). (*A* 2)

Nietzsche describes the gift-giving virtue as a "power" (*Macht*), a "dominant thought" (*herrschender Gedanke*) that is inseparable from a will "to command all things" (*Z*: 1 "On the Gift-Giving Virtue"; see, in comparison, *Z* "On Self-Overcoming"). Zarathustra sees this will in his disciples for they "must approach all values as a robber"; they "force [*zwingt*] all things to and into themselves," but only so that they can flow back out of their "wells [*Borne*]" as "the gifts of their love" (*Z*: 1 "On the Gift-Giving Virtue"). Nietzsche contrasts their will to power with that of the "small men [*Menschen*] of virtue" who steal because they cannot rob: "And when you receive it is like stealing, you small men of virtue; but even among rogues, *honor* says: 'One should steal only where one cannot rob'" (*Z*: 3 "On Virtue That Makes Small"). The virtuous are creators of values who confront the task of giving a new "meaning to the earth" (*Z*: 2 "On the Gift-Giving Virtue").[62] This task requires them to be courageous, to be "fighters" who break old tablets and replace them with new ones (*Z*: 2 "On the Gift-Giving Virtue"). The striving for power reflected in the gift-giving virtue, however, is not a striving for power over others. On the contrary, the gift-giving virtue overcomes such forms of power and domination toward greater freedom.

According to Nietzsche, a bond that inspires the other's liberation is achieved by offering oneself as an example of life and thought. In *Thus Spoke Zarathustra*, Nietzsche recounts that it is the sight of Zarathustra's gift-giving virtue that inspires the higher human beings (*Z* "The Welcome"). Zarathustra inspires by making others see how he lifts himself up. The aim is not to directly impose a message upon the other, but to content oneself with the offering of an image of an admirable way of life, such that only those who have the eyes to see it are those who also have the hands to receive it. The figure of the self-healing physician exemplifies this idea: "Physician, help yourself: thus you help your patient too. Let this be his best help that he may behold with his own eyes the one who heals himself" (*Z*: 2 "On the Gift-Giving Virtue"). Gift-giving does not generate dependency but freedom in the other; it thus conflicts with both giving alms and begging: "But beggars should be abolished entirely! Verily, it is annoying to give to them and it is annoying not to give to them" (*Z* "On the Pitying"; see also *Z* "The Last Supper"). Both giving alms and begging are practices that bind those who receive in such a way that they remain dependent on those who give or, rather, on those whose gifts are poisoning them. Ultimately, their charity fails to be giving.

In order that the gift not become part of the logic of power and domination, or of appropriation and exploitation, it is necessary for the gift-giving virtue to pass unrecognized. The sign of virtue is that "it does not desire to be recognized" (*WP* 317). The figure of Zarathustra, the giver of gifts, illustrates this idea when he addresses his disciples by saying that: "I like to give as a friend to friends. Strangers, however, and the poor may themselves pluck the fruit from my tree: that will cause them less shame" (*Z* "On the Pitying").[63] For there to be a gift, giving and receiving should not be perceived either by the giver or by the receiver. The image of the tree and the plucking of its fruits shows that the giver of gifts gives without causing shame, without humiliating and without belittling, because she gives without being recognized (ibid.; see also *D* 464). In accordance with this idea, Derrida holds that a true gift "ought not appear as gift: either to the donee or to the donor."[64] The problem of recognition, the perception of the meaning or the intention of the gift, is that it reflects a movement of temporalization that "always sets in motion the process of the destruction of the gift: through keeping, restitution, reproduction, the anticipatory, expectation or apprehension that grasps or comprehends in advance."[65] This is yet another reason why there can be no gift without what Derrida calls "excessive forgetting or the forgetful excess";[66] or without what I refer to as the forgetfulness of the animal in Nietzsche.

In Chapter 1, I argued that the recovery of animality and animal forgetfulness should not be confused with the voluntary act of bringing back the animal. Rather, it must be understood in terms of a chance encounter that requires patience, readiness, and attentiveness, so that animality may be grasped when it comes forward to be encountered. In *Thus Spoke Zarathustra*, Nietzsche calls this chance encounter "the great *Hazar*" (*Z* "The Honey Sacrifice"). Zarathustra's waiting for the advent of an event, for the moment when he will go under like the sun, exemplifies the idea that the gift is an event, or, in the words of Derrida, that there is "no gift without the advent of an event, no event without the surprise of the gift."[67]

At the end of the first book, Zarathustra separates from his friends and returns to solitude. He still has things to tell them and give them, and he asks himself, "[w]hy do I not give it? Am I stingy?" (*Z* "The Stillest Hour"). The reason for not giving what he has to give is not that Zarathustra is stingy, but that the right moment for giving has not yet come. He described this moment earlier as the "great noon," "when the human being stands between the animal and the overhuman" (*Z*: 3 "On the Gift-Giving Virtue"). Later, in "The Honey Sacrifice," Zarathustra follows the suggestion of his animal friends and climbs up the mountain to offer the honey sacrifice. Once he has climbed the mountain, Zarathustra confirms that he is waiting for the sign that the time has come for his descent and going-under. He describes himself as patient and impatient at the same time, as oversaturated with gifts. He is like the cup that wants to overflow but lacks what will finally make it flow over (Z: 1 "Prologue"). Zarathustra knows that it all depends on the "great *Hazar*" (Z "The Honey Sacrifice"). He reassures himself that "[o]ne day it must yet come and may not pass. . . . Our great *Hazar*: that is our great distant human kingdom [*Menschenreich*], the Zarathustra kingdom of a thousand years" (Z "The Honey Sacrifice"). In Zarathustra's kingdom of freedom and justice, human beings will relate to each other through gift-giving; but since gift-giving is a contingent event, the freedom and justice generated by gift-giving lack an absolute foundation. Consequently, freedom and justice cannot be achieved once and for all, but call for an open-ended struggle undertaken by those who are willing to fight to attain this goal.

5

Animality, Creativity, and Historicity

In this chapter, I consider one of Nietzsche's untimely considerations (*Betrachtung*), "On the Use and Disadvantage of History for Life," in order to explain the importance of animality and animal forgetfulness in Nietzsche's conception of history.[1] In the recent literature on this essay, one can distinguish two basic interpretative approaches to Nietzsche's remarks on animality and animal forgetfulness. The first emphasizes the difference between human and animal life, contrasting the animal's forgetfulness and a-historicity with the human being's memory and historicity. The second emphasizes the continuity between animal and human life, linking animal forgetfulness and a-historicity to human memory and historicity.[2] The interpretation I offer falls within the second approach, according to which a consideration (*Betrachtung*) of human life is inseparable from a consideration (*Betrachtung*) of animal life. The historicity of the human life form and the human being's memory are neither radically distinct nor separable from the a-historicity and forgetfulness of the animal. In fact, they reveal human life to be an instance of the historical becoming of the totality of life.

In the recent reception of "On the Use and Disadvantage of History for Life," commentators have generally emphasized the conception of memory and history put forth by Nietzsche without paying much attention to his conception of forgetfulness. My interpretation of "On the Use and Disadvantage of History for Life" is new in the sense that it is centered on forgetfulness rather than on memory. I contend that the novelty of Nietzsche's essay is contained in his assertion that animal forgetfulness is prior and primordial to human memory, and that life is historical through and through because it is forgetful through and through.[3] Forgetfulness precedes memory in the sense that one remembers because one can forget, rather than the other way around. Accordingly, what makes for the human being's historicity is not, as one may assume, its memory, but rather, its forgetfulness. Thus, the historical is engendered by the a-historical and memory by forgetfulness. Animal forgetfulness is not dependent upon human memory; but human memory is dependent upon animal forgetfulness.

Because commentators generally pay greater tribute to memory, they often miss the central role played by forgetfulness in Nietzsche's new conception of historiography as an art of interpretation.[4] In my reading of the relationship between animality and historicity, the transformation of history into an art of interpretation depends on the return of animal forgetfulness. I argue that Nietzsche holds animal forgetfulness responsible for the artfulness of history writing and the unhistorical animal sensibility, exemplified by the Greeks, responsible for the greatness of their culture. Nietzsche confronts the human being's memory with animal forgetfulness in order to stimulate a new awareness and self-awareness within the human being that will lead it, first, to affirm itself as animal, as a forgetful and historical being; and, second, to see in its memory a creative life force. This perspective on animal forgetfulness reveals that memory is an artistic force (*Kunsttrieb*). As a consequence, historiography must be understood as artwork (*Kunstwerk*) rather than as science (*Wissenschaft*), concerned with interpretation rather than with a factual representation of the past.

During a period when the dominant view of history was that it ought to be concerned with the factual reconstruction of the past, whether in the form of an a priori narrative, a positivistic science, or a realistic representation of historical reality, Nietzsche's untimely claim that history is an art initiated a debate on the question of the scientific value of the historical sciences. In this ongoing debate, historical and natural sciences are typically considered to be distinct because of their different methodologies. The historical sciences are understood to be part of the human and social sciences, while the natural sciences are understood to be part of the physical and mathematical sciences. Nietzsche instead groups the historical and natural sciences together because he considers them both to be based on a fundamental misperception, namely, the belief that life can be made transparent through rational explanations that objectively reproduce the world as it really is. Nietzsche holds that any science, whether historical or natural, has to give up this notion of "objectivity" and content itself with hypothetical interpretations; he believes that this is the only way that the natural and historical sciences can be truly scientific and objective. Nietzsche's new insight raises the question of whether a truly effective history may actually be found in the works of an artist rather than in those of a historian, even if the latter is artistic and not scientific.[5]

In order to show that, first, animal forgetfulness is the crucial discovery Nietzsche makes in "On the Use and Disadvantage of History for Life" and, second, that the return of animal forgetfulness generates an artistic approach to history, I begin with the encounter of animal forgetfulness. I then give several reasons why the human being needs the forgetfulness of the animal and show how an involvement with that forgetfulness gives rise to an artistic notion of history, and historical writing in particular. In the period from 1886 to 1888, Nietzsche reedited each of his books and added new prefaces. In these prefaces, Nietzsche tells the story of how he came to write these books and how he would like them to be read. The chapter ends with an interpretation of Nietzsche's prefaces, focusing on "An Attempt at Self-Critique." I argue that the prefaces provide us with an example of how Nietzsche envisages artistic historiography.

The Encounter with the Animals' Forgetfulness

In "On the Use and Disadvantage of History for Life," Nietzsche's approach to the animals is not that of a scientist who desires to know about the animals, but that of a poet who imagines the life of the animals, whose thoughts on the animals are imaginary, illusory, and fantastic rather than scientific, rational, and true.[6] It does not seem to be a coincidence that the opening scene of Nietzsche's historical essay—which describes the image of the grazing cattle who cannot understand the meaning of yesterday or today and are neither bored nor melancholic—was inspired by a poet, Leopardi (*HL* 1).[7] Nietzsche's animal imaginary raises the question of whether a history that understands itself as a science should not, like Nietzsche himself, let itself be inspired by images and illusions, or let itself be carried away by forgetfulness and become an art, an art of interpretation. Moreover, it raises the question of whether dreams, illusions, and images, rather than truth and knowledge, are in fact the enhancing and invigorating carriers of future life. And finally, from the beginning of the text, it suggests that history's and memory's artistic transformations are tied to the human being's becoming-animal.

Nietzsche follows the poet's animal imaginary and ironically draws the picture of the human being's tragic suffering in a world of memory as he contemplates the animal's idyllic happiness in a world of forgetfulness.

Secretly admiring the animals and their harmonious oneness with nature, envious of their perfection, honesty, beauty, and innocence, humans want to live happily like the animals. But tied to a world of memory and memories, the bliss of forgetfulness seems forever inaccessible to the animal who has learned how to be human, how to remember, speak, and reason, and has forgotten how to be animal, how to forget, keep silent, sense, and intuit. Compared with the animal's happiness, human happiness can at best be a pretense of *Heiterkeit*, an illusion and a simulacrum of the animal's happiness. Further, the human's pride in its own distinction now seems all too human and a source of shame rather than honor or gratification, for its distinction from the animal is its relative vulnerability rather than its relative superiority. Nietzsche's reconstruction of the animal imaginary de-centers the *anthropos* and problematizes the human imaginary of the world. From such a dislocated perspective, the possession of human memory no longer establishes humans as superior to animals and their forgetfulness but, in fact, makes them weaker and less capable of generating the lives they desire.

In their happiness and forgetfulness, the animals resemble children. The comparison of animals to children suggests that humans are animals that have lost their animality, their forgetfulness, just as they have lost their childlike innocence and happiness. The encounter with the animals reminds the human being of this irrevocable loss. It is suffused with nostalgic longing and a desire to return to a lost childhood, a "lost paradise" (*HL* 1).[8] Nietzsche rejects this fantasy as naïve and romantic. As he says in *Philosophy in the Tragic Age of the Greeks*, "the way to the beginnings leads everywhere to the barbaric" and every return to the beginning, hence, is horrifying rather than soothing and pacifying (*PTA* 1).[9] The forgetfulness of animals and children needs to be disrupted, even if it is indispensable to life, because humans also need memory and knowledge of the past. Despite the human being's need for history, Nietzsche holds on to the belief that the human being's animal beginning reveals something essential and necessary that belongs to the human being, something which the human being has lost and needs to recover in order to enhance the future of its life form.

Historicity, Suffering, and Struggle

Animals live a-historically, entirely absorbed by and identified with the present moment. They are one with the movement of becoming. They do not suffer from the past and they do not fear the future. Animals, as Nietzsche pictures them, perceive only the timeless beauty and harmony of things. Their vision of the world is purely aesthetic. As Nietzsche later re-marks in *Thus Spoke Zarathustra,* for animals, "all things themselves are dancing" (*Z*: 2 "The Convalescent"). The encounter with the animal makes the human being "wonder at itself, that it cannot learn to forget but clings relentlessly to the past: however far and fast it may run, this chain runs with it" (*HL* 1). Next to the animal's lightness of being, the human being's life is heavy, split, torn, and in need of remedy. Incapable of forget-fulness, of undoing the chains of the past, humans are doomed to live in unredeemable suffering and struggle, for freedom and happiness are acces-sible only through forgetfulness: "It is always the same thing that makes happiness: the ability [*Vermögen*] to forget or, expressed in more scholarly fashion, the capacity to feel *unhistorical* during its duration" (*HL* 1).

Nietzsche confronts the human being's suffering with the animal's for-getful happiness in order to make the human question the source of its suffering. Suffering, it turns out, is the result of a particular conception of the past: one that ignores the ways in which the human animal needs forgetfulness. Without forgetfulness, the human animal "braces itself against the great and ever greater pressure of what is past: it pushes it down or bends it sideways, it encumbers its steps as a dark, invisible burden which it can sometimes appear [*zum Scheine*] to disown [*verläugnen*]" (*HL* 1). When the past cannot be dissolved, its weight on the present increases. Being bound to the past in such a way generates feelings of impotence and imprisonment. The past becomes something one renounces and resents, something one "is too glad to disown [*verläugnen*]," such as a crime or a bad conscience (*HL* 1).[10] Confronted with the impossibility of undoing the past and desiring to bring back forgetfulness and freedom from the past, the human being turns away from life and toward death as the only possible relief: "Death at last brings the desired forgetting" (*HL* 1).

The idea that suffering comes from adopting a perspective on the past that ignores the ways in which the human animal needs forgetfulness has, as I have pointed out in previous chapters, strong affinities with what Nietzsche identifies as slave morality in *On the Genealogy of Morals* (*GM* I: 10). Nietzsche defines slave morality as a moral perspective on the past that does not know how to forget and, therefore, generates feelings of resentment, hatred, and revenge for the past. In contrast, noble morality exemplifies a perspective on the past that is defined by the power of for-getfulness. Those who know how to forget do not dwell on the past and, hence, do not "disown [*verläugnen*]" the past. Knowing how to forget leads one to experience historicity not only as something that continu-ously brings back the past but also as something that carries the past be-yond itself and toward the future. Animal forgetfulness subverts a historical perspective that considers the past to be necessary, stable, and fixed. It makes possible a historical perspective that considers the past to be contingent, fluid, and reversible. Such a perspective is not closed unto itself, but looks out toward the future. Animal forgetfulness opens up the possibility of a liberating intervention into the past. It reverses the flow of time: instead of having the past impose itself on the future with necessity, the future imposes itself on the past with necessity.[11] I will return to this aspect of animal forgetfulness below in the section on "Counterhistory."

Despite the "conflict, suffering and satiety" stirred up by the "it was" (*HL* 1), Nietzsche does not suggest abstaining from history and memory altogether.[12] Instead, he argues for a refinement of the human animal's historical sensibility and a receptiveness of the value and significance of animal forgetfulness for life. It is only when the human being learns again how to forget and become animal that it can overcome the abyss between the animal's lightness of being and the human's tragedy of becoming. In the end, however, there can be no final overcoming of suffering from the past, but always only a provisional and illusory one. Nietzsche's pessimism leads him to question whether final redemption would, in fact, be desirable. Opposed to the idea of a final redemption from suffering, Nietzsche affirms suffering as a source of life that inspires future life, for he sees, in a difficult past, something that challenges the human animal to become and overcome itself. Nietzsche approvingly cites the words of Meister Eckhart: "The animal that bears you fastest to perfection is suffering" (*SE* 4).

Why Humans Need Forgetfulness

In "On the Use and Disadvantage of History for Life," rather than establishing a new hierarchy that favors forgetfulness, Nietzsche dissolves any possible hierarchic ordering between humans and animals or between memory and forgetfulness and establishes them both as necessary to the enhancement of human animal life:

Cheerfulness, the good conscience, the joyful deed, confidence in the future—all of them depend . . . on one's being just as able to forget [*zu vergessen weiss*] at the right time as to remember at the right time; on the possession of a powerful instinct [*kräftigem Instincte*] for sensing [*herausfühlt*] when it is necessary to feel historically and when unhistorically. This, precisely, is the proposition the reader is invited to meditate upon: the unhistorical and the historical are necessary in equal measure for the health of an individual, of a people and of a culture. (*HL* 1)[13]

From this new perspective, becoming human is not a movement against or away from the animal, but a return of and to the animal and of and to forgetfulness as a force indispensable to human animal life and becoming. Because Nietzsche values forgetfulness and memory equally, he rejects both the suprahistorical and the historical perspective on life, although he considers the former to be a useful antidote to the latter (*HL* 10). Whereas the suprahistorical is rejected for being too a-historical, the historical is rejected for being too historical. Nietzsche suspects that behind the suprahistorical denial of the historicity of human life, there hides a metaphysical longing for eternal being, for a life similar to that of the animals, above and beyond a life in indefinite becoming.[14] He defends history against the suprahistorical precisely because the latter ignores the ways in which human animal life is historical in its becoming and, at least to some extent, dependent upon history: "History for the purposes of life has more future than the wisdom of the suprahistorical and their disgust for history" (*HL* 1).[15] Nietzsche praises the human animal's power to make what is unhistorical, exceeding human life, into something that is historical, constituting human animal life (*HL* 1).[16] But, at the same time, he rejects the historical perspective insofar as the latter ignores the value and significance of animal forgetfulness for life: "they have no idea that, despite their preoccupation with history, they in fact think and act unhistorically" (*HL* 1). The key question, therefore, remains: How can forgetfulness enable memory, how can the a-historical enable the historical?

Nietzsche emphasizes the need for the human being to affirm itself as animal and as forgetful, for he perceives too much memory to be a threat to life: "with an excess of history, the human being ceases to exist" (*HL* 1).[17] Only on the basis of the animal's forgetfulness does human life and culture become possible at all: "without that envelope of the unhistorical it would never have begun or dared to begin" (*HL* 1). Nietzsche rejects and condemns the prejudice that sees, in the animal, only past and, in the human, only future. He proposes, instead, that what is promising in the human are its animality and its forgetfulness rather than its so-called humanity and memory.[18] Forgetfulness is, therefore, necessary to life—as a soothing remedy against the indigestion of too much history,[19] for example—and also more essential to life than memory. As the animal proves, it is possible to live with almost no memory, but not without forgetfulness:

> We shall thus have to account the capacity [*Fähigkeit*] to feel to a certain degree unhistorically as being more vital and more fundamental [*wichtigere und ursprünglichere*], inasmuch as it constitutes the foundation upon which alone anything sound, healthy and

great, anything truly human can grow. The unhistorical is like an atmosphere within which [*umhüllenden*] alone life can germinate [*erzeugt*] and with the destruction of which it must vanish again. (*HL* 1)

Human life begins with the forgetfulness of the animal and, moreover, continues to become and grow thanks to that forgetfulness.[20] Forgetfulness and the veil of the unhistorical are no longer reduced to exclusively animal traits but are now established as inherently belonging to the human animal.

Nietzsche claims not only that forgetfulness is inseparable from that which constitutes human animal life but also, more importantly, that the historical itself is engendered by the unhistorical. Forgetfulness is the ground on which the historical event is built, the birthplace of all great deeds (*rechte Tat*), and the source of a creative and passionate life:

> It is the condition in which one is least capable of being just [*der ungerechteste Zustand von der Welt*]; narrow-minded, ungrateful against the past, blind to [*gegen*] dangers, deaf to [*gegen*] warnings, one is a little vortex of life in a dead sea of darkness and forgetfulness: and yet this condition—unhistorical, counter-historical [*widerhistorisch*] through and through—is the womb not only of the unjust but of every just deed too. (*HL* 1)[21]

Forgetfulness is a blind passion, a kind of frenzy and stupidity. Without forgetfulness, the human animal would not dare take risks; it would not give itself and throw itself into its life and its actions. It is a frenzy (*Wahn*) that enhances the human animal's activity and increases its vitality.[22] Forgetfulness narrows down, centers, and concentrates the perspective: to "forget most things so as to do one thing" (*HL* 1). In the human animal, forgetfulness gives rise to a higher, more virtuous, and more generous form of human animal life than an all-too-human memory.[23] It leads the human animal to its highest purpose, which is, according to Nietzsche, to perish in the pursuit of one's dearest values and highest aims (*HL* 9).[24] Forgetfulness deviates the glance away from becoming and provides the human animal with illusions of something fixed and absolute, something which has being and is not subject to becoming. Without these illusions of stability to provide a point of orientation, a where-from and a where-to, human life and action are inconceivable: "Forgetting is essential to action of any kind" (*HL* 1). Nietzsche imagines that someone who would be fully aware of and accept life as an indefinite becoming ("an imperfect tense that can never become a perfect one" [*HL* 1]) would be incapable of sustaining one's own life:

such a person would no longer believe in its own being, would no longer believe in itself, would see everything flowing asunder in moving points and would lose itself in this stream of becoming. Like the pupil of Heraclites it would not even dare lift a finger. (*HL* 1)

Forgetfulness opens time to what is outside of time. It produces illusions of eternity, which the human animal needs so as to keep on creating forms of life that transcend the flow of becoming and appear to be of eternal value and worth.[25]

Nietzsche praises forgetfulness so highly because he sees in forgetfulness not only a force that stabilizes memory for the sake of action but also a force that disrupts memory for the sake of the further becoming of life. Contrary to a memory directed exclusively toward the past, forgetfulness intervenes in order to de-center, disorient, and reorient the human animal. This displacement allows for the overcoming of an illusion of stability that has forgotten its own illusory character and has become too static, rigid, and dogmatic. What is needed, then, is animal forgetfulness understood as that force which disrupts the continuity of time in order to generate a new beginning. Animal forgetfulness allows the past to become the other of the past and transform the past into something that can no longer be identified with the past. As such, animal forgetfulness affirms the human animal as the center of the unexpected, the unpredictable, and the miraculous, a form of life characterized by the freedom to begin and rebegin.[26]

It is in this function that animal forgetfulness is also indispensable to the philosopher: "Many a man fails to become a thinker only because his memory is too good" (*AOM* 122).[27] The animal's forgetfulness stands at the beginning and rebeginning of philosophy. In this context, it is interesting to note that Nietzsche himself, throughout his writing life, seemed to forget most of his writings. He confesses in his letters to have forgotten most of his books, including his history essay.[28] Perhaps this is the only way to do justice to his books, as Nietzsche recalls in *Ecce Homo*: "In order to be just to 'The Birth of Tragedy' [*um gegen die 'Geburt der Tragödie' gerecht zu werden*], one will have to forget a few things" (*EH* "Books" 1).

Counterhistory

From the perspective of life, forgetfulness is not a force that inhibits memory, but is actively involved in the becoming of memory.[29] Conversely, memory is not opposed to the animal's (or the child's) forgetfulness but stands for an involvement with forgetfulness. When memory is set against forgetfulness, memory brings forth a past that undermines the becoming of life. However, when involved with forgetfulness, memory establishes a life-enhancing relationship with the past. Nietzsche, therefore, argues for a new form of memory that is not antithetical to forgetfulness. He believes, first, that an involvement with forgetfulness would allow for memory to be redirected away from the past and toward the future. Second, he argues that it is only through opening up the future that history can become valuable to human animal life.[30] Nietzsche's formula for untimeliness confirms this idea:

> for I do not know what meaning classical studies could have for our time if they were not untimely—that is to say, acting counter to our time and thereby acting on our time and, let us hope, for the benefit of a time to come. (*HL* "Preface")

An involvement of memory with forgetfulness gives rise to a form of history that turns what is dead (the past) into something that is alive (the future). Nietzsche calls his new conception of history "counterhistorical" because it reverses the flow of time:[31]

> Fortunately, however, [history] also preserves the memory of the great fighters *against history* . . . precisely, those are the real historical natures who bother little with the "thus it is" so as to follow "thus shall it be" with a more cheerful pride. (*HL* 8)[32]

According to this new meaning given to history, history is what turns past contingencies into future necessities. Counterhistory sees necessity not in what was and is, but in what shall be and shall become in the future. From the perspective of counterhistory, the past is not a given with which one has to come to terms, but something that has to be formed and transformed, interpreted and reinterpreted until it fulfills the terms determined for it. Counterhistory reveals that, at the beginning, there are dreams and illusions, not truth; the past is illusory and contingent rather than factual and necessary. This frees the human animal's creative potential to produce a past from which it may spring forth, rather than one from which it may have been derived (*HL* 3).[33] Counterhistory liberates the human animal's creativity from the ties of an all-too-historical perspective on the past. It allows the human animal to experience its life forces as creative and artistic, rather than as moral and rational. In counterhistory, memory and forgetfulness become forces of overcoming invested in future life rather than in the preservation of past life. They do not stand for a return to the past that is a return to the origin as what is necessary and true, or as what deserves to be imitated and admired; instead, they point to the infinite number of ways of deferring from the past, of rebeginning their beginning.[34] As such, counterhistory is inherently revolutionary.

Counterhistory trespasses on the past insofar as it reorients the human animal toward what is to come rather than toward what has been. Counterhistory, instead of producing a pure and objective knowledge of the past, falsifies the past, uses and abuses it: "As long as the study of history serves life and is directed by the vital drives of life [*Lebenstriebe*], the past itself suffers" (*HL* 2). For Nietzsche, it is questionable whether a pure and objective knowledge of the past is possible at all, since this would depend on an objective and "disinterested" perspective on the past. But, as Nietzsche convincingly shows, such a perspective is impossible, because it would not be a perspective of life.[35] As a consequence, the injustice counterhistory commits against the past cannot be redeemed: it always acts in the service of life as an inherently violent and cruel force, interested only in its own enhancement.[36] The only "consolation [*merkwürdigen Trost*]" is that every beginning is a rebeginning and that every beginning can be returned to its beginnings (*HL* 3). History then becomes an infinitely open movement of revolutions where every beginning announces the possibility of its rebeginning, that is, of its being overthrown by another future beginning.

Monumental, antiquarian, and critical history are forms of counterhistory insofar as they exemplify future-oriented involvements of memory with forgetfulness. Like counterhistory, they are all inherently destructive, but it is only on the basis of this violence that they can engender life: their cruelty accounts for their creativity. Monumental, antiquarian, and critical history use those portions of the past that can be transfigured into future life and forget the rest. They are not forms of history in service of the past, rather their use of the past responds to a need of life:

> History pertains to the living in three respects: it pertains to him as a being who acts and strives [monumental history], as a being who preserves and reveres [antiquarian history], as a being who suffers and seeks deliverance [critical history]. (*HL* 2)

Whenever a form of history is cut off from the basic life need that generated it, it inevitably declines as a form of life (*HL* 2).[37] The intimate linkage between the form historiography takes and the life need to which it corresponds stresses the idea that history is not an abstraction from life, but a form of life, just like philosophy and truth in Nietzsche are also not abstractions of life but forms of life.[38]

Monumental history grows out of the "man of action's [*Tätigen und Mächtigen*]" need for encouragement, for the company and example of the great heroes of the past. From the perspective of monumental history, only the true hero, the one who refuses to live at any price, deserves to be remembered (*HL* 2).[39] Monumental history radically forgets everything else. In fact, monumental memory is so forgetful that Nietzsche sees, in the monumental vision of the past, nothing but mythical fabulation (*HL* 2).[40] Due to its incapacity to remember, monumental history resembles the prehistorical and unhistorical more than the historical, the animal more than the human, enclosed in the moment rather than aware of becoming. For Nietzsche, however, the problem of the monumental is not its a-historicity, but its depreciation of what cannot be universalized, of the individual, the detailed, the marginal, and the peripheral. Nietzsche warns of monumental history's violence against what is different and distinct:

How much of the past would have to be overlooked if it was to produce that mighty effect, how violently what is individual in it would have to be forced into a universal mold and all its sharp corners and hard outlines broken up in the interest of conformity. (*HL* 2)

This danger immanent to monumental history is counteracted by antiquarian history, which preserves and conserves human life against the violence of an overly forgetful monumental history.

Antiquarian history caters to those in need of the preservation and conservation of their life forces. Its premise is that life needs a firm ground to grow; this ground can take the form of tradition, for example. Whereas monumental history is, above all, concerned with the future, antiquarian history reflects a way of life that values only the old and despises the new. Like the monumental, the antiquarian perspective also has a blind spot. Whereas the first sees only the universal form of the heroic act, the second preserves and reveres everything and anything beyond distinction:

The antiquarian sense of an individual, a community, a whole people, always possesses an extremely restricted field of vision; most of what exists it does not perceive at all, and the little it does see, it sees much too close up and isolated; it cannot relate what it sees to anything else and it therefore accords everything it sees equal importance and therefore to each individual thing too great importance. (*HL* 3)

This limitedness of the antiquarian perspective is comparable to that of the scientists (*Gelehrte*): "sharp-sightedness for things close up, combined with great myopia for distant things and for what is universal" (*SE* 6). Both translate into an inability to distinguish between what is and what is not important for the enhancement of life. As a consequence, antiquarian history brings with it the danger of mummifying life. Since the antiquarian lacks the life-engendering instinct of the monumental, it can carry the same consequences as scientific and historical culture: too much history, too much past, too much knowledge, too much impotence. Like the scholar (*wissenschaftliche Gelehrte*), a servant of science, the practitioners of antiquarian history can become passive and retrospective: "It paralyses the historical agent who, as one who acts, will and must offend some piety or other" (*HL* 3).[41] Antiquarian history can only preserve life if it reverses its perspective on the past. Instead of indiscriminately revering and admiring everything that is past, it has to let go of the past. Temporarily letting go of the past is the only way in which antiquarian history can preserve its memory of the past. If antiquarian history cannot forget, it ends up destroying the force which brought it forth, namely, animal forgetfulness, and thereby risks the loss of its memory of the past.

Critical history counteracts antiquarian history when its reverence for the past becomes too oppressive. It belongs to those who suffer from the past and need to be freed from the past. Critical history dissolves and forgets the past in favor of a new beginning. Its premise is that everything in the past deserves to be denied and that life gains life through the continuous negation, destruction, and contradiction of itself.[42] What is critical in the struggle against the past is to know how far one must carry out the denial of the past without completely destroying one's own life (*HL* 3).[43] Nietzsche warns against an overly strong aggression toward the past because it undermines the most important task of critical history, which is to "implant in ourselves a new habit, a new instinct, a second nature [the future], so that our first nature [the past] withers away" (*HL* 3).

Critical history negates the past because of a judgment it pronounces against an injustice committed in the past. As such, critical history keeps the memory of suffering from injustice alive:

> Sometimes, however, this same life that requires forgetting demands a temporary suspension of this forgetfulness; it wants to be clear as to how unjust the existence of anything—a privilege, a caste, a dynasty, for example—is, and how greatly this thing deserves to perish. (*HL* 3)

Critical history sets out to condemn the past in the name of justice. But its judgment of the past is, itself, unjust because it does not operate in the name of some abstract principle of morality, truth, or justice, but in the name of a need of life: the need to forget, to overthrow and to overcome the past in view of life to come.[44] Despite this conflict, critical history must hold on to a belief in justice, at least momentarily, so as to be able to keep on counteracting the past. Ultimately, however, confronted with its own injustice, every second nature has to give up the belief in final justice. The only consolation for second natures is that their injustice will be remembered by a critical history to come, and that the latter will hopefully give rise to future second natures that will redeem their injustice by overthrowing it.[45]

Artistic Historiography

Nietzsche's counterhistorical conception of history, a history that knows how to forget portions of the past for the sake of the future, subverts an understanding of history that wants to remember everything for the sake of a greater knowledge of the past.[46] This leads him to the insight that history in the service of life is an art and not a science, and that the drive to form and transform the past is artistic and not epistemological: "Thus the human being spins its web over the past and subdues it, thus it gives expression to its artistic drive, but not to its drive towards truth or justice" (*HL* 6). Accordingly, the artifacts of history should be recognized as interpretations rather than truths, and memory should be recognized as a force of illusion and imagination rather than as an instrument of knowledge and truth (*HL* 1).[47] Nietzsche warns against scientific culture because it denies that creativity is essential to human animal life and history (*HL* 10).[48] It is interesting in this context to mention that in "On Truth and Lies in an Extra-Moral Sense," Nietzsche argues in similar fashion that the perspective of forgetfulness reveals the intellect to be creative rather than rational, and truth to be metaphorical rather than epistemological. Both "On Truth and Lies in an Extra-Moral Sense" and "On the Use and Disadvantage of History for Life" oppose the artistic to the scientific and epistemological. They define the artistic as a process that brings forth something that cannot be reduced to and induced from factual knowledge.

In "On the Use and Disadvantage of History for Life," the artistic, in contrast to the scientific, refers to a forgetful activity that is brought forth in the absence of reason and consciousness. Nietzsche describes historicity as a haunting: "A moment, now here and then gone, nothing before it came, again nothing after it has gone, nonetheless returns as a ghost and disturbs the peace of a later moment" (*HL* 1). The haunting of history reveals that memory and forgetfulness are not capacities under the human being's conscious control. As Nietzsche points out in a later text, it is not within the power of the human will to determine when to remember and when to forget: "the act of recollection does not lie within our power" (*D* 126) and, therefore, "one may want to forget but one cannot" (*D* 167).

This haunting of history disturbs historical scientists by pushing them to the limits of their rationality. The past resists the grip of the scientists' memory. The haunting of history brings into doubt the possibility of mastery over the past by means of reason and historical consciousness. It directly threatens the historical scientists' world view. To protect their belief in a scientific and rational conception of history, the historical scientists have to "disown [*verläugnen*]" and forget their having been haunted by the past. This is the only way they can keep their scientific world-view intact.[49] In contrast, artistic historians affirm the contingencies of time as a source of strength, as something that challenges their virtuosity and the refinement of their historical sensibility.[50] Artistic historians do not confuse memory with a conscious act of bringing back the past. Artistic memory is not a means of mastery and domination. Instead, for artistic historians, it is the past that erupts in the face of memory, which is beyond its control. Remembering is surprised by that which exceeds the capacity to remember. Artistic memory becomes a form of attentiveness, a readiness to grasp the past when it comes forward to the encounter. It means to encounter the past as much as being encountered by the past; it is a return to the past as much as a return of the past. Artistic historians welcome the return of animal forgetfulness as a force that enhances their ability to capture the meaning of the past.

Artistic historians know what in the past is truly great and needs to be preserved because they imagine the past to be like an oracle that speaks a secret language decipherable only by those who are "architects of the future" (*HL* 6).[51] Only to them does the past return. However, the past refuses to offer itself to those who lack a surplus of strength and virtue and have nothing to give in return. The oracle of the past reveals artistic historians to be powerful and creative beings, driven by the desire to increase and multiply the expressions of life.[52] However, it also reveals scientific historians' need for knowledge of the past to be symptomatic of a weakness that forecloses the possibility of a fruitful encounter with the past. The scientists' insatiable desire for knowledge (of the past) points to their lack of a mythical past, that is, a past taken up by the human being's animal imaginary. The image of starving historians desperately digging up the roots in search of nutrition illustrates this idea. Their "knowledge" of the past reflects the greediness with which they grasp for food: "Now mythless the human being stands there, surrounded by every past there has ever been, eternally hungry, scraping and digging in a search for roots . . . this [scientific] culture is anything other than the greedy grabbing and chasing after nourishment of the hungry—" (*BT* 23). The figure of the starving historians demonstrates the dilemma presented by a modernity that fails to bring forth a form of memory on which it can live (*HL* 10).

History as a pure science is a kind of conclusion of life for humankind (*HL* 7). It carves out human animal life, eats it up, and makes it collapse onto itself. What remains are shadows of life, pale reflections that hide behind the decoration of so-called historical education (*historische Bildung*):

> The reason is that it has lost and destroyed its instincts and having lost its trust in the "divine animal," it can no longer let go the reins when its reason falters and its path leads it through deserts. Thus the individual grows fainthearted and unsure and dares no longer believe in itself: it sinks into its own interior depths, which here means into the accumulated lumber of what it has learned but which has no outward effect, of instruction which does not become life. (*HL* 5) [53]

Nietzsche questions whether the forms of life brought forth by modern historicism can, in fact, be called human. He concludes that historicism produces not humans, not gods, not animals, but forms of historical pseudo-education (*historische Bildungsgebilde*), "thinking-, writing-, and speaking-machines [*Denk- Schreib- und Redemaschinen*]" (*HL* 5).[54] Contrary to the destructive impact of history as a science on modern culture, Nietzsche wants to bring back the forgetfulness of the animal so as to open up, to those who have been alienated by their historical education, the possibility of becoming human again (*HL* 10). Only that form of history which allows a promising future culture to emerge, whose education is a liberation rather than a suffocation and which is artistic and forgetful, can be called distinctly human (*HL* 6, 7; *SE* 2). Nietzsche believes, like the scientific scholar (*wissenschaftliche Gelehrte*), history is necessary to life. He also believes, however, that if history wants to become the carrier of future life, it needs to overcome itself as a pure science and adopt the status of an art form: "Only if history can endure to be transformed into a work of art, that is, to become a pure artistic form [*reines Kunstgebilde*], will it perhaps be able to preserve instincts or even evoke them" (*HL* 7). History has to turn against itself so that the age of historicism can be overcome and bring about a "new age," a "powerful" and "original" age, that promises "more life" (*HL* 8).[55]

Nietzsche himself attempts an artistic and counterhistorical overcoming when he tries to bring back what is gone and reintroduce the Greeks and their historical animal sensibility into modernity. The return of Greek thought aims to turn a history saturated with knowledge into one bursting with creativity.[56] The example of the Greeks, like that of the animal's forgetfulness at the beginning of the second *Untimely Consideration*, is meant to show that what is responsible for the greatness of culture is unhistorical animal sensibility. The Greeks' unhistorical animal sensibility allows them to determine when the appropriation of the past is life-enhancing and when it is life-diminishing. Nietzsche underlines that "with the word 'the unhistorical' I designate the art and power of *forgetting* and of enclosing oneself within a bounded *horizon*" (*HL* 10). Modern culture has lost this art, has lost its unhistorical animal sense and, thus, risks being drowned in either too much history or too much forgetfulness (*HL* 1). Modern culture lives off the illusion that science and knowledge have a redeeming power.[57] As such, the moderns stand at antipodes with the Greeks, who moderate their desire for knowledge in the name of increasing their vitality: "The Greeks have bound their insatiable desire for knowledge by an ideal desire for life [*ein ideales Lebensbedürfniss*]—because they immediately want to live what they learn" (*PTA* 1). Memory for the Greeks is a plastic,[58] artistic, and forgetful force that uses the past as a nutrient for the future, but forgets everything else that it cannot draw into its horizon (*HL* 10).[59] Culture for the Greeks, therefore, neither confounds itself with an accumulation of knowledge, nor with imitation and repetition. Instead, it stands for a pluralization of life that "augments nature with new living nature" (*SE* 6). Consequently, "humanity" for the Greeks is not something added to life, like a dress veiling the body, but rather signifies an affirmation of their animality as an inherently cultural force (*HL* 10).[60]

Nietzsche's Prefaces as Examples of Artistic Historiography

Nietzsche's project of reediting his entire body of work started in 1886 with "An Attempt at Self-Criticism," prefacing *The Birth of Tragedy*, and ended in 1888 with the writing of *Ecce Homo*. During this period Nietzsche reread all of his pre-*Zarathustra* books and added new prefaces to their original editions.[61] These prefaces provide us with examples of artistic historiography insofar as they are constituted by a return to the past that breaks open the past and reorients it toward the future. The underlying premise of Nietzsche's project was that the past is not yet defined, determined, and fixed, but open to "an attempt to give oneself, as it were a posteriori, a past in which one would like to originate in opposition to that in which one did originate" (*HL* 3).[62] Such an attempt requires adopting the perspective of the artistic historian who knows not only how to remember but also how to forget, and who can therefore supply artistic formations and transformations of the past, which are carriers of future life.

Nietzsche emphasizes the future directedness of his writings when he says retrospectively about *The Birth of Tragedy* that "everything in this essay is predicting the future [*vorherverkündend*]" and that "a tremendous [*ungeheure*] hope speaks out of this writing" (*EH* "Books" BT: 4). In the preface to *Beyond Good and Evil*, he illustrates this idea using the image of the bending of the bow (*BGE* "Preface"). The image of the bending bow reflects the relationships between the present time of writing the preface, the past book, and its future reading. Like the bending of a bow, the present time turns itself upon the past, returns to the past. The return of the past effects a countermovement that redirects the past toward the future, like an arrow. The further the bow can be bent, the more the past can be appropriated and the further it can spring forward into the future. The image of the jump in Nietzsche also illustrates this idea:

> Bad! Bad! What? Isn't he going—back?—Yes! But you understand him badly when you complain. He is going back like anybody who wants to attempt a big jump. (*BGE* 280)[63]

The preface's aspiration toward the future calls for a form of counter-memory, an involvement of memory with forgetfulness, which disrupts, displaces, and overthrows a book of the past for the sake of a new beginning. The prefaces are artistic and creative interventions into the past that have the power to revive the life of his books by supplying them with new interpretations.

Nietzsche's prefaces are critical readings guided by the question of whether his books still contain life and, thus, are able to inspire new life:

> That author has drawn the happiest lot who as an old man can say that every life-creating, invigorating, elevating, enlightening thought and feeling in him still lives on in his writings and that he himself now signifies only the gray ashes, while the fire has everywhere been saved and carried on. (*HH* 208)

In "An Attempt at Self-Criticism," Nietzsche confirms that *The Birth of Tragedy* passes this critical test insofar as whatever underlies that book, "it must be a most stimulating and supremely important question [*eine Frage ersten Ranges und Reizes*]" ("An Attempt at Self-Criticism" 1). *The Birth of Tragedy*, despite being a highly "questionable [*fragwürdiges*] book" (I return to this aspect below), is "a book which has *proved* itself" meaning that it "satisfied 'the best of its time'" and, thus, deserves to be treated "with some consideration [*Rücksicht*] and reticence [*Schweigsamkeit*]," at least in this respect ("An Attempt at Self-Criticism" 2).

The critical questioning of his past writings occasions an agonistic encounter between Nietzsche-reader-prefacer and Nietzsche-writer-author. For Nietzsche, reading involves a secret antagonism (*Entgegenschauen*) and a conspiracy against the author. The writing of prefaces provides an occasion "to take sides against himself [*gegen sich Partei ergreifen*]" (*AOM* 309), to think against himself (see also *AOM* "Preface" 1 and 7; *AOM* 191). This is how Nietzsche hopes to elevate the value of his past books: "Advantage for the opponent.—A book full of spirit communicates some of it to its opponents too" (*AOM* 160). The practices of reading and writing exemplified in the prefaces constitute the opening of a public space where "free spirits" meet to confront their different and opposing views. The function of the preface is, in this respect, comparable to the function assigned to the artistic historian, namely, to transform the past into a medium through which exceptional individuals can challenge each other: "It is the task of history to be the mediator between [great individuals] and thus again and again to inspire and lend the strength for the production of greatness [*Erzeugung des Grossen*]" (*HL* 9). For Nietzsche, not only the practices of reading and writing, but all public matters in general, are unthinkable outside of an arena of competition. In matters of public concern, he follows the advice of Stendhal: "to make one's entry into society with a *duel*" (*EH* "Books" UB: 2). In "An Attempt at Self-Criticism," this "duel" features a competition between the "young" Nietzsche, a devoted disciple of Wagner and Schopenhauer, and the "older" yet in many ways "younger" Nietzsche. The idea of competition (agon) is important because Nietzsche sees in the latter a force of overcoming: The direct confrontation with his past is the only way to overcome and redeem an "impossible book" of the past ("An Attempt at Self-Criticism" 2 and 3). The agonistic struggle between Nietzsche-the-prefacer and Nietzsche-the-author is intended to reverse the reader's perspective on his books so as to provoke a renaissance and rebirth of his books.[64] As such, the prefaces exemplify the idea that every beginning is a rebeginning and every beginning can be returned to its beginning.

In "An Attempt at Self-Criticism," the rebirth of tragedy is not considered apart from the rebirth of comedy. The seriousness of the philosopher's critical investigation has to be disrupted by the laughter of the comic philosopher, as the co-author of the preface. The human being's need for laughter is comparable to its need for animal forgetfulness. Contrary to "young" Nietzsche's "memory brimming over with questions, experiences, hidden things to which the name Dionysus has been appended as yet another question mark" ("An Attempt at Self-Criticism" 3), Nietzsche as the writer of the preface counters with Dionysian laughter. Dionysian laughter disrupts the otherwise burdening pursuit of the philosopher and prevents her from understanding herself in exclusively tragic terms. At the end of "An Attempt at Self-Criticism," Nietzsche also advises his readers to laugh themselves out of their need for "metaphysical consolation [*Trösterei*]" ("An Attempt at Self-Criticism" 7). While, in "On the Use and Disadvantage of History for Life," Nietzsche prescribes animal forgetfulness as an antidote to too much history, in "An Attempt at Self-Criticism," he prescribes laughter against too much metaphysics: "you should learn to *laugh*, my young friends, if you are really determined to remain pessimists. Perhaps then, as those who laugh, you will some day send all attempts at metaphysical solace to Hell—with metaphysics the first to go!" ("An Attempt at Self-Criticism" 7).

The project of preface-writing contests the idea that a book's content has a definite meaning determined by the author. Instead, meanings emerge from the interaction between the book and the reader's interpretative intervention of reading. Nietzsche as the writer of the preface does not conceal the irreducible incompleteness of his books or their dependence on an encounter with a reader to come. Certainly, the prefaces are concerned with the selection and seduction of the "good reader"; the themes of seduction and selection run throughout the discourse of Nietzsche's prefaces (*GM* "Preface" 8; *BGE* "Preface"). Nietzsche recounts, for example, that he addressed *The Birth of Tragedy* only to "the initiated" and shut it off "from the *profanum vulgus* of the 'educated' even more than from the 'common people,'" which proves that the "young" Nietzsche already knew "well enough how to seek out its [the book's] fellows" ("An Attempt at Self-Criticism" 3).

In the end, however, Nietzsche as the preface writer acknowledges that the future readings of his books cannot be manipulated. They exceed the project of preface-writing because the future of the book, just like that of the preface itself, is inherently dependent upon readers to come. The significant role assigned to the reader reveals the indeterminacy of the meaning of his books. Their meanings do not deploy from the past (the written book) in a linear, teleological movement of time. Nietzsche no longer conceives either the written book or the author as the causal origin of the future readings of the book. But, if the meaning of the book is no longer determined by the author, then the possibility of a renewal of meaning lies entirely in the hands of the reader. The book to come pushes its author to disappear, to dissimulate himself, to absent himself from the writing.[65] The practice of reading and writing exemplified in Nietzsche's prefaces exposes his books to what is outside, such that this exteriority can become the source of their meanings.

Kofman argues that what disappears with the idea of the author, represented by the father who immortalizes himself in the child, is an idea of culture that recognizes in the past the sole model for the determination of absolute, normative evaluations.[66] According to her, interpretation is a practice of reading and writing that circumscribes the realms of culture and self-culture. There is no culture without writing, and if nature has to be interpreted, it is because nature itself is not a presence of meaning, but of writing.[67] When the author disappears from her writing, then culture, the practice of reading and writing, becomes a continuous formation and transformation of new meanings through interpretation. Interpretation, rather than absolutizing the book's meaning, twists it free to a plurality of meanings. What immortalizes the book, what rekindles its life, is no longer the name and fame of the author, but the continuous movement of interpretation and reinterpretation of the book by readers to come:

> Now if we reflect that every human action, and not only a book, in some way becomes the cause of other actions, decisions, thoughts, that every thing that happens is indissolubly tied up with everything that will happen, then we recognize the real *immortality* that exists, that of movement: anything that has ever moved is included and eternalized in the total union of all that exists [*in dem Gesamtverbande alles Seienden*], like an insect in amber. (*HH* 208)

Interpretation as the practice of reading and writing cultivates the reader and the written simultaneously because each interpretation reflects the invention of a new meaning as a unique way of affirming a certain irreducible possibility of life and thought.

Ecce Homo concludes the project of preface-writing. It reflects Nietzsche's attempt to articulate the irreducible possibilities of life and thought exemplified in his own philosophy.[68] *Ecce Homo* is, in this sense, paradigmatic of Nietzsche's attitude as a preface writer toward himself as a book writer. In *Ecce Homo*, Nietzsche wants to recollect himself, to show the coherence of his work and to affirm it as such. However, this self-concentration can only be expressed by a rupture and a confusion between Nietzsche and Nietzsche. To consider himself identical to himself is impossible, and he therefore rejects the idea that a philosophical work must be systematic and closed. Instead, a philosophical work should reflect a plurality of views that neither exclude nor complement each other, but are a reflection of the philosopher's self-overcomings:

> *We incomprehensible ones.*—. . . We are misidentified—because we ourselves keep growing, keep changing, we shed our old bark, we shed our skins every spring, we keep becoming younger, full of future [*zukünftiger*], taller, stronger . . . . Like trees we grow—this is hard to understand, as is all life—not in one place only but everywhere, not in one direction but equally upward and outward and inward and downward . . . we are no longer free to do only one particular thing [*etwas Einzelnes*], to *be* only one particular thing [*etwas Einzelnes*]. (*GS* 371; see also *GM* "Preface" 1)

In accordance with this conception of self-overcoming, the prefaces do not ground Nietzsche's identity, but rather fragment what pretends to be unified. Contrary to the idea of an anonymous, metaphysical subjectivity dissolved in an ideal continuity, teleological movement, or natural linkage, *Ecce Homo* affirms the author as a living, speaking fragment. Nietzsche's preferred metaphor of "self-identity" is "dynamite" or "explosive material" (*EH* "Books" UB: 3): "I am not a human being. I am dynamite" (*EH* "Destiny" 1). Both metaphors illustrate the explosive birth of Nietzsche's manifold identities. Nietzsche rejects the pretension of a proper identity, stable and folded over itself, built on the illusion of personal identity as a fixed property. His "proper" name and identity are the name and identity of multiple Nietzsches. Consequently, as Derrida points out, the signatures of Nietzsche-prefacer and Nietzsche-author do not reveal one and the same Nietzsche. Rather, they are the revealing signs of his multiple identities.[69]

From "An Attempt at Self-Criticism" to *Ecce Homo,* Nietzsche's prefaces trace the becomings and overcomings of his multiple identities. They show that the project of becoming what one is should not be confused with the realization of an ideal self, which is projected into the future according to a predetermined teleology provided by an authority outside or inside the self. Nietzsche's prefaces demonstrate that becoming what one is arises from neither self-knowledge nor self-mastery. On the contrary, it requires loosening oneself and deappropriating oneself, since becoming what one is always occurs through something other than the self, something that remains, like the animal, at an irreducible distance from the self:

> We remain strange to ourselves out of necessity, we do not understand ourselves, we *must* confusedly mistake who we are, the motto:

"everyone is furthest from himself" applies to us for ever,—we are not "knowers" [*Erkennenden*] when it comes to ourselves. (*GM* "Preface" 1)

Becoming what one is necessitates an overcoming of oneself that is inseparable from an experience of self-alienation and self-forgetfulness, an experience that results from an exposure of the self to the (animal) otherness of the self. As such, becoming what one is undermines the idea that identity and self-identity are something to be realized through one's life. For Nietzsche, life is a series of experiments and experiences where the aim is not to find out who one truly is, but who else one could be.[70] The intention behind the writing of prefaces is not to identify who the author truly was but what else he could become.

Nietzsche understands history and historiography as a haunting (*D* 307; *HL* 1). The artistic historiographer haunts the past and is haunted by the past. The reconstruction of the past, as Nietzsche imagines it, is therefore neither an attempt to gain control over one's work, nor an attempt to manipulate the contingencies of its reception. "An Attempt at Self-Criticism" exemplifies that the past returns to Nietzsche and haunts him; the past imposes itself on him as the necessity for self-criticism. Nietzsche cannot but attempt self-criticism in light of a past that keeps returning to and disturbing him.[71] From the perspective of the artistic historian, the fact that Nietzsche is subject to the necessity of self-criticism is a sign that his return to the past actually corresponds to a need of life, specifically, the need to be freed from a past that has become too oppressive. If Nietzsche as preface writer was not practicing artistic history as a response to a need of life, his critical reconstruction of the past could not "grow" into a carrier of future life, but would risk growing into a "devastating weed" (*HL* 2).

The idea that the past exceeds the artistic historian's capacity to capture its meaning is exemplified in "An Attempt at Self-Criticism." In this preface, Nietzsche recalls that, to him, *The Birth of Tragedy* is an "odd [*wunderlich*] and rather inaccessible [*schlecht zugängliches*] book," a book that he finds highly "questionable [*fragwürdig*]" ("An Attempt at Self-Criticism" 1). In *Ecce Homo*, Nietzsche reconfirms that *The Birth of Tragedy* is "awkward [*merkürdig*] beyond all measure [*über alle Maassen*]" (*EH* "Books" BT: 2). The double meaning of the adjectives Nietzsche uses to describe his book of the past—*fragwürdig* (questionable/question-worthy), *wunderlich* (odd/remarkable), and *merkwürdig* (awkward/noteworthy)—may indicate that his attempt at self-criticism has led him into an aporia. It confronts him with a book that he no longer recognizes as his and cannot reappropriate for himself. In *Human, All Too Human*, Nietzsche describes such an experience as follows:

> *The book become almost human.*—It surprises every writer anew how a book lives on with a life of its own as soon as it has been detached from him; he feels as if one part of an insect had been separated and was now going its own way. Perhaps he almost completely forgets it, perhaps he raises himself above the views set down there, perhaps he no longer even understands it and has lost the updraft on which he flew when he devised that book: meanwhile it seeks out its readers, ignites life, causes happiness or fear, begets new works, becomes the soul of projects and of actions—in short: it lives like a being provided with spirit and soul and yet is not a human being. (*HH* 208)

Rereading *The Birth of Tragedy* is an uncanny (*unheimliche*) experience.[72] Nietzsche is disturbed by the "strange voice [*fremde Stimme*]" that speaks out of his past book ("An Attempt at Self-Criticism" 3); he revisits the awkwardness of his own beginning: "I shall not suppress [*unterdrücken*)] entirely just how unpleasant [*unangenehm*] it now seems to me, how alien [*fremd*] it seems, standing there before me 16 years later" ("An Attempt at Self-Criticism" 2). In *Ecce Homo*, he recalls, as mentioned above, that "this beginning is awkward beyond all measure" (*EH* "Books" BT: 2). The experience as a preface writer confirms Foucault's insight that "the human being began with a grimace of what it was to become."[73] Reappropriating *The Birth of Tragedy* is an impossible task because, as Nietzsche repeatedly insists in his preface-writing, "I find it an impossible book today" ("An Attempt at Self-Criticism" 2 and 3). For the later Nietzsche, *The Birth of Tragedy* remains a "questionable [*fragwürdige*] book" ("An Attempt at Self-Criticism" 5), in spite of the fact that its goal, examining science from the perspective of the artist and the artist from the perspective of life, has persisted over time, and is a goal that Nietzsche still identifies with at the end of his writing career.

Just like the project of artistic historiography, the project of preface-writing is indeterminable and open insofar as there can be no final interpretation of the past, but always only an infinite number of possible reinterpretations. Nietzsche's critical and self-critical return to the past does not operate in the name of a progression toward an ultimate truth, narrowing and closing off the past, but in the name of a pluralization of the possible meanings of his books. In "An Attempt at Self-Criticism," Nietzsche confirms this idea when he says that the philosophical questions treated by the author of *The Birth of Tragedy* remain open questions, and he singles out the Greek question as one that is still unanswered:

> [E]ven today everything is still there for a philologist to discover and excavate in this area! Above all the problem *that* a problem exists here—and that, for as long as we do not have an answer to the question, "What is Dionysian [*dionysisch*]?", the Greeks will remain as utterly unknown [*unerkannt*] and unimaginable as they have always been. ("An Attempt at Self-Criticism" 3)

For Nietzsche as a writer of prefaces, the fact that he still cannot provide a definite answer to the question "What is Dionysian [*dionysisch*]?" is neither a dilemma nor a defeat. On the contrary, it is a hint that, in philosophy, the task is not to solve problems and close off questions, but to keep them open for further questioning. Philosophical questions are like an animal that cannot be tamed insofar as their nature requires that they be challenged, deepened, and refined. Nietzsche's reply to the question "What is Dionysian [*dionysisch*]?" exemplifies this idea. After having raised the question "What is Dionysian [*dionysisch*]?" he responds with an unending series of questions that multiply and pluralize the question of the beginning:

> "Birth of Tragedy from the Spirit of Music"—from music? Music and tragedy? Greeks and the music of tragedy [*Tragödien-Musik*]? Greeks and the pessimistic work of art [*Kunstwerk des Pessimismus*]? The finest [*wohlgerathensten*], most beautiful, most envied [*bestbeneidete*] kind of human being [*Art der bisherigen Menschen*] ever known, the people who made life seem most seductive, the Greeks—what, they of all people needed tragedy? Or even more—art? For what [*wozu*]—Greek art?" ("An Attempt at Self-Criticism" 1 and 4)[74]

The practice of multiplying and pluralizing questions distinguishes Nietzsche's style of philosophical investigation throughout. His practice of self-criticism demonstrates that there can be no final critique of the self, because the self, as Nietzsche imagines it, always remains open to the possibility of a future reevaluation. Furthermore, Nietzsche's practices of reading and writing show that there can be no final reading of his books and prefaces, because books always remain open to the possibility of future reinterpretation. Finally, it seems that the ultimate purpose of Nietzsche's preface-writing is to preserve the openness of his books, to assure that his own philosophy will always be understood as provisional and in becoming, never final, but always only a preface for a philosophy to come (*BGE* 42).[75]

Animality, Language, and Truth

Nietzsche is often perceived as being most radical when he articulates his views on truth. On these occasions, he is seen as the anti-metaphysician, the "denier of truth."[1] Interpretations oscillate between ascribing to him a self-refuting, relativistic doctrine of truth and claiming that Nietzsche's idea of truth remains the traditional one of correspondence to facts.[2] Such divergent and often mutually exclusive readings fail to acknowledge that his writings on truth cannot be reduced to a single, homogenous discourse which assumes that truth is an elementary concept, an irreducible predicate that applies in the same way to every proposition. I shall argue, by way of contrast, that Nietzsche articulates his treatment of truth in three distinct and incommensurable genres or types of discourses. These genres may all be found in a particular book or text, but they receive different degrees of attention from Nietzsche as his writing develops.

The first discourse on truth is theoretical and belongs to the genre of a critique of metaphysics. Through this genre, Nietzsche approaches the question of truth from the vantage points of ontology and cosmology, pursuing the question of "what there is." But Nietzsche's early (and also late) ontology turns out to be a me-ontology, an ontology of lack of being.[3] In other words, the investigation of "what there is" reveals the world to be lacking in metaphysical reality, that is, a world without a "highest" being or a "most real" being which functions as the "ground" of beings in their totality.[4] Nietzsche's theoretical treatment of truth corresponds to this perspective of "the world well lost."[5]

This chapter approaches Nietzsche's treatment of truth within the genre of a critique of metaphysics through a reading of "On Truth and Lies in an Extra-Moral Sense." My reading of this text is centered on the notion of *Anschauungsmetapher* (intuited metaphor).[6] I seek to show that through this notion Nietzsche not only advances a critique of metaphysics but also offers a new conception of philosophy understood as an art in pursuit of singular truth. In the existent readings of Nietzsche's treatment of truth, "On Truth and Lies in an Extra-Moral Sense" is considered in one of two ways. The first holds that this early text by Nietzsche represents a "confused," even "self-contradictory" denial of truth, which undergoes a radical change in his late writings, when he settles on a consistent, coherent theory of truth.[7] The second position maintains the centrality of "On Truth and Lies in an Extra-Moral Sense" for an understanding of Nietzsche's early, middle, and late treatments of truth.[8]

I offer a reading of "On Truth and Lies in an Extra-Moral Sense" that seeks to establish the validity of the second position. I argue that *Anschauungsmetapher* is the name Nietzsche gives to an idea of truth as singularity. The possibility of singular truth calls forth Nietzsche's "denial" of metaphysical truth—though this does not mean that Nietzsche is denying all kinds of truth. The idea of singular truth introduces a new, positive idea of truth as well as a novel way to understand the pursuit of truth. *Anschauungsmetapher* are brought forth by what Nietzsche refers to as pictorial thinking (*Bilderdenken*), thinking in pictures rather than in concepts.[9] *Bilderdenken*, or pictorial thinking, is a form of thought humans share with other kinds of animal life. This return of and to the form of thought of the animal (of and to *Anschauungsmetapher* and *Bilderdenken*) is essential to Nietzsche's attempt to renew philosophy as a life-affirming form of thought. I argue that this return allows philosophy to overcome its understanding of itself as metaphysics and to embrace "postmetaphysical" thinking, which is life-affirming rather than ascetic, productive rather than nihilist.

This reading of "On Truth and Lies in an Extra-Moral Sense" complements the reading of "On the Use and Disadvantage of History for Life" provided in the previous chapter. While that chapter showed that a return of and to the forgetfulness of the animal is essential to the future of history, the objective of this chapter is to show that a return of and to *Anschauungsmetapher* is essential to the future of philosophy understood as a "pure and honest drive to truth" (*TL* 1). The appropriation of animal forgetfulness and pictorial thinking allows philosophy to overcome its understanding of itself as a science, entirely motivated by the drive to acquire knowledge and, instead, move toward the affirmation of itself as an art motivated by the drive to illusion. While a return of and to animality allows history to become an art of interpretation, the same return allows philosophy to become an art of transfiguration.

A common shortcoming of those interpretations that simply see Nietzsche as a "denier" of truth is their failure to distinguish his practical discourse on truth from his theoretical treatment of truth. Nietzsche's practical treatment of truth belongs to the genre of social criticism, or what has come to be called a "critical theory" of society. Here "truth" refers to a basic, normative presupposition of all social beings living together and all communicative action among human beings. "Truth" in this practical sense, therefore, needs to be distinguished from both metaphysical and singular truth. Beginning with an evaluation of "On Truth and Lies in an Extra-Moral Sense," I demonstrate that Nietzsche's critique of metaphysics is joined together with what I refer to throughout this book as his critique of civilization. Through social criticism, Nietzsche investigates the operation of a "will to truth" in the constitution of social order and political power. With this kind of discourse on truth, Nietzsche resembles an Enlightenment (*Aufklärung*) thinker, seeking to unmask power-formations and ideological constructs by exposing how the domination and exploitation of the human being's animality is central to the establishment of a "truth" that can function as the basis of civil society and is understood as the highest achievement of abstract and conceptual thinking.[10]

Finally, this chapter thematizes what I refer to as Nietzsche's biopolitical treatment of truth. This genre is guided by the question of what value truth (in its various senses) holds for life. In other words, what kind of truth, if pursued, leads to an ascending form of life, and what kind of truth, if pursued, brings about decadent forms of life? I argue that Nietzsche's biopolitical treatment of truth aims at the renewal of a "pure and honest drive for truth" (*TL* 1). Nietzsche returns to the pre-Socratic ideal of philosophical life as an example of how to rethink the role that truth has in a life of the mind that overcomes not only the domination and exploitation of animality found at the basis of "truth" in civilization but also the "errors" inherent in a metaphysical world view. I argue that such an overcoming requires a return of and to the animality of the human being. Here, animal forgetfulness and pictorial thinking are understood not only as the source of pluralization of inherently singular forms of life but also as the source of honesty (*Redlichkeit*) and truthfulness (*Wahrhaftigkeit*). The ideas of honesty (*Redlichkeit*) and truthfulness (*Wahrhaftigkeit*) are now exemplified by the irreducibly singular entanglements of life with thought that characterize a philosophical life. These concepts, honesty and truthfulness, overcome the domination and exploitation of animal life occasioned by the metaphysical, epistemological, and psychological requirements of a "will to truth" that strives to provide unquestionable foundations for social order and political power. In this chapter I argue that overcoming the "will to truth" in the name of philosophical truthfulness and honesty is what Nietzsche refers to in his later work as "great politics," a task that lies with the "philosopher of the future."

The Encounter with the Silent Truth of the Animal

In "On the Use and Disadvantage of History for Life," Nietzsche claims that animals live in truth because their life is inherently unhistorical:

> Thus the animal lives *unhistorically*: for it is contained [*geht auf*] in the present, like a number without any awkward [*wunderlicher*] fraction left over; it does not know how to dissimulate [*verstellen*], it conceals [*verbirgt*] nothing and at every instant appears [*erscheint*] wholly as what it is; it can therefore never be anything but honest. (*HL* 1)

The unhistoricity of animal life, as discussed in the previous chapter, is due to its forgetfulness. Forgetfulness draws the animal into the moment; it absorbs the animal in the singular instant of time. As such, animals always live in the truth of the moment. The way they appear (*Erscheinen*) always truthfully reflects the way they are (*Sein*). As a result of their forgetfulness, animals can never deceive themselves or others. The opposite is the case for humans. They do not live in truth because their life is inherently historical. Their existence is an "imperfect tense," "an uninterrupted has-been, a thing that lives by negating, consuming and contradicting itself" (*HL* 1). As such, humans live not in the truth of the moment, but always in its falsification.

Humans experience their historicity, their memory of the past, as a burden (*HL* 1). Nietzsche notes that, as a consequence, humans like to deceive themselves and others with respect to their past. They envy the animal who does not know the "it was," the "password which gives conflict, suffering and satiety" (*HL* 1). Nietzsche imagines that a human being might ask an animal:

> "Why do you not speak to me of your happiness but only stand and gaze at me?" The animal would like to answer, and say "The reason is I always forget what I was going to say"—but then he forgot this answer too, and stayed in silence: so that the human being was left wondering [*verwundert*]. (*HL* 1)

Nietzsche's animal imaginary introduces a fissure, a break with respect to the main tradition of Western metaphysics according to which the human being's capacity for truth is inseparable from its capacity for language.[11] Truth, in this tradition, is something that exclusively belongs to the human being insofar as humans are animals who possess *logos.*[12] In contrast to humans, animals merely possess a voice *(phone).* Animals make sounds, but because they lack *logos,* these sounds do not communicate anything more than feelings of pleasure and pain, foreclosing the possibility of representing reality as it is.[13] In contraposition to the long-standing tradition of humanism in philosophy, Nietzsche separates truth from language and, aligning the former with silence, associates it with the animals. By identifying animals as thinking but silent beings, Nietzsche does not mean to silence them.[14] Rather, the silence of the animals stands for the manifestation of an alterity that does not express itself in conceptual language.[15] The silent presence of the animal not only offers, as I shall argue below, another paradigm of truth (connoting the idea of singular truth rather than metaphysical truth), but also it is on the basis of continuity with this animal silence that human language and communication can be understood.

In the imaginary encounter between the human and the animal, the animal does not respond to the human being's questioning with a comforting answer. Instead, it remains silent and leaves the human being wondering. The silence of the animal provokes questions in the mind of the human being. Faced with the animal's silent gaze, the human being experiences a state of embarrassment (*Verwunderung*), which it cannot fully express in its language.[16] The animal's silence implies a truth inaccessible and inexpressible in human language. Compared to the animal's silent proximity to truth, human language now seems inadequate and false, perhaps constituted by nothing but untruth and lies (*TL* 1).

Intuited Metaphors (*Anschauungsmetapher*) and Singular Truths

In "On the Use and Disadvantage of History for Life," truth, silence, and animal forgetfulness stand in clear opposition to lies, language and human memory. This opposition shares a strong affinity with the distinction found in "On Truth and Lies in an Extra-Moral Sense" between intuited metaphors (*Anschauungsmetapher*) and pictorial thinking (*Bilderdenken*) on the one hand, and conceptual language and abstract thinking (*Begriffsdenken*) on the other. A study of intuitive metaphor and pictorial thinking is of particular interest to an investigation of the relationship between animality and truth because it provides insight into what Nietzsche refers to as the silent truth of the animal in "On the Use and Disadvantage of History for Life" (*HL* 1).

In "On Truth and Lies in an Extra-Moral Sense," Nietzsche contrasts intuited metaphors (*Anschauungsmetapher*), pictures (*Bilder*), and dreams (*Traum*) with concepts (*Begriffe*), metaphors (*Metapher*), and schemes (*Schemata*). While the former uses pictorial thinking (*Bilderdenken*) to generate a world of first impressions (*anschauliche Welt der ersten Eindrücke*), the latter uses conceptual thinking (*Begriffsdenken*) to create an abstract world of regulating and imperative (linguistic) laws (*TL* 1; 2). In this text, conceptual thinking separates the human from the animal, just as memory establishes a distinction between human and animal forms of life in "On the Use and Disadvantage of History for Life." The abstract world of regulating and imperative (linguistic) laws constituted by conceptual thinking is a distinctly human world: "[e]verything which distinguishes [*abhebt*] human beings from animals depends on this ability [*Fähigkeit*] to displace [*verflüchtigen*] intuitive metaphors [*anschauliche Metapher*] into a scheme, in other words to dissolve a picture [*Bild*] into a concept [*Begriff*]" (*TL* 1). In contrast, thinking in terms of pictures confirms the continuity between human and animal life much like forgetfulness confirms the continuity between human and animal life. The intuitive world of first impressions brought forth by pictorial thinking is a world the human animal shares with other animals insofar as pictorial thinking pertains, generally speaking, to the eye: "There exists no form in nature because there exists no inner and outer. All art rests on the mirror of the eye" (*KSA* 7:19[144]).[17] Nietzsche considers the primordial drive (*Fundamentaltrieb*) to bring forth intuited metaphors and pictures more essential to life than the drive to displace intuited metaphors into concepts and schemes (*TL* 2), just as he considers the forgetfulness of the animal more essential than the memory of the human being (*HL* 1).

Pictorial thinking constitutes a "primitive world of metaphors [*primitive Metapherwelt*]," which arises from the "primal power of the human imagination [*Urvermögen menschlicher Phantasie*]" and its "overflowing [*hervorströmende*]" of a "mass of images [*Bildermassen*]" (*TL* 1). These intuited metaphors and pictures capture "unique, utterly individualized, primary experiences [*einmalige, ganz und gar individualisierte Urerlebnis*]" (*TL* 1). Through intuited metaphors humans access "what is individual [*Individuelle*] and real [*Wirkliche*]," for each intuited metaphor is itself "individual and incomparable [*ohne ihres Gleichen*]" (*TL* 1). Intuited metaphors do not contain knowledge of "essential qualities [*wesenhaften Qualität*]," but of "numerous individualized [*individualisierten*] and hence non-equivalent [*ungleichen*] actions" (*TL* 1). As such, intuited metaphors express what I call "singular truth" insofar as each and every intuited metaphor is singular and unique in an absolute sense, a product of the human animal's irreducibly singular experience and vision of the world.[18] This is why truth in the singular is inherently plural. The intuited world of first impressions is not composed of one universal truth, but of an infinite plurality of singular truths.[19]

What distinguishes intuited metaphors, pictures, and dreams from concepts, metaphors, and schemes is the immediacy with which they transpose the singular and distinct without consequently destroying it. Like the forgetfulness of the animal, intuited metaphors draw the human being into the moment, into the singular instant of time. As such, they can be understood in terms of the animal's forgetfulness, which, likewise, draws them into the moment, into the singular instant of time. In the immediacy of intuition, the human being recovers the silent truth of the animal. In contrast, concepts (*Begriffe*), metaphors (*Metapher*), and schemes (*Schemata*) cannot be understood in terms of the animal's forgetfulness or silent truth. They are not carriers of singular truths, of the individual (*Individuelle*) and the real (*Wirkliche*), but are instead displacements (*Verflüchtigung*) from intuited, incomparably singular pictures to abstract, universal concepts.

Concepts (*Begriffe*), metaphors (*Metapher*), and schemes (*Schemata*) attribute a deceiving generality (*Allgemeine*) and equality (*Gleiche*) to that which is inherently unequal (*ungleich*). Accordingly, while in the intuited world of first impressions one finds the silent truth of the animal, in the abstract world of regulating and imperative (linguistic) laws one encounters only errors and lies:

> Let us consider in particular how concepts are formed; each word immediately becomes a concept, not by virtue of the fact that it is intended to serve a memory of the unique, utterly individualized, primary experience to which it owes its existence [*Entstehen*], but because at the same time it must fit countless other, more or less similar cases, i.e., cases which strictly speaking, are never equivalent [*gleiche*], and thus nothing other than non-equivalent [*ungleiche*] cases. Every concept comes into being by making equivalent that which is non-equivalent [*Gleichsetzten des Nicht-Gleichen*]. (*TL* 1)[20]

In the process of concept formation, equality (*Gleichheit*) is assigned to what is merely similar (*das Ähnliche*) and, strictly speaking, nonequal

(*Nicht-Gleich*).[21] Whereas intuited metaphors express, like the forgetfulness of the animal, an experience and vision of the singular and the real, concepts establish an unfaithful equality and generality on the basis of forgetting the singular and real. While every concept stands for the loss and forgetting of the irreducibly singular and unique experiences that underlie its formation, every intuited metaphor serves as a "memory of the unique, utterly individualized, primary experience" (*TL* 1). In other words, whereas the formation of concepts exemplifies civilizational forgetfulness, the formation of intuited metaphors constitutes a cultural memory.[22]

Insofar as intuited metaphors trace the experience of the singular and the real, they are themselves inherently "individual and incomparable [*ohne ihres Gleichen*]" (*TL* 1). This is why intuited metaphors and pictures do not make up a (conceptual) language. What distinguishes language is, precisely, the displacement (*Verflüchtigung*) from intuitions and pictures of the singular and the real to general, common, and communicable concepts: "a metaphorical transposition into a different language and sphere that is unfaithful through and through" (*PTA* 3). That conceptual language is structured by signifying or sense-producing displacements highlights the fact that its symbols have always already lost the singular and the real.[23] In contraposition to language and speech, Nietzsche privileges the noble ways of silence for preserving the irreducible singularity of every experience. In comparison to conceptual language, intuited metaphors are noble and refined. They distinguish the unique, exceptional, and distinct but always only at a distance and in silence.[24]

Intuited metaphors offer pictures that express the singular and the real in such a way that their secret remains protected at a distance:

> No regular way leads from these intuitions [*Intuitionen*] into the land of the ghostly schemata and abstractions; words are not made from them; the human being is struck dumb when he sees them, or he will speak only in forbidden metaphors and unheard-of combinations of concepts so that, by at least demolishing and deriding the old conceptual barriers he may do creative justice to the impression [*Eindruck*] made on him by the mighty [*mächtigen*], present [*gegenwärtigen*] intuition [*Intuition*]. (*TL* 2)

When pictorial thinking does break into linguistic expression, it produces a counterlanguage that questions and ultimately destroys the regulative and imperative order established by abstract thinking. In this sense, pictorial thinking is honest like the animal: It cannot but remain faithful to its vision and experience of the singular and the real. Hence, it cannot but undo and dissolve the constructions of abstract thinking:

> It [the drive to form intuited metaphors] constantly confuses the cells and the classifications of concepts by setting up new translations, metaphors, metonymies; it constantly manifests the desire to shape the given world of the waking human being in ways which are just as multiform, irregular, inconsequential, incoherent, charming, and ever-new, as things are in the world of dream. Actually the waking human being is only clear about the fact that he is awake thanks to the rigid and regular web of concepts, and for that reason he sometimes comes to believe that he is dreaming if once that web of concepts is torn apart by art. (*TL* 2)

The difference between the intuited world of first impressions brought forth by pictorial thinking and the abstract world of regulating and imperative (linguistic) laws reflects the distinction between dreaming and waking life introduced in Chapter 1. Nietzsche privileges pictorial thinking over abstract thinking because it affirms the human being's continuity with the totality of life. It reconnects the human being with life's fundamental drive to bring forth dreamlike images and illusions. Pictorial thinking shows not only that human life is deeply involved and dissolved in dreams and illusions but also that dreams and illusions are the only condition under which life can strive and thrive.

In Nietzsche, the ability to dream manifests itself in the ability to create. Life is a dream that lives by imagining and reimagining, creating and recreating itself. As such, the creation of intuited metaphors, dreamlike images and illusions is inherently tied to the possibility of future life. In contrast to concepts, metaphors, and schemes, which are always already "old" (*TL* 2), intuited metaphors, pictures, and dreams are rejuvenating and "ever-new" (*TL* 2). When life is understood as an inherently artistic process, intuited metaphors and pictorial thinking are of greater value than universal concepts and abstract thinking. Whereas the former are, like the forgetfulness of the animal, carriers of the pluralization and singularization of life, the latter are, like the memory of the human, carriers of its equalization and uniformization. Intuited metaphors and pictorial thinking overflow with life while universal concepts and abstract thinking exercise restriction and control over the artistic expression of animal life.

The Question of Metaphysical Truth

Despite the differences between the intuited world of first impressions and the abstract world of regulating and imperative (linguistic) laws, it is important to emphasize that these worlds are not entirely disconnected because they both result from the human animal's artistic drive to form metaphors. Whereas the former is constituted by the transposition (*Übertragung*) of nerve stimuli into pictures, which Nietzsche also refers to as "first metaphor" (*TL* 1), the latter is generated when sounds and words imitate pictures, which Nietzsche also refers to as "second metaphor": "The stimulation of a nerve is first translated [*übertragen*] into an image: first metaphor! The image is then imitated [*nachgeformt*] by a sound: second metaphor!" (*TL* 1). However, what distinguishes the transposition of nerve stimuli into pictures from sound's imitation of pictures is that while the latter is inherently anthropocentric and anthropomorphic because it reflects a projection of the human onto the world, the former is free from such anthropocentrism and anthropomorphism. The intuited world of first impressions is, in this sense, a world that comes toward the human rather than one that is projected by the human or conceived according to human measure.

Since, for Nietzsche, conceptual language is human, subjective rather than objective, he contends that it can teach us nothing about the world as it is "in itself": "words are only symbols for the relation of things among themselves and of things to us and touch nowhere an absolute truth" (*PTA* 11). Conceptual language constitutes a self-referential whole, a symbolic system closed unto itself, failing to lead out to a world understood as the "thing in-itself," "pure truth," "truth without consequences," the "essence of things," a *qualitas occulta* (hidden property), the "mysterious X of the thing-in-itself;" and so on (*TL* 1). Nietzsche repeatedly insists that:

> Through words and concepts we will never reach behind the wall of relations some kind of primal mythical origin of things [*fabelhaften Urgrund der Dinge*], and even through the pure forms of sensibility and understanding, through space, time and causality, we gain nothing which would resemble a *veritas aeterna*. (*PTA* 11)

Nietzsche's critique of metaphysical truth ("absolute truth" or *veritas aeterna*) is not only intended to deny that conceptual language can "correspond" to the world understood as "thing-in-itself," "pure truth," the "essence of things," the "mysterious X of the thing-in-itself," but it also denies that such entities exist in the first place. Nietzsche's so-called denial of (metaphysical) truth, then, in no way presupposes his belief in metaphysical realism.[25]

That the abstract world of regulating and imperative (linguistic) laws is a world constituted by anthropomorphic projections is best illustrated by an analysis of the formation of human language (*Sprachbildung*). For instance, the concept "being" (*Sein*) can be etymologically traced back to human respiration, which humans then metaphorically transfer to all other things:

> The concept of being! As if the merely empirical origin of this concept would not already be revealed by its etymology! For *esse* essentially means "breathing": if humans apply this word to other things, then all they do is transfer by means of metaphor, that is by means of something illogical, the fact that they are breathing and alive, to other things and understand their existence as a breathing analogous to theirs. (*PTA* 11)

Since all objective or scientific knowledge of the world relies on conceptual language and is, therefore, based on anthropomorphic projections, Nietzsche denies that the scientific knowledge humans possess is " 'true in itself' and independent from the humankind" (*TL* 1).

> Anyone [*Forscher*] who searches for truths of that kind is basically only seeking the metamorphosis of the world in human beings; he strives for an understanding of the world as something which is similar in kind to humanity [*der Welt als eines menschenartigen Dinges*]. . . . His procedure is to measure all things against the human being, and in doing so he takes as his point of departure the erroneous belief that he has these things directly before him, as pure objects. Thus, forgetting that the original intuited metaphors [*Anschauungsmetapher*] were indeed metaphors, he takes them for the things in themselves. (*TL* 1)

The anthropomorphism of human conceptual language depends on mistaking the intuited metaphors for representations of "things in themselves." The very idea that an objective world exists apart from human thought and can be represented through concepts only becomes possible by forgetting the human animal's drive for metaphor creation.[26]

For Nietzsche, the possibility of a "pure and honest drive for truth" must begin with a denial of metaphysical truth or, in other words, with the recognition that conceptual language is inherently metaphorical and created and, therefore, does not correspond to things in and of themselves.[27] Whereas metaphysical truth exemplifies the forgetfulness of the original intuited metaphors, a "pure and honest drive for truth" exemplifies the memory of intuited metaphors. It affirms that conceptual language is metaphorical and, hence, the concept of truth itself is nothing but a metaphor:

> What then is truth? A mobile army of metaphors, metonymies, anthropomorphisms, in short a sum of human relations which have been subjected to poetic and rhetorical intensification, translation, and decoration, and which, after they have been in use for a long time, strike people as firmly established, canonical, and binding; truths are illusions of which we have forgotten that they are illusions, metaphors which have become worn by frequent use and have lost all sensuous vigor, coins which, having lost their stamp, are now regarded as metal and no longer as coins. (*TL* 1)

Nietzsche conceives conceptual language as a realm of metaphor formation where words and their meanings reflect metaphorical transpositions, first and second metaphors rather than truthful representations of the world as it is "in itself." Conceptual language is constituted by an infinite play of interpretations, where the meanings of words are never absolute or fixed, but always only provisory and open to new metaphorical transpositions.[28] Rather than attempting to stabilize conceptual language into fixed and absolute meanings, Nietzsche advocates breaking open conceptual language and releasing its "fixed" and "absolute" meanings into the flow of the continuous formation and transformation of intuited metaphors.

This does not mean that Nietzsche gives up on science or on the scientific pursuit of knowledge. Rather he holds that if the pursuit of knowledge is to be scientific, then it must begin by giving up on the idea of metaphysical truth and recognize that its conceptual tools are composed of "metaphors which have become worn by frequent use and have lost all sensuous vigor, coins which, having lost their stamp, are now regarded as metal and no longer as coins" (*TL* 1). Science must abandon the notion of representing the world "as it is in itself" and instead pursue experimental, tentative attempts (*Versuch*) at transposing the "coins" of intuited metaphors and pictures which have been "stamped" in the visions and experiences of the singular and the real. From this perspective, the function of science is primarily a critical one. Rather than being invested in the dishonest pursuit of metaphysical truth, science needs to invest itself in the "pure and honest" pursuit of "untruth" [*Falschheit*]. Science, whether philosophical or natural, has its greatest moments when critically questioning the pursuit of metaphysical truth.

The idea of the pursuit of truth as a tentative, indeterminate, and incomplete translation of intuited metaphors into conceptual language resonates with Nietzsche's later vision of the "philosophers of the future" as attempters:

> A new species [*Gattung*] of philosophers is coming up: I venture to baptize them with a name that is not free of danger. As I unriddle them, insofar as they allow themselves to be unriddled—for it belongs to their nature to *want* to remain riddles at some point—these philosophers of the future may have a right [*Recht*], it might also be a wrong [*Unrecht*], to be called attempters [*Versucher*]. This name is itself in the end a mere attempt and, if you will, a temptation [*Versuchung*]. (*BGE* 42)

The double meaning of attempt (*Versuch*)—as experiment and as seduction/temptation (*Versuchung*)—indicates that philosophy as Nietzsche envisages it in the future is an experimental attempt to approach truth with the awareness that one will never fully grasp or possess it: "The novelty of our current views on philosophy is the conviction which no other age had before us: *that we do not possess truth*" (*KSA* 12:9[91]). The pursuit of truth as an experimental play of seduction and temptation requires the philosopher to become a seducer (*Versucher*) and experimenter; someone who does not reveal truth but conceals it.

The Question of Correct Sense Perception

Although intuited metaphors, unlike conceptual language, provide access to the singular and the real, the singular and the real as they are metaphorically transposed in pictorial thinking do not correspond to a "primal mythical origin of things [*fabelhafter Urgrund der Dinge*]" (*PTA* 11). When Nietzsche insists that nature is inaccessible and indefinable (*TL* 1) he does not suggest that Kant was right to presuppose the existence of a "mysterious X of the thing-in-itself" behind the world of "appearance" (*TL* 1). From the beginning, Nietzsche rejects both the notion of the "mysterious X of the thing-in-itself" and that of "appearance":

> The word appearance [*Erscheinung*] contains many seductions, and for this reason I avoid using it as far as possible; for it is not true that the essence of things appears in the empirical world. (*TL* 1)

Accordingly, Nietzsche's critique of metaphysical truth in "On Truth and Lies in an Extra-Moral Sense" should not be confused with a Schopenhauer-influenced radicalization of a Kantian critique of metaphysics.

Rather, Nietzsche's critique breaks with the fundamental assumptions of the Kantian critique because it rejects not only the notion of the "thing in-itself" but also a "world of appearance [*Phenomena*]."[29] Nietzsche replaces this pair of concepts, and the dualism of worlds that they conjure, with the notion of intuited metaphor. The priority of metaphor means that there can be no truthful representation (*Vorstellung*) of the world but always only an illusory dissimulation (*Verstellung*). The notion of metaphoric dissimulation (*Verstellung*) deprives the idea of representation (*Vorstellung*) of any "reality" [*Gegenstände*], whether the latter be understood as noumenal or phenomenal.[30] As a consequence of the shift from *Vorstellung* to *Verstellung*, the question of whether there could be correct or objective sense perception—whether our perceptions can be regimented (a priori or a posteriori) so as to provide a representation of "mind independent objects" (of an "objective world")—becomes meaningless. In other words, the idea of intuited metaphor, of the transposition of the singular and the real into pictures, calls into question the very idea of "correct perception" (*TL* 1).

Once again, Nietzsche uses the perspectives of other animals as vantage points from which the existence of criteria for correct perception become questionable:

> He [the human being] even has to make an effort to admit to himself that insects or birds perceive a quite different world from that of human beings, and that the question as to which of these two perceptions of the world is the more correct is quite meaningless, since this would require them to be measured by the criterion of the *correct perception*, i.e., by a *non-existent* criterion. (*TL* 1)

It makes no sense to speak of the human being's perception of the world as the correct or objective way of perceiving the world because its relation to the world is not fundamentally representational.[31]

Nietzsche here makes another break from the main tradition of Western metaphysics. While this tradition holds that correct perception provides a solid basis for an epistemological, cognitive relation to the world, Nietzsche asserts the human animal's relation to the world is not primarily epistemological, but aesthetical:

> But generally it seems to me that the correct perception [*richtige Perception*]—which would mean the full and adequate expression [*adäquate Ausdruck*] of an object in the subject—is something contradictory and impossible [*ein widerspruchsvolles Unding*]; for between two absolutely different spheres, such as subject and object

are, there is no causality, no correctness, no expression, but at most an *aesthetic* way of relating [*ein ästhetisches Verhalten*], by which I mean an allusive transference [*andeutende Uebertragung*], a stammering translation [*eine nachstammelnde Uebersetzung*] into a quite different language [*fremde Sprache*]. For which purpose a middle sphere and mediating force is certainly required which can freely invent and freely create poetry. (*TL* 1)[32]

From this perspective, perception belongs to a "middle sphere," a "mediating force" that "freely invents and freely creates poetry," thereby excluding the possibility of correct representation understood as "the full and adequate expression of an object in the subject" (ibid.). Humans are "deeply immersed in illusions and dream-images; their eyes merely glide across the surface of things and see 'forms'; nowhere does their perception [*Empfindungen*] lead into truth; instead it is content to receive stimuli and, as it were, to play with its fingers on the back of things" (ibid.).

Generally speaking, the transposition of nerve stimuli into pictures (intuited metaphors) and the imitation of pictures by sounds (concepts) both reflect an aesthetic relationship, "an allusive transference [*andeutende Übertragung*], a stammering translation [*eine nachstammelnde Übersetzung*] into a quite different language [*fremde Sprache*]" (ibid.). Still, it is important to note that while the transpositions reflected in intuited metaphors are characterized by the forgetfulness of the animal, the transpositions reflected in concepts are characterized by what I refer to as civilizational forgetfulness. Consequently, while the imitations reflected in concepts are constituted by deceiving generalizations, the translations reflected in intuited metaphors are irreducibly singular expressions of the singular and the real. They reveal the singular truth of a vision or experience of the world in a picture without dissolving, losing, and ultimately destroying its singularity.[33]

In the end, however, the translations reflected in intuited metaphors are always only tentative attempts (*Versuche*). They are by definition indeterminate and incomplete, for in every experience (of the outside world) something withdraws itself from being transposed and translated into another sphere, whether of pictures or of concepts. It resists being captured in a picture or imitated by a concept, and thus always remains secret and silent, certainly withdrawn from the concept, but perhaps also hidden somewhere in the picture.

Philosophy and Tragedy

The notions of intuited metaphor and pictorial thinking not only allow Nietzsche to redetermine the status of philosophy in relation to art and science, but also offer him a new basis for questioning philosophy's relationship to the "honest and pure drive for truth" (ibid.). Nietzsche holds that when philosophical intuitions are translated into abstract reflections, their vision of singular truths is lost. A passage from *Philosophy in the Tragic Age of the Greeks* illustrates this idea:

> And like for the playwright words and verses are only stammering in a strange language which he employs to say what he lived and saw, so the expression of each deep philosophical intuition in dialectics and scientific reflection are on the one hand the only means to communicate what is seen, but a poor means, at bottom a metaphorical transposition in a different language and sphere that is unfaithful through and through. (*PTA* 3)

Nietzsche understands philosophical intuition as a "lightning-like grasping and illuminating of similarities [*Ähnlichkeiten*]" (ibid.). Philosophical intuitions share these features with intuited metaphors and the silent truth of the animal's forgetfulness: they grasp and illuminate singular truths without reducing them to sameness and equality. In contrast, abstract reflection substitutes a posteriori by means of conceptual language "similarity [*Ähnlichkeiten*]" by "sameness [*Gleichheiten*]," a "vision of a next-to-each-other [*Nebeneinander-Geschaute*]" by causality (ibid.).

Philosophical intuitions, like intuited metaphors, are characterized by their sensibility for the singular and the real. From this viewpoint, philosophy is not concerned with objective knowledge or metaphysical truth, but with wisdom and taste:

> The Greek word which designates the "wise" belongs etymologically to *sapio* (I taste), *sapiens* (the one who tastes), *sisyphos* (the human being with the sharpest taste); a discriminatory taste and capacity for meaningful distinctions characterizes, according to the common sense of the people, the rare art of the philosopher. . . . It is such a selection and distinction of the uncommon, surprising, difficult, divine which separates philosophy from science, just as its emphasis of the useless separates it from cleverness [*Klugheit*]. (ibid.)

In his early writings, Nietzsche contrasts the philosopher's pictorial thinking with the scientist's conceptual thinking. Whereas the scientists, due to their lack of taste and sense of distinction, arrive only at general abstractions, the intuitive philosophers distinguish an infinite plurality of irreducibly singular truths. Their sensibility for singular truths is revelatory of their nobility and pathos of distance. They do not want to share their experience and vision of truth because to do so would undermine its singularity. This is why they are not dogmatists seeking to impose their truth on others. A citation from *Beyond Good and Evil* shows that the figure of the intuitive philosopher in Nietzsche's early writing stands in continuity with his later conception of the philosopher of the future:

> That is probable enough, for all philosophers so far have loved their truths. But they will certainly not be dogmatists. It must offend their pride, also their taste, if their truth is supposed to be a truth for everyone—which has so far been the secret wish and hidden meaning of all dogmatic aspiration. "My judgment is *my* judgment": no one else is easily entitled to it—that is what such a philosopher of the future may perhaps say to himself. One must shed the bad taste of wanting to agree with many. "Good" is no longer good when one's neighbor mouths it. And how should there be a "common good"! The term contradicts itself: whatever can be common always has little value. In the end it must be as it is and always has been: great things remain for the great, abysses for the profound, nuances and shudders for the refined, and, in brief, all that is rare for the rare. (*BGE* 43)

[margin annotation: ≠ Common Good]

Intuitive philosophers, as Nietzsche imagines them, do not see metaphysical truth as the ultimate object(ive) of philosophy. Rather they understand philosophy as an art, a continuation of the mythical drive:

> Great dilemma: is philosophy an art or a science? Both in its purposes and its results it is an art. But it uses the same means as science—conceptual representation. Philosophy is a form of artistic invention [*Dichtkunst*]. . . . He knows in that he invents, and he invents in that he knows [*er erkennt in dem er dichtet und er dichtet in dem er erkennt*]. Philosophy is invention beyond the limits of experience; it is the continuation of the mythical drive. It is thus essentially pictorial [*in Bildern, Bilderdenken*]. Mathematical expression is not a part of the essence of philosophy. Overcoming of knowledge by means of the powers that *fashion myth*. (*P* 53)

[margin annotation: PHIL =]

Responding to the dilemma of whether philosophy is art or science, Nietzsche asserts that philosophy is an art insofar as it gives up on a metaphysical idea of reality and truth, recognizing the priority of dissimulation in relation to a conceptual language that always claims to "represent" reality "as it is in itself." Following its "pure and honest drive for truth," philosophy must not only affirm "reality" as an illusion (an intuited world of first impressions brought forth by pictorial thinking) but also will this illusion by creating and continuing to create new illusions (intuited metaphors). The will to illusion defines the tragic dimension of Nietzsche's vision of philosophy as an art, for to will honesty and truthfulness now means to will illusion and deception.[34]

For Nietzsche, it is essential that philosophy operate a return to intuited metaphors, "overcoming of knowledge," or the idea of a "representational" access to the world, "by means of the powers that fashion myth," that is, by recovering the lived contact with the world given through intuited metaphors and pictorial thinking.[35] In fact, the future of philosophy depends on its ability to dismiss itself as a science in pursuit of metaphysical truth and, instead, to embrace itself as a "pure and honest drive" for singular truths. Just as history has to overcome itself as a science and become an art of interpretation, so philosophy must become an art of transfiguration in the service of life.

In more general terms, Nietzsche's distinction between philosophy as intuitive, pictorial thinking and philosophy as abstract, conceptual thinking reflects the distinction between philosophy's role in the tragic age of Greek culture and its role in post-Socratic scientific culture in *The Birth of Tragedy*. Whereas Greek culture in the tragic age understands philosophy as an art guided by intuitions and a refined sensibility for singular truth, Socrates is accused of introducing a scientific idea of culture that envisions philosophy as a science guided by abstractions and a pursuit of metaphysical truth. According to Nietzsche's analysis, under the rule of scientific culture, philosophy takes on forms that are distinctly hostile to life. In order to overcome these life-denying forces, Nietzsche advocates a return to a tragic conception of culture and philosophy (*EH* "Books" BT: 4).

> *The philosopher of tragic knowledge.* He masters the uncontrolled knowledge drive [*entfesselten Wissenstrieb*], though not by means of a new metaphysics. He establishes no new faith. He considers it *tragic* that the ground of metaphysics has been withdrawn, and he will never permit himself to be satisfied with the motley whirling game of the sciences. He cultivates a new *life*; he returns art to its rights. . . . When carried to its limits the knowledge drive turns against itself in order to proceed to the *critique of knowing*. Knowledge in the service of the best life. One must even *will illusion*—that is what is tragic. (*P* 37)

The tragic philosopher offers no new metaphysics: she pursues truth following her *Wissenstrieb*, her "pure and honest drive for truth," but is aware that such a pursuit is "tragic" because there is no longer any meta-physical "reality" that could give meaning to metaphysical truth. In other words, there is no longer a ground for metaphysics: Its ground has been withdrawn by the idea of intuited metaphor as the primary way of being in contact with the world. Likewise, science is no comfort for the tragic philosopher. Because there is no in-itself, there is also no appearance that can be regimented into objective knowledge.[36] Tragic philosophers affirm the metaphoric character of truth: Their drive for truth is a drive for illu-sion.[37] As such, the tragic philosopher overcomes the distance between the silent truth of the animal and the lies inherent to human conceptual lan-guage. When philosophy regains the silent truth of the animal, it becomes the artistic expression of singular rather than metaphysical truths.

The intimate relationship between the "drive to form [intuited] met-aphors" and the "honest and pure drive for truth" reveals that "On Truth and Lies in an Extra-Moral Sense" is not simply concerned with a critique of metaphysical truth but with how to give new and positive meaning to the "honest and pure drive for truth." Here the guiding question is not "What is truth?" but "What are the uses and disadvan-tages of truth with respect to life?" In other words, the question is not whether intuited metaphors, dreamlike images, and illusions are more truthful than metaphors, concepts, and schemata, or whether they reflect a more correct perception of the word, but whether they are more life-enhancing or life-diminishing.[38]

Given the importance of this question, it is hardly surprising that Nietzsche not only distinguishes between dreamlike images, intuited met-aphors, and illusions and concepts, metaphors, and schemata but between two corresponding ways of life (and culture), namely, that of the intuitive human being (tragic or Dionysian culture) and that of the abstract human being (scientific or Socratic culture):

> There are epochs in which the rational human being and the in-tuitive human being stand side by side, the one fearful of intuition, the other filled with scorn for abstraction, the latter as unreasonable as the former is unartistic. They both desire [begehren] to rule [herr-schen] over life; the one by his knowledge of how to cope with the chief calamities of life by providing for the future, by prudence and regularity, the other by being an "exuberant hero [überfroher Held]" who does not see those calamities and who acknowledges life as real when it is disguised as beauty and appearance. Where the intuitive human being, as was once the case in ancient Greece, wields his weapons more mightily and victoriously than his contrary, a culture

can take shape, given favorable conditions, and the rule [*Herrschaft*] of art over life can become established; all the expressions of a life lived are accompanied by pretense, by the denial of neediness, by the radiance of metaphorical intuition [*metaphorischen Anschauung*], and indeed generally by the immediacy of deception. . . . Whereas the human being who is guided by concepts and abstractions only succeeds thereby in warding off misfortune, is unable to compel the abstractions themselves to yield him happiness, and strives merely to be as free as possible from pain, the intuitive human being, standing in the midst of a culture, reaps directly from his intuitions not just protection from harm but also a constant stream of brightness, a lightening of the spirit, redemption, and release. (*TL* 2)

Whereas the abstract human being reflects a form of life that needs to believe in the illusion of scientific knowledge and metaphysical truth—which is, in fact, the only illusion of truth with which one can cope (*GS* 121)—the intuitive human being reflects a form of life that pursues the pluralizing augmentation of life through the seeking of singular truths. Nietzsche acknowledges the achievements of science and civilization insofar as they solve the problem of the human animal's need for security and stability. Still, he considers a culture exclusively based upon science and rationality to be dangerous because it undermines the singular in the name of the universal, the animal in the name of the (all too) human, and the forgetfulness of culture in the name of the memory of civilization.

In order to adequately address the question of whether intuited metaphors, dreamlike images, and illusions are more life-enhancing than metaphors, concepts and schemata, it is necessary to distinguish a third, biopolitical sense in Nietzsche's treatments of truth. At the center of this third genre is the representation of the philosopher's life and thought as an example of singular truth: "The challenge is to bring to light what we must always *love* and *admire* and what no posterior knowledge can rob from us, namely, the great human being" (*PTA* "Preface"). But, before I move on to a discussion of Nietzsche's biopolitical discourse on truth, it is necessary to deepen our understanding of how the shift from *Vorstellung* to *Verstellung* affects Nietzsche's conception of the intellect. Rather than seeing the intellect as an instrument of knowledge in the service of the "will to truth," Nietzsche sees the intellect as an instrument of dissimulation (*Verstellung*) in the service of life. But if the intellect acts in the service of life then it must also be investigated from the perspective of life. Nietzsche's critique of metaphysics, therefore, must be considered within his larger conception of life. One of the great novelties of "On Truth and Lies in an Extra-Moral Sense" is that it investigates the human intellect as an artistic and creative force, which is then examined as a force of life. What is at stake in "On Truth and Lies in an Extra-Moral Sense" is an investigation of knowledge (science) from the perspective of art and of art from the perspective of life. In "An Attempt at Self-Criticism," Nietzsche claims to have remained faithful to this task throughout his writing career ("An Attempt at Self-Criticism" 2).

The Dissimulations of the Intellect

within? nature!

"On Truth and Lies in an Extra-Moral Sense" begins with the provocative claim that when considered from the perspective of the totality of life, the intellect is a "pitiful [*kläglich*]," "insubstantial [*schattenhaft*]," "transitory [*flüchtig*]," "purposeless," and "arbitrary" entity (*TL* 1).[39] Nietzsche ironically contrasts this perspective with the traditional view of the intellect as an emblem of the human being's distinction from and superiority to other forms of life because of its purported capacity to represent reality correctly. Nietzsche casts doubts on these claims by adopting the perspective of other animals, wondering whether the human being's sentimental pride in its intellectual capacities can be compared to that of a midge:

> If we could communicate with a midge we would hear that it too floats through the air with the very same pathos, feeling that it too contains within itself the flying center of this world. (*TL* 1)

He draws a pitiless caricature of human beings inflating themselves like balloons, exploding with pride in their intellectual achievements. In order to deflate their self-image, he recounts the following disenchanting fable, which suggests that the human intellect is nothing but a contingent and ephemeral phenomenon, insignificant beyond the bounds of human life:

myth of conse.

> In some remote corner of the human universe, flickering in the light of the countless solar systems into which it happened to be poured, there was once a planet on which clever animals invented cognition [*Erkennen*]. It was the most arrogant and most mendacious minute in the "history of the world"; but a minute was all it was. After nature had drawn just a few more breaths the planet froze and the clever animals had to die. (*TL* 1)[40]

TL

Far from marking the human being's superiority over other forms of life, its reliance on the intellect is revelatory of its inferiority and relative weakness with respect to other forms of life. In fact, from the perspective of life, the intellect fulfills primarily a life-preserving function. It is the "aid supplied to the most unfortunate, most delicate and most transient beings so as to detain them for a minute within existence" (*TL* 1).

In accordance with this early consideration of the intellect Nietzsche argues, in *The Gay Science*, that contrary to the belief that consciousness denotes the human being's superiority with respect to other forms of life, consciousness in the human animal is a relatively young, insufficiently developed organ, which, as such, can even be dangerous (*GS* 11; 354).[41] Nietzsche esteems unconsciousness above consciousness for the simple reason that most of the human animal's vital functions operate without consciousness. Unconsciousness is more essential to life than consciousness because human animals have, thus far, preserved themselves due to their unconsciousness rather than their consciousness. In a passage from the *Nachlass*, Nietzsche claims that what is commonly referred to as memory is only the surface of many physiological, nervous, and entirely unconscious processes:

> There exists no proper organ of "memory": all nerves, for example in the leg remember prior experiences. Every word, every number is the result of a physical process and somewhere fixed in the nerves. Everything which has been organized in the nerves continues to live on in them. There are waves of stimulation, where this life becomes *consciousness*, we remember. (*KSA* 9:2[68])

In comparison to the unconscious memory of life, what is commonly referred to as memory reflects only an insignificant and ephemeral portion of that which is remembered unconsciously. The extension of the unconscious memory of organic life signals that the distance between what the human animal knows and what it ignores about itself is infinite.[42]

In "On Truth and Lies in an Extra-Moral Sense," Nietzsche claims that the intellect is not only an instrument for the preservation of human animal life but, more radically, that it generates illusory dissimulations (*Verstellungen*) rather than truthful representations (*Vorstellungen*) of the world.

> As a means for the preservation of the individual, the intellect shows its greatest strength in dissimulation [*Verstellung*], since this is the means to preserve those weaker, less robust individuals, who, by nature, are denied horns or the sharp fangs of a beast of prey with which to wage the struggle for existence. (*TL* 1)

What distinguishes the human being from other animals is not the capacity of its intellect to produce a correct representation of the world as it is "in-itself," or, as Rorty refers to it, a "mirror nature." Instead, what makes the human animal unique is its ability to invent deceiving dissimulations (*Verstellung*).[43] This talent takes the form of an art rather than a science, an "art of dissimulation [*Verstellungskunst*]" that reaches its peak in humankind (*TL* 1):

> Deception, flattery, lying and cheating, speaking behind the back of others, keeping up appearances [*Repräsentieren*], living in borrowed finery, wearing masks, the drapery of convention, play-acting for the benefit of others and oneself—in short, the constant flattering of human beings around the flame of vanity is so much the rule and the law that there is virtually nothing which defies understanding so much as the fact that an honest and pure drive towards truth should ever have emerged in them. (*TL* 1)

Nietzsche does not reject the intellect due to its incapacity to provide anything "substantial," such as metaphysical truth. On the contrary, he praises the intellect's talent for dissimulation because it preserves the life of the individual. Seen from the perspective of life, the human animal's intellect is an inherently artistic force, a drive to bring forth distorted images, illusions, and dissimulations of the world which are life-enhancing.[44] Therefore, the human animal should be conceived of as an "artistically creative subject" (*TL* 1), an animal that dissimulates (*verstellen*) rather than represents (*vorstellen*) everything it encounters. And, hence, the human being is an animal that is not cut off from the totality of life due to its so-called intellectual capacities but, on the contrary, stands in continuity with other forms of life insofar as they too are "artistically creative subjects":

> A more advanced [*höhere*] physiology will surely confirm that the artistic force inheres our becoming, not only in that of the human being, but also in that of the animal: it will say that the *artistic begins* with the *organic*. (*KSA* 7:19[50])[45]

It is important to note that the shift from *Vorstellung* to *Verstellung* in Nietzsche's treatment of truth signals more than just a shift from understanding the intellect as an instrument of knowledge and metaphysical truth in the service of science to understanding it as an artistic force in the service of the creative transfiguration of life. More importantly, it signals a shift from the genre of critique of metaphysics to the genre of social criticism. Accordingly, one should not be misled into thinking that philosophy in Nietzsche is being reduced to an aesthetic activity practiced at the margin of society. On the contrary, I hold that the transformation of philosophy into an art goes hand in hand with assigning a new role of social and political significance to the "pure and honest drive for truth." By prioritizing art over science, Nietzsche does not obey Nehamas's ideal of "life as literature" but, rather, renews the tradition of Enlightenment by recovering the intellect's ability to critique society.

The affinity between the intellect as an artistic force of dissimulation and the intellect as a force of critical evaluation is shown when one takes into account how Nietzsche distinguishes between the two different kinds of dissimulations of the intellect. On the one hand, there are those dissimulations that preserve the life form of the group and, on the other hand, there are those that foster the cultivation of the irreducible singularity of each individual's life and thought. In the former case the intellect functions as a tool for the preservation of society: In this function the intellect is inherently unfree and captured by the rule of civilization. In the latter case the dissimulations of the intellect become vehicles of critical thinking (that is, freedom of thought). This freedom of thought primarily constitutes a counterforce to the rule of civilization but, beyond critique, it also manifests itself as a source for the pluralizing singularization of forms of life and thought. To better understand how the intellect's artistic and creative talent for dissimulation (*Verstellung*) is linked with the preservation of human life as a whole, it is necessary, first, to address the relationship Nietzsche sees among human memory, conceptual language, and abstract thinking, and, second, to examine how this relationship fits with Nietzsche's treatment of truth in the genre of critique of civilization.

Conceptual Language and Abstract Thought

The relationship that I establish between intuited metaphor and the forgetfulness of the animal also applies to the relationship between conceptual language and human memory insofar as Nietzsche conceives of the process of concept formation in the same way he conceives of the process of memory formation:

> We have to revise our views on memory: it is the quantity of all experiences of all organic life, alive, self-ordering, mutually forming each other, competing with each other, simplifying, condensing and transforming into many different unities. There must exist an inner *process*, which proceeds like the formation of concepts [*Begriffsbildung*] out of many singular cases [*Einzelfällen*]: the emphasizing and continuous new underlining of basic schemes and the omission of marginal traits [*Weglassen der Nebenzüge*]. (*KSA* 11:26[94])[46]

The formation of language and memory are both processes of establishing deceiving simplifications, generalizations, and universalizations constituted by movements of "seeing as equal [*Gleichsehen*]" and "taking as equal [*Gleichnehmen*]" what is inherently "unequal [*ungleich*]":

> Our *memory* relies on a seeing as *equal* and a taking as equal: it thus relies on an *imprecise* seeing; originally it is of the greatest *coarseness* and sees almost everything as *equal*.—That our representations [*Vorstellungen*] act as stimulating impulses is due to the fact that we always imagine and feel many representations [*Vorstellungen*] as being the same, that is, due to our coarse memory which sees as equal and due to our imagination, which, out of laziness, poetizes as equal what in truth is different. (*KSA* 9:11[138])

Memory establishes sameness and identity between what is singular and distinct. As such, memory is based on the same imprecision as the process of concept formation. Both subsume the singular and the real under a more general unity according to the criterion of sameness or equality (*Gleichheit*). Furthermore, both memory and concept formations are defined by civilizational forgetfulness: concepts are formed "by dropping these individual differences arbitrarily, by forgetting those features which differentiate one thing from another" (*TL* 1). Whereas intuited metaphors are defined by the forgetfulness of the animal as a carrier of silent truth, the civilizational forgetfulness inherent to the formation of memory and concepts is inseparable from a loss of singular truth or, in other words, from a dissimulating transposition (*Übertragung*) of an intuited metaphor into a word.

Speaking in more general terms, the processes of both concept and memory formation are a reflection of the civilizing processes of socialization. What distinguishes socialization, as I have argued in Chapter 2, is a "seeing as equal [*Gleichsehen*]" and a "taking as equal [*Gleichnehmen*]" of what is irreducibly singular and distinct.[47] In the processes of civilization and socialization, the singular and distinct are "forgotten," excluded, and left over for the sake of the formation of greater, more general unities under which they can be subsumed. The singular and distinct remain over at the margin of society just as they remain over at the margin of the concept. According to Nietzsche's critique of civilization, just as modern egalitarianism needs to be made sensitive to the values of aristocratic culture, so too does conceptual language need to be made sensitive to the silent picturing of the singular and distinct.

Nietzsche recognizes that "seeing as equal [*Gleichsehen*]" and "taking as equal [*Gleichnehmen*]" play significant roles in the preservation of human

Abstract thinking

animal life and, therefore, need to be recognized as praiseworthy.[48] In "On Truth and Lies in an Extra-Moral Sense," he claims that abstract thinking (that is, the substitution of the similarity between singulars by equality and sameness) is life-preserving. Abstract thinking protects the human animal from being swept away by "sudden impressions [*plötzliche Eindrücke*]" and "intuitions [*Anschauungen*]" (*TL* 1). Abstract thinking produces a world in which humans can live harbored by the illusion of safety and stability. This view stands in continuity with the thesis Nietzsche defends in his later work, namely, that "the falseness of a judgment is for us not necessarily an objection to a judgment":

> The question is to what extent it is life-promoting, life-preserving, species-preserving, perhaps even species-cultivating [*Art-züchtend*]. And we are fundamentally inclined to claim that the falsest judgments (which include the synthetic judgments *a priori*) are the most indispensable to us; that without accepting the fictions of logic, without measuring reality [*Wirklichkeit*] against the purely invented world of the unconditional and self-identical [*Sich-selbst-Gleichen*], without a constant falsification of the world by means of numbers, the human being could not live,—that renouncing false judgments would mean renouncing life and a denial of life. To recognize untruth as a condition of life—that certainly means resisting accustomed value feelings in a dangerous way; and a philosophy that risks this would by that token alone place itself beyond good and evil. (*BGE* 4)[49]

In accordance with this view, "truth" is life-preserving not because it correctly represents reality (whether phenomenal or in-itself) but because it is an illusion that artistically transforms the world in such a way that humans can live in it. Abstract thinking produces a regular and imperative order of concepts, which imbues the human animal with feelings of safety and stability. Moreover, it allows humans to understand themselves and their actions as moral and rational: "As creatures [*Wesen*] of *reason,* human beings now make their actions subject to the rule of abstraction [*Herrschaft der Abstraktion*]" (*TL* 1). For abstract thinking provides, like the memory of the will discussed in Chapter 2, a basis for the preservation of life in society with others.

Nietzsche compares the abstract world of regulative and imperative (linguistic) laws to a Roman columbarium, a burial site of the intuition (*der Begräbnisstätte der Anschauung*) (*TL* 2). This architectural metaphor illustrates the cruelty and violence with which the abstract world of regulating and imperative linguistic laws imposes itself on and rules over the intuited world of first impressions:

[S]omething becomes possible in the realm of schemata which could never be achieved in the realm of intuited first impressions, namely, the construction of a pyramidal order based on castes and degrees, the creation of a new world of laws, privileges, subordinations, definitions of borders, which now confronts the other intuited world of first impressions as something firmer, more general, more familiar, more human, and hence as something regulatory and imperative. Whereas every intuited metaphor [*Anschauungsmetapher*] is individual and unique and is therefore always able to escape classification, the great edifice of concepts exhibits the rigid regularity of a Roman *columbarium*, while logic breathes out that air of severity and coolness which is peculiar to mathematics. (*TL* 1)[50]

Nietzsche appreciates the ability to dissolve pictures into concepts, for he recognizes the merits of founding a human world of concepts upon the intuited world of first impressions. However, he remains critical of this ability insofar as the abstract world of regulating and imperative (linguistic) laws undermines and, ultimately, destroys the vision and experience of singular truths reflected in each and every intuited metaphor.

The problem of abstract thinking is that it forecloses the possibility of an experience and vision of the singular and the real. It not only cuts off human life from the totality of life but, more importantly, it loses touch with the drives of life, such as the drive to bring forth intuited metaphors and pictures which enhance the becoming of future life. In contrast to the freedom and fullness of life characteristic of pictorial thinking, abstract thinking essentially reflects an impotent way of life and thought which is incapable of engendering new life, just as the way of life and thought of the scientific scholar (*Gelehrte*) produces knowledge of the past but does not carry future life. Separated from the life-engendering force of pictorial thinking, abstract thinking misses the encounter with otherness that the human animal experiences in those primal visions expressed in intuited metaphors. In this sense, abstract thinking is self-referential and closed unto itself. It produces nothing but cold shadows of life that reflect unfruitful ways of relating to life. This is why abstract thinking generates feelings of imprisonment and hostility toward life. When the human animal relies on abstract thinking alone it becomes the prisoner of its own conceptual constructions, just as it becomes a hostage to the past when it relies only on its memories, cutting itself off from animal forgetfulness as the force that redirects the past toward the future (*HL* 1). Given the dangers inherent to abstract thinking, the enhancement of human life and the increasing pluralization of irreducibly singular forms of life depend on the recovery not only of the forgetfulness of the animal but also of the animal's power to bring forth intuited metaphors, pictures, and dreamlike illusions.

"Truth" and the Critique of Civilization

One of the great merits of "On Truth and Lies in an Extra-Moral Sense" is that it shows how the pursuit of "truth" is inseparably linked with the project of civilization. Within this project, "truth" is understood as a set of regulative and imperative (linguistic) laws which form the institutional, conventional basis of society:

> Insofar as the individual wishes to preserve itself in relation to other individuals, in the state of nature it mostly uses its intellect for concealment and dissimulation [*Verstellung*]; however, because necessity and boredom also lead the human beings to want to live in societies and herds, they need a peace treaty, and so they endeavor to eliminate from their world at least the crudest forms of the *bellum omnium contra omnus*. In the wake of this peace treaty, however, comes something which looks like the first step towards the acquisition of that mysterious drive for truth. For that which is to count as "truth" from this point onwards now becomes fixed, i.e., a way of designating things is invented which has the same validity and force everywhere, and the legislation of language also produces the first laws of truth. (*TL* 1)[51]

In what follows I use "truth" in quotations to refer to Nietzsche's sociopolitical treatment of institutionalized "truth." "Truth" understood as the basis of society has to be distinguished, first, from the notion of singular truth revealed and concealed in intuited metaphors and, second, from the notion of metaphysical truth rejected by Nietzsche. Unlike singular or metaphysical truth, "truth" is invented in order to constitute and secure a social and political order that guarantees the preservation of human life. "Truth" as a normative concept fulfills the criteria of a morally and legally binding standard to which individuals must submit themselves if they want to enjoy the privileges of a secure life in the society of others.

When "the drive for truth [*Wahrheitstrieb* or *Trieb zur Wahrheit*]" contributes to the foundation and preservation of a set of legally and morally binding rules of societal living, it pursues a political interest and fulfills an ideological function (*TL* 1). "Truth" surely preserves the life of the group: it is useful but not truthful. When "the drive for truth" refers to the invention of a rational and moral order whose principles serve as guidelines

for the social and political organization of human life, then this drive is *conversly*
no longer a "pure [*reine*] and honest [*ehrlich*] drive for truth" but rather
something that satisfies the need to stabilize and secure the rule of civilization. "Truth" then is nothing but the "obligation to lie in accordance
with a firmly established convention, to lie en masse and in a style that is
binding for all" (*TL* 1).

The relationship between the institution of "truth" and the rule of civilization in "On Truth and Lies in an Extra-Moral Sense" is analogous to
the relationship between the memory of the will and the rule of civilization developed in *On the Genealogy of Morals*. In Nietzsche's genealogical
discourse, the foundation of society is inseparable from the institution of
a memory of the will. In both texts, the notions of the memory of the will
and "truth" determine a fixed set of rules and norms intended to guarantee the orderly functioning of society. Both constitute moral and legal
guidelines that are imposed on every member of society so as to secure the
well-being of the group. Moreover, the idea of "truth" as a normative
standard (*TL* 1) is analogous to the idea of the memory of the will (*GM*
II: 1) because both institute general norms by means of violence and domination. The violence and domination involved in the process of civilization and socialization are, as I argue throughout, directed against the
human being's animality. The institution of "truth," just like the institution of the memory of the will, is dependent upon the successful "taming"
(*bändigen*) and "defeating" (*bezwingen*) of the human animal's artistic
drive to transpose nerve stimuli into pictures and intuited metaphors (*TL*
2).

Life in society requires that the human animal learn to think abstractly
and use abstract concepts as moral and epistemological guidelines. In *On
the Genealogy of Morals*, the taming and breeding of the human animal
intentionally eliminates its forgetfulness. The underlying idea is that only
when the human animal can remember (the moral and legal norms of
society) is it apt to live peacefully in society with others. In both cases, the
objective of breeding and taming is to imbue (*einverleiben*) the human
animal with a particular sensibility for "right" and "wrong," "error" and
"truth," "justice" and "injustice" (*TL* 1; *GM* II: 1–3). It is only through
the bodily incorporation (*Einverleibung*) of such a moral sensibility that
the memory of the will (*GM* II: 1) and "truth" (*TL* 1) become effective
as morally and legally binding norms. The project of breeding and taming
has been successful when "truth" is linked with a moral feeling deeply
inbred into the human animal:

> The feeling that one is obliged to describe one thing as red, an-
> other as cold, and a third as dumb, prompts a moral impulse which

pertains to truth [*erwacht eine moralische auf Wahrheit sich bezie-hende Regung*]; from its opposite, the liar whom no one trusts and all exclude, human beings demonstrate to themselves just how hon-orable, confidence-inspiring and useful truth is. (*TL* 1)

One important aspect of the institution of "truth" is its coincidence with the institution of language. Nietzsche shows that the grammatical laws and rules of conceptual language directly correspond to the moral and legal rules and norms of "truth." The "drive for truth," when it is aimed at providing the foundation and preservation of society, is essential to the formation of a language [*Sprachbildung*], which is accepted by all who use it as veridical, that is, capable of saying the truth as it appears to common sense: "the invincible faith that *this* sun, *this* window, *this* table is truth in itself [*Wahrheit an sich*]" (*TL* 1). From this perspective, the institution of political rule depends upon the institution of a language. Conversely, to overthrow a language is to overthrow a rule; to alter meaning is to alter rule. In order to gain political control over life it is crucial to gain control over language, that is, to gain control over the animal's drive to bring forth intuited metaphors, pictures, and dreamlike illusions.

Nietzsche compares conceptual language to the architectural structure of the Roman columbarium, the burial site of intuition. In the architec-tural structure of conceptual language, all concepts and their meanings are univocal, absolute, determined, and fixed. Their use and application are not subject to interpretation but are generally and universally binding. This is because only a language whose meanings are absolute and impera-tive can provide a stable structure for the moral, legal, and political order-ing of society. Seen from within the sociopolitical discourse on truth, Nietzsche's claim that conceptual language and its meanings are merely metaphorical and contingent, that is, formed, formable, and transforma-ble, is intended to unmask the contingency and reversibility of the social and political order. As such, the assertion of the metaphorical nature of language and "truth" constitutes a direct threat to political power, to the stability of rule. As a consequence, from the perspective of civilization, it is crucial that the metaphorical character of language and "truth" be for-gotten. It is only when the human being forgets that it is an animal im-mersed in an intuited world of first impressions, constituted by the continuous formation and transformation of intuited metaphors, pictures, and dreamlike illusions, that it can come to understand itself as a rational and moral agent living in accordance with "truth." Furthermore, it is pre-cisely because of this unconsciousness and forgetting that the human ani-mal arrives at the feeling of truth:

Only by forgetting this primitive world of metaphors, only by virtue of the fact that a mass of images, which originally flowed in hot, liquid stream from the primal power of the human imagination, has become hard and rigid, only because the invincible faith that *this* sun, *this* window, *this* table is truth in itself [*Wahrheit an sich*]—in short only because the human being forgets itself as a subject and indeed as an artistically creative subject, does the human being live with some degree of peace, security, and consistency; if he could escape for just a moment from the prison walls of this faith, it would mean the end of his "consciousness of self [*Selbstbewußtsein*]." (*TL* 1)

Forgetting the primitive world of intuited metaphors means not only forgetting that life is a dream, which lives off the continuous formation and transformation of intuited metaphors, pictures, and dreamlike illusions, but also that the human animal is an "artistically creative subject," an animal whose primordial drive is to continuously create intuited metaphors, pictures, and dreamlike illusions.

The intimate relationship that Nietzsche sees among "truth," conceptual language, and the normative foundations of social existence in "On Truth and Lies in an Extra-Moral Sense" has a strong affinity with his later analysis of "consciousness" and its relationship to communication and the normative foundations of society in *The Gay Science*. There Nietzsche shows that the emergence of consciousness coincides with the foundation of society, just as in "On Truth and Lies in an Extra-Moral Sense" he shows that the emergence of "truth" coincides with that of society. Nietzsche argues that consciousness must be understood as a response to the human animal's relative inferiority with respect to other forms of life. Hence, like the intellect and abstract thinking in "On Truth and Lies in an Extra-Moral Sense," consciousness is nothing but a means for the preservation of human life. In both texts consciousness, intellect, and abstract thinking are analyzed from the greater perspective of life.

The analysis of consciousness in *The Gay Science* particularly emphasizes the human animal's need for communication.[52] In order to preserve themselves, humans had to be able to communicate their respective needs to one another. Nietzsche argues that consciousness has developed only in response to the need to communicate:

Consciousness is really just a net connecting one human being with another—only in this capacity did it have to develop; the solitary and predatory human being would not have needed it. That our actions, thoughts, feelings, and movements—at least some of them—even enter into consciousness is the result of a terrible "must" which has ruled over the human being for a long time: as the most endangered animal, he *needed* help and protection, he needed his equals; he had to express his neediness and be able to make himself understood—and to do so, he first needed "consciousness." (*GS* 354)

Analogous to "truth" in "On Truth and Lies in an Extra-Moral Sense," consciousness in *The Gay Science* is a function of the group because it reflects a universal, absolute norm that is morally and legally binding for all. Both consciousness and "truth" thus undermine what cannot be shared, namely, the irreducibly singular truth (genius) reflected in each and every intuited vision and experience of the world:

> My thought is evidently that consciousness actually belongs not to the human being's existence as an individual but rather to the community and herd-aspects of his nature; that accordingly, it is finely developed only in relation to its usefulness to community or herd; and that consequently each of us, even with the best will of the world to *understand* ourselves as individually as possible, "to know ourselves," will bring to consciousness precisely that in ourselves which is "non-individual," that which is "average"; . . . At bottom, all our actions are incomparably and utterly personal, unique, and boundlessly individual, there is no doubt; but as soon as we translate them into consciousness, *they no longer seem to be.* . . . This is what *I* consider to be true phenomenalism and perspectivism: that due to the nature of *animal consciousness*, the world of which we can become conscious is merely surface- and sign-world turned into generalities and thereby debased to its lowest common denominator— that everything which enters consciousness thereby *becomes* shallow, thin, relatively stupid, general, a sign, a herd-mark; that all becoming conscious involves a vast and thorough corruption, falsification, superficialization, and generalization. (*GS* 354)[53]

Singular truth does not manifest itself as consciousness for it withdraws itself from being communicated: It always remains at a distance, secret, and silent, concealed in the sphere of intuited metaphors rather than revealed in the realm of consciousness. It resists being subsumed under more general and universal entities such as those constituted by conceptual language, consciousness, and "truth" understood as regulative and imperative standards of collective life.

After having introduced the idea of "truth" as a set of moral and legal norms required by human social existence, Nietzsche notes that although he discovered "truth" at the origin of the foundation of society, "we still do not know where the drive to truth [*Trieb zur Wahrheit*] comes from, for so far we have only heard about the obligation to be truthful which society imposes in order to exist" (*TL* 1). In my reading of "On Truth and Lies in an Extra-Moral Sense," the institution of "truth" also designates the origin of the "pure and honest drive for truth" as a means of critiquing "truth," that is, as a counterforce to the convention of standing in accordance with a determined set of regulative and imperative (linguistic) laws. The "pure and honest drive for truth" begins with the critical task of unveiling the institution of "truth" as a lie and as an ideology. It shows that the institution of "truth" is inherently interested rather than pure; that it denies the illusory character of "truth" for the sake of the preservation of the rule of civilization. Interestingly, in Nietzsche, this social critique operates from the perspective of life. It is guided by the question of whether instituted "truth" is life-enhancing or life-diminishing, of whether it generates greater health and future life. Should "truth" turn out to be life-diminishing, the task of the philosopher becomes a distinctly positive one, namely, to provide a new truth, an example of life and thought that promises greater health. The latter falls under the genre of Nietzsche's biopolitical treatment of truth: here philosophy takes on the challenge of great politics.

The Philosophical Life

Throughout his work, Nietzsche cites the figure of the philosopher as a promising example of life. In his early work, the pre-Socratic philosopher demonstrates a form of life for which the intellect is not an abstract or empty (metaphysical) category, but the reflection of an indisputable and irrefutable "piece of personality" where "strict necessity rules between thought[s] and character" (*PTA* 1). In "Schopenhauer as Educator," Nietzsche adds:

> But this example must be supplied by his outward life and not merely in his books—in the way, that is, in which the philosophers of Greece taught, through their bearing, what they wore and ate, and their morals [*Sitte*], rather than by what they said, let alone what they wrote. (*SE* 3)

Following their example, Nietzsche considers his own philosophy and life to be inseparably superposed, dissolved into each other such that life and thought become indistinguishable. There exist no purely spiritual problems, for Nietzsche believes that the life of the philosopher is never accidental or external to his philosophy. Rather, he conceives of philosophy as a kind of unconscious and involuntary memoir of the philosopher's life (*BGE* 6; *EH* "Preface"). The intimate link between life and philosophy is, as discussed in the previous chapter, best illustrated by Nietzsche's prefaces. For example, in "An Attempt at Self-Criticism," Nietzsche recounts how and under what circumstances *The Birth of Tragedy* was written: "Whatever underlies this questionable book, it must be a most stimulating and supremely important question, and furthermore a profoundly personal one—as is attested by the times in which it was written, and *in spite of which* it was written, the turbulent period of the Franco-Prussian War of 1870/1" ("An Attempt at Self-Criticism" 1). The imagery of war indicates that philosophy requires effort and courage, risk-taking and sacrifices, which fully involve the life and body of the philosopher. The stages of the Franco-German War, in which Nietzsche directly participated, further describe how his ideas emerged from the battle, infused with the philosophical questions once raised by the Greeks. After peace was declared at Versailles and Nietzsche was literally healed from the injuries of war, he could finally deliver *The Birth of Tragedy out of the Spirit of Music*. Nietzsche ends his narrative with a reference to a corner of the Alps where, aside and apart from his time, he ultimately could complete his untimely book ("An Attempt at Self-Criticism" 1).

The figure of the philosopher stands for a lived singular truth that represents a "pure and honest drive for truth," which is inseparable from the striving for greater freedom, a freedom that directly conflicts with the objection to conform to a determined set of rules.[54] A passage from "Schopenhauer as Educator" illustrates this idea:

> Where there have been powerful societies, governments, religions, public opinions, in short wherever there has been tyranny, there the solitary philosopher has been hated; for philosophy offers an asylum to the human being into which no tyranny can force its way, the inward cave, the labyrinth of the heart [*Brust*]: and that annoys the tyrants. (*SE* 3)

Contrary to the institution of an absolute, normative, and universally binding standard of "truth," the philosopher upholds her example of a lived singular truth as an alternative to the form of life determined by institutionalized "truth." Against the claim that there exists only one "truth," she affirms the possibility of a plurality of singular truths. Singular truths are neither universally binding, nor generally applicable. Instead, there are as many singular truths as there are examples of life and thought. The affirmation of a plurality of singular truths contests the institution of "truth" as one way of life according to which all ought to live.

As such, singular truth constitutes a threat to the fabric of the group. Society, therefore, stands in need of protecting itself against the honest and pure drive for singular truth.[55]

Nietzsche claims that singular truth can be harmful for it stands in opposition to the established conventional "truth" accepted by all and, hence, always calls for conflict and struggle. Singular truth is therefore inherently antipragmatic, contesting the view that the truthful is always necessarily also the useful. Generally speaking, humans prefer those truths that are comforting and have pleasant, profitable consequences, such as the idea of metaphysical truth and the idea of "truth" as the basis for society:

> They desire the pleasant, life-enhancing consequences of truth; they are indifferent to pure knowledge [*reine, folgenlose Erkenntnis*] if it has no consequences, but they are actually hostile towards truths which may be harmful and destructive. (*TL* 1)

The example of the artist is supposed to encourage the philosopher not to give up on the struggle for singular truth against the institution of "truth":

> Our artists live more boldly and more honestly; and the mightiest example we have before us, that of Richard Wagner, shows how the genius must not fear to enter into the most hostile relationship with the existing forms and order if he wants to bring to light the higher order and truth that dwells within him. (*SE* 3)

The example of the artist signals the intimate link between an "honest and pure drive to truth" and the affirmation of the human animal as an "artistic and creative subject" whose creativity stands in continuity with that of all other forms of life. Lived singular truth allows not only for a different self-understanding of the human being but also for a new understanding of society: It shows that "truth" is nothing but an inherently contingent set of rules that are formable and transformable rather than necessary or morally and legally binding.

In *The Gay Science*, Nietzsche argues that the "pure and honest drive for truth" emerges only long after "truth" had established itself as the most useful and preserving form of life. This idea that "truth emerges as the weakest form of knowledge [*Erkenntnis*]" (*GS* 110) coincides with the thesis he defends in "On Truth and Lies in an Extra-Moral Sense," namely, that the institution of "truth" precedes the emergence of an "honest and pure drive for truth" (*TL* 1). In comparison with "truth," the "pure and honest drive for truth" seems to reflect a weaker and less future promising form of life:

> Through immense periods of time, the intellect produced nothing but errors; some of them turned out to be useful and species-preserving; those who hit upon them or inherited them fought their fight for themselves and their progeny with greater luck. Such erroneous articles of faith, which were passed on by inheritance further and further, and finally almost became part of the basic endowment of the species . . . . Only very late did the deniers and doubters of such propositions emerge; only very late did truth [that is, the "pure and honest drive for truth"] emerge as the weakest form of knowledge [*Erkenntnis*]. It seemed that one was unable to live with it; that our organism was geared for its opposite: all its higher functions, the perception of senses and generally every kind of sensation, worked with those basic errors that had been incorporated since time immemorial. . . . Thus the *strength* of knowledge lies not in its degree of truth, but in its age, its embodiment [*Einverleibtheit*], its character as a condition of life. (*GS* 110)

From the perspective of life, the question is not how can singular truth be known, but how can singular truth be lived, or, in other words, "to what extent can truth stand to be incorporated [*Einverleibung*]?" (*GS* 110). This question stands at the center of Nietzsche's biopolitical discourse on truth:

> Truth does not designate the opposite [*Gegensatz*] of error, but the position of certain errors [*Irrthümer*] in relation to other errors [*Irrthümer*], for instance, that they are older, deeper, more embodied, that we could not live without them, and the like. (*KSA* 11:34[247])

Rather than instituted, incorporated "truth," the philosopher of the "pure and honest drive for truth" has to show that his or her singular truth and irreducibly unique example of life and thought are more life-enhancing than "truth," that they carry "greater health" than "truth." The philosopher succeeds in this enterprise only if he or she can demonstrate that the need for "truth" can be overcome. "Overcoming" here literally means to overcome a form of life and to bring forth a new, alternative form of life, thereby proving that living according to one's irreducibly singular truth (genius) is more life-enhancing than living according to the instituted "truth" that one embodies (*einverleibt*).

The difficulty of the philosopher's new task becomes even more apparent when one considers that the "pure and honest drive for truth" produces nothing but another dissimulation (*Verstellung*) and, hence, nothing "substantial" to hold against "truth." In order to solve this problem, the philosopher must have faith in his or her singular truth. This faith is supposed to encourage and strengthen the philosopher in his or her defense of singular truth (*GS* 347). However, Nietzsche recognizes that this faith always also entails the danger of falling back into a dogmatic pursuit of (metaphysical) truth. In order to prevent the philosopher from falling back into shaping herself like the metaphysician, she must give up this faith in singular truth as soon as she has gained enough strength to declare her own faith as dogmatic, perhaps metaphysical. Nietzsche sees in such a declaration an example of genuine truthfulness (*Wahrhaftigkeit*) and honesty (*Redlichkeit*): the sign that "truth" has been overcome.[56]

In "On Truth and Lies in an Extra-Moral Sense," this genuine truthfulness is reflected in the freedom of the intellect. Under the rule of civilization, the intellect's capacity for dissimulation, its artistic drive for the creation of intuited metaphors, is unfree, not an end in itself, but an instrument for the achievement of "higher," life- and group-preserving ends. Despite civilization's effort to dominate and control the human being's artistic animal drives, this effort is in vain, for these drives escape from the captivation of civilization into the spheres of culture, art, and myth:

> That drive to form metaphors, that fundamental human drive which cannot be left out of consideration for even a second without also leaving out human beings themselves, is in truth not defeated [*bezwungen*], indeed hardly even tamed [*gebändigt*], by the process whereby a regular and rigid new world is built from its own displaced [*verflüchtigen*] products—concepts—in order to imprison it in a fortress [*Zwingburg*]. The drive seeks out [*flüchtet*] a channel and a new area for its activity, and finds it in myth and in art generally. (*TL* 2)[57]

In the realm of culture, art and myth, the intellect recovers its artistic animal drive from the oppressiveness of civilization. Under the rule of intuition (*Herrschaft der Anschauung*), the intellect is no longer bound by the regulative and imperative (linguistic) laws of the abstract world of reason, but it is free to artistically form and transform all it encounters. The liberation of animality as it is reflected in the free dissimulations of the intellect manifests itself in the human animal's recovery of the vigor and strength of the animal:

Art reminds us of conditions of animal vigor; it is sometimes an excess and effusion of burgeoning corporality in the world of images and desires; at other times, an arousal of animalistic functions through images and illusions of intensified life, a heightening of the sensation of life and its stimulant. (*KSA* 12:9[102])

The intellect no longer needs the protections provided by conceptual language and abstract thinking. It is now free to affirm human life not only as continuous with other forms of animal life but also as inherently artistic and creative, a form of life which lives off the continuous formation and transformation of intuited metaphors, pictures, and dreamlike illusions.

Freed from the obligation to conform to a determined set of regulative and imperative (linguistic) laws, the intellect's talent for dissimulation is no longer reduced to an instrument for the preservation of life:

> The vast assembly of beams and boards to which the needy human being clings, thereby saving himself on his journey through life, is used by the liberated intellect as a mere climbing frame and play-thing on which to perform its most reckless tricks, and when it smashes this framework, jumbles it up and ironically re-assembles it, pairing the most unlike things and dividing those things which are closest to one another, it reveals the fact that it does not require those makeshift aids of neediness, and that it is now guided not by concepts but by intuitions. (*TL* 2)

The free intellect now views life as a dream, as a creative and artistic power, and language as a set of metaphors with which it plays. From this perspective, "[b]ecoming is not a moral but an artistic phenomenon" (*PTA* 19).

Interestingly, in "On Truth and Lies in an Extra-Moral Sense," just as in *On the Genealogy of Morals*, Nietzsche posits the freedom of the intellect as the direct opposite of slavery and domination. When the free intellect is at its height, its power overcomes the need to dominate others:

> The intellect, that master of dissimulation [*Verstellung*], is free and absolved of its usual slavery for as long as it can deceive without *doing harm*, and it celebrates its Saturnalian festivals when it does so; at no time is it richer, more luxuriant, more proud, skilful, and bold. Full of creative contentment, it jumbles up metaphors and shifts the boundary stones of abstraction. . . . The intellect has now cast off the mark of servitude; where as it normally labors, with dull-spirited industry, to show to some poor individual who lusts after life the road and the tools he needs, and rides out in search of spoils

[*Raub*] and booty [*Beute*] for its master, here the intellect has become the master itself and is permitted to wipe the expression of neediness [*Bedürftigkeit*] from its face. (*TL* 2)

The freedom of the intellect, as well as its sovereignty and power, are expressed in liberating and elevating dissimulations that enchant and seduce others without consequently harming them. The free intellect generates feelings of elevation and joy in those who contemplate its talent for dissimulation (*Verstellung*). As such, the rule of culture facilitates a free relationship with the other, a relationship that is not subject to the utilitarian calculus that defines the struggle to preserve life under the rule of civilization. Rather, these free relationships with the other make up a whole which does not stand for the totalization of its parts but, like a work of art, is exceeded by the plurality of its parts.

For Nietzsche, as I have argued before, this free relationship with the other is figured by the idea of a responsibility to the other which is accrued through this freedom. It therefore follows that the intellect's freedom from the process of civilization calls forth a new and greater responsibility. This responsibility is nothing short of the cultivation of a higher type of humanity:

> Let us suppose that my *attentat* on two millennia of anti-nature and the violation of human kind succeeds. That party of life which takes in hand the greatest of all tasks, the higher cultivation of humanity[*Höherzüchtung der Menschheit*], together with the remorseless destruction of all degenerate and parasitic elements, will again make possible on earth that *over-abundance of life* [*Zuviel von Leben*] out of which the Dionysian condition must again proceed. (*EH* "Books" BT: 4)[58]

This responsibility corresponds to what Nietzsche calls "great politics,"[59] a consciously ironic appropriation of a Bismarckian formula that he puts to very anti-Bismarckian, indeed, anti-German, uses:

> The Germans with their "Wars of Liberation" deprived Europe of the meaning, of the miracle of meaning of the existence of Napoleon—they thereby have on their conscience everything that followed, that exists today, this sickness and unreason the *most inimical to culture* that is nationalism. . . . that eternalizing of the petty-state situation of Europe, of *petty* politics. (*EH* "Books" CW: 2)[60]

But what kind of politics could achieve the "higher cultivation of humanity" and "the remorseless destruction of all degenerate and parasitic elements,"[61] while avoiding nationalism and its associated sicknesses of racism and imperialism? What "great politics" could not be "inimical to culture"? I suggest that Nietzsche's notion of "great health" and his characterization of the philosopher as a physician might provide an answer to this question.

Nietzsche's shift to a biopolitical treatment of truth, in which the criterion for truth is "greater health," has puzzled recent commentators. According to Roberto Esposito, Nietzsche's attempt to "select," "separate," and "destroy" what he calls "degenerate and parasitic elements" in order to protect health places him in an autoimmunitary predicament whereby the "health" he is looking for is achieved by the very means that characterize sickness, weakness, resentment, and decadence.[62] Yet, Nietzsche himself indicates that the attempt to separate health from sickness is not only impossible but also counterproductive (GS 382). Perhaps the best way to understand this apparent tension in Nietzsche's discourse on health is to pursue his reading of Plato. Nietzsche calls Plato the "greatest" philosopher,[63] who had previously considered the pursuit of truth and health in relation to the problem of politics and culture. What led Plato astray was Socrates, who seduced Plato into comparing the task of the philosopher to that of the physician by establishing an analogy between the physician as the healer of the body and the philosopher as the healer or "improver" of the soul (TI "Socrates" and "Improvers"). Nietzsche thinks Plato is "better" than Socrates and, in fact, appropriates the Socratic analogy by ironically overturning it.[64] Nietzsche's attempt to draw Plato away from Socrates, to separate the strong philosopher from his ascetic and weak counterpart, to make Plato into the last of the pre-Socratic, tragic philosophers of intuitive thinking, indicates how one should interpret Nietzsche's claim that the philosopher is no longer responsible for the health of the soul, but for the health of the body. From this perspective, the philosopher acts in the service of life and health rather than in the service of (metaphysical) truth and (scientific) knowledge.[65]

The philosopher as physician does not separate truth from life in an attempt to gain an objective perspective on life, but abandons herself to life in an attempt to attain truthfulness. For her, health is not a final state. From time to time, health must be given up to attain greater health in the future:

> The great health, a health that one does not only have, but also acquires [erwirbt] continually and must acquire [erwerben] because one gives it up again [preisgiebt] and again, and must give it up [preisgeben]! (GS 382)

Abandoning one's self (*Selbst*) to sickness is a tempting experiment (*Selbst-Versuchung*). From it, one learns that philosophy's aim is not to find (metaphysical) truth, but to find health and future life.

The new task of the philosopher is to diagnose sickness and health by experiencing both, analogous to the way in which Plato experienced both the pre-Socratic and Socratic traditions in order to determine the doses of (singular) truth someone can be exposed to without diminishing her life forces (*GS* "Preface"). The degree to which one needs (singular) truth to be thinned, sweetened, and falsified is dependent upon one's physical constitution (*BGE* 39), just as one's exposure to knowledge of the past is dependent upon one's physical constitution (*HL* 5). Nietzsche distinguishes between philosophy (metaphysical truth) as a response to a weak state of health, that is, philosophy as "a prop, a sedative, medicine, redemption, elevation, or self-alienation" (*GS* "Preface" 2) and philosophy (singular truth) as "only a beautiful luxury, in the best case the voluptuousness of a triumphant gratitude" (*GS* "Preface" 2). Although Nietzsche recognizes that philosophy in both of the above cases serves life, he privileges the latter over the former insofar as it leads beyond the mere preservation of life and toward the creation of new life.

Conclusion

Biopolitics and the Question of Animal Life

While it has been widely accepted that Foucault's notions of sovereign and disciplinary power have their conceptual origin in Nietzsche's genealogy of morals, the relation between Foucault's notion of biopolitics and Nietzsche's political thought has only recently entered the scholarly debate.[1] In conclusion, I would like to make a few remarks about how biopolitics can be approached through Nietzsche's treatment of the question of animal life.[2] This question centers on whether (and, if so, how) the recovery of animality in Nietzsche's philosophy contributes to an understanding of what Foucault calls the "biological threshold of modernity."[3] In my view, Nietzsche provides a way to understand the relationship between animality and humanity, which can be given a new and productive interpretation by seeing it as developing an affirmative sense of biopolitics. Positive biopolitics sees in the continuity between human and animal life a source of resistance to the project of dominating and controlling life-processes. Whereas the latter divides life into opposing forms of species life, the affirmative biopolitics I lay out subverts such a division and replaces it with the project of cultivating inherently singular, nontotalizable forms of animal life.

In Foucault, the term "biopolitics" designates the historical discontinuity through which "for the first time in history, no doubt, biological existence was reflected in political existence; the fact of living was no longer an inaccessible substrate that only emerged from time to time, amid the randomness of death and its fatality; part of it passed into knowledge's field of control and power's sphere of intervention."[4] The Foucaultian idea that biological existence is "reflected" in political existence should not be confused with either the view that biopolitics means understanding the state as an organism, or with the view that biopolitics simply designates the entrance of issues concerning biological life into the sphere of political discussion and decision-making. Both views presuppose an external and hierarchical relationship between life and politics.[5] In contrast, Foucault holds that biopolitics constitutes a transformation in the nature of political power itself: "For millennia, man remained what he was for Aristotle: a living animal with the additional capacity for a political existence; modern man is an animal whose politics places his existence as a living being in question."[6] This definition of biopolitics is crucial in several respects. First, Foucault clearly adopts the view that "modern man is an animal." Second, this animal's politics concerns not only its "way of life" or *bios*, but also its biological life, what the Greeks call *zoe*.[7] While, for Aristotle, the political existence of the human being both presupposes and transcends its animality, Foucault claims that, at least for modern men, the essential concern of political life lies in the status of their animality, of their biological existence: "Western man was gradually learning what it meant to be a living species in a living world."[8] Foucault's notion of biopolitics depends on understanding the animality of the human being in terms of "the life of the body and the life of the species."[9] The transformation of the human being's animal life into species life is the leitmotif of Foucault's genealogy of modern political science's emergence from the classical and especially Christian theme of "pastoral power."[10] But Foucault also shows that this biopolitical regulation of life gives rise to resistance, to what he calls "contre-conduites," which seeks to free the individual from being led (dominated) by others and instead to "search for ways to conduct one's own life."[11] This resistance to biopower does not transcend the horizon of "a living species in a living world"[12] but, rather, "life as a political object was in a sense taken at face value and turned back against the system that was bent on controlling it."[13] Resistance counteracts the constitution of the subject in and through its transformation into a species by cultivating or caring for the self thus redefining the status of the human being's animality.

Foucault's critique of biopolitics as a politics of domination over the human being's animal life seeks to create a different relationship with the self, one that separates the self from the "herd" without isolating the self from others or from one's own animal life. The formula for this other relationship with the self passes through culture, through a cultivation of nature, which does not dominate nature or animal life but, to the contrary, emphasizes its creative potential: "We should not have to refer the creative activity of somebody to the kind of relation he has to himself, but should relate the kind of relation one has to oneself to a creative activity."[14] The important point here is that Foucault understands the life of the self as a function of creativity rather than understanding creativity as a particular quality of the self.

Foucault clearly states that the only way to resist negative biopolitics is to care for the self by cultivating the human being's existence as a living animal through understanding the self as a function of creativity. Foucault, however, does not explain how creativity is related to animal life. In this book I have argued that Nietzsche's philosophy provides us with the missing link between animality and creativity. A return to Nietzsche's philosophy, therefore, makes a significant contribution to the contemporary debate on the relationship between biopolitics and animal life because it provides a conception of culture which articulates the relationship among animal life, culture, and politics. Furthermore, it offers an account of how animality engenders culture, of how animal life becomes the source of creativity.

Nietzsche addresses the relationship among animality, culture, and politics through the fundamental "antagonism between culture and civilization" (*KSA* 13:16[10]). By civilization, Nietzsche means the emergence of forms of social and political organization that are based on the disciplining and taming of the human being's animality. Civilization constitutes an economical approach to animality, whose aim is the preservation of the group at the cost of the normalization of the individual. By culture, on the other hand, Nietzsche means the critique of civilization that liberates animal life from being the object of political domination and exploitation.[15] Culture reflects openness to animality which is directed toward the pluralization of inherently singular forms of life, forms of life which resist being subsumed under a totality. Culture and civilization constitute two distinct and antagonistic ways in which animal life can be politicized. Whereas the politics of civilization reflects what Foucault calls biopolitics, or what I refer to as negative biopolitics, the politics of culture reflects what Foucault defines as new forms of resistance against biopolitics, or what I refer to as affirmative biopolitics. While the objective of a politics of civilization is to produce a normalized society through the violent means of taming and breeding, the objective of a politics of culture is to cultivate forms of sociability and community through the practice of individual self-responsibility, or, in Foucault's terms, through "care of the self."[16]

Nietzsche understands civilization as a politics of moral improvement that requires the separation of human life from animal life (*TI* "Morality"; "Improvers"). Its objective is to impose a "second" nature on the human being which is, morally speaking, "superior" to its "first" animal nature. The project of civilization represents the humanist and Enlightenment belief that humanity will be free only when it emancipates itself from animality through a disciplining process directed against, for example, the forgetfulness of the animal articulated in the memory of the will (*GM* II: 1). But, since this process depends on dividing and imposing a hierarchy on the continuum of life, it also betrays its affinity with racism, which, according to Foucault, relies on this same division and hierarchy. Nietzsche, on the contrary, proposes to investigate culture as part of the continuum of life, as constituted out of animal life. From the perspective of this continuum, the challenge is to bring forth forms of life that are not separated from, but rather, embodied by animality: to bring forth a second nature that is a more "natural naturalness" (*HL* 10). Here, culture stands for "the longing for a stronger nature, for a healthier and simpler humanity" (*SE* 3). In this capacity, culture seeks to stimulate the pluralization of inherently singular forms of life, which I take to be the supreme aim of Nietzsche's affirmative biopolitics of culture. However, the question remains: How can culture bring forth such a "second nature" without relying on the civilizing techniques of taming and breeding?

Nietzsche's answer depends on the link he establishes between creativity and animality through a new conception of animal forgetfulness. Nietzsche praises animal forgetfulness so highly because it enhances the human being's creativity while increasing its vitality. Forgetfulness is not only "essential to actions of any kind" (*HL* 1), but also indispensable to the philosopher: "many a man fails to become a thinker only because his memory is too good" (*AOM* 122). Forgetfulness defines the creativity of the genius of culture who "uses himself up, who does not spare himself" for the sake of culture (*TI* "Skirmishes" 44). It is also the source of virtue exemplified by the tragic hero whose "strength lies in forgetting himself" (*SE* 4), in perishing in "the pursuit of his dearest values and highest aims" (*HL* 9). Forgetfulness, moreover, belongs to the sovereign individual who enjoys the privilege of making promises but who "fully appreciates the countervailing force, forgetfulness" (*GM* II, 1). Finally, it belongs to the giver of gifts who Zarathustra loves, "whose soul is overfull so that it forgets itself" (*Z*: 3 "Prologue"). What distinguishes this plurality of individual figures in Nietzsche—the historical agent, the philosopher, the genius of culture, the tragic hero, the giver of gifts, the sovereign individual—is that it is composed of singular individuals in whom animality, "their existence as a living being," has become creative and productive, providing examples of what Foucault refers to as new practices of freedom.

Both Hannah Arendt and Michel Foucault point out that totalitarian ideologies are directed at "the fabrication of mankind" and, to that end, "eliminate individuals for the sake of the species, sacrifice the parts for the sake of the whole."[17] Analogously, Foucault says that: "If genocide is indeed the dream of modern powers . . . it is because power is situated and exercised at the level of life, the species, the race, and the large-scale phenomena of population."[18] The emergence of totalitarian biopolitics in the twentieth century challenged contemporary political philosophy to conceive of the relationship between political life and animal life beyond the "biological threshold" of species life. What is needed is a new awareness of the artificial character of the very idea of species life. Arendt sought to move beyond this idea by showing how political acts create a discontinuity or break with what she calls the "cycle of life," thereby bringing about radical novelty while manifesting the singularity of the actor. I have shown how Nietzsche's (animal) philosophy opens up another possibility for moving beyond species life by emphasizing the continuity, rather than the discontinuity, between political and animal life. The affirmation of the continuum of animal and human life is grounds for denying validity to the division among species. In this sense, Nietzsche's recovery of the animality of human beings is far more conducive to undermining rather than underpinning the foundations of totalitarian ideology. Furthermore, the affirmation of animality in Nietzsche is oriented toward pluralization. From this perspective, it seems the uncontrollable plurality and singularity of life forms that Arendt was seeking to counteract totalitarian politics and provide the foundation of a new humanism may result from affirming, rather than denying our dependence on animality.

Notes

Introduction: The Animal in Nietzsche's Philosophy   *ANIMAL in N*

1. For a treatment of the animal theme in Nietzsche, see Christa D. Acampora and Ralph Acampora, *A Nietzschean Bestiary: Becoming Animal Beyond Docile and Brutal* (New York: Rowman and Littlefield, 2004); Adrian Del Caro, *Grounding the Nietzsche Rhetoric of Earth* (Berlin: De Gruyter, 2004), 401–16; Peter Atterton and Matthew Calarco, *Animal Philosophy* (London and New York: Continuum Press, 2004), 1–14; Cary Wolfe, *Zoontologies: The Question of the Animal* (Minneapolis: University of Minnesota Press, 2003), 93–96; Akira Mizuta Lippit, *Electric Animal* (Minneapolis: University of Minnesota Press, 2000), 55–73; Jennifer Ham, "Taming the Beast: Animality in Wedekind and Nietzsche," in *Animal Acts*, ed. Jennifer Ham and Matthew Senior (London and New York: Routledge, 1997), 145–63; Michel Haar, "Du symbolisme animal en général, et notamment du serpent," *Alter: Revue de Phénoménologie*, no. 3 (1995): 319–45; Margot Norris, *Beasts of Modern Imagination: Darwin, Nietzsche, Kafka, Ernst, and Lawrence* (Baltimore: Johns Hopkins University Press, 1985), 1–25, 53–100; T. J. Reed, "Nietzsche's Animals: Idea, Image and Influence," in *Nietzsche: Imaginary and Thought*, ed. Malcolm Pasley (Berkeley and Los Angeles: University of California Press, 1978), 159–219.

RANDOM theme

2. For the view that the animal is a random theme in Nietzsche's philosophy, see Martin Heidegger, *Nietzsche* vols. 1 and 2 (Stuttgart: Verlag Günter Neske, 1998). For the view that the animal is a metaphorical device in Nietzsche's philosophy, see Monika Langer, "The Role and the Status of the Animals in Nietzsche's Philosophy," in *Animal Others: On Ethics, Ontology and Animal Life*, ed. Peter Steeves (New York: State University of New York Press, 1999), 75–91.

3. According to Norris, "[t]his movement has two major, related consequences: a subversive interrogation of the anthropocentric premises of Western philosophy and art, and the invention of artistic and philosophical strategies that would allow the animal, the unconscious, the instincts, the body, to speak again in their work" (Norris, *Beasts of Modern Imagination*, 5).

4. For an example of this view, see Alexander Nehamas, *Nietzsche: Life as Literature* (Cambridge, Mass.: Harvard University Press, 1985).

5. For an example of this view, see Gregory Moore, *Nietzsche, Biology and Metaphor* (Cambridge, Mass.: Harvard University Press, 2002). Stiegler argues that Nietzsche's notion of life should not be reduced to a mere metaphor but has to be taken seriously as an attempt to provide a properly biological conception of life. Nevertheless, she underlines that Nietzsche's conception of life as will to power exceeds a biological, Darwinian notion of life insofar as it cannot be reduced to a struggle for survival. Barbara Stiegler, *Nietzsche et la biologie* (Paris: PUF, 2001), 7–8.

6. "I presuppose memory and some kind of spirit in everything organic: the apparatus is so subtle, that for us it does not seem to exist. What foolishness on Haeckel's part, to equate two embryos with each other! One should not be deceived by the smallness of size" (*KSA* 11:25[403]). With the exception of occasional emendations, throughout this book I rely on the following translations: Friedrich Nietzsche, *Thus Spoke Zarathustra*, trans. Walter Kaufmann (New York: Modern Library, 1995); Friedrich Nietzsche, *Human, All Too Human*, trans. R. J. Hollingdale (Cambridge: Cambridge University Press, 1986); Friedrich Nietzsche, *The Gay Science*, trans. J. Nauckoff (Cambridge: Cambridge University Press, 2001); Friedrich Nietzsche, *The Birth of Tragedy*, trans. R. Speirs (Cambridge: Cambridge University Press, 1999); Friedrich Nietzsche, *On the Genealogy of Morals*, trans C. Diethe, ed. Keith Ansell-Pearson (Cambridge: Cambridge University Press, 1994); Friedrich Nietzsche, *Untimely Meditations*, trans. R. J. Hollingdale (Cambridge: Cambridge University Press, 1997); Friedrich Nietzsche, *Daybreak*, trans. R. J. Hollingdale (Cambridge: Cambridge University Press, 1997); Friedrich Nietzsche, *Twilight of the Idols*, trans. R. J. Hollingdale (London: Penguin Books, 1968); Friedrich Nietzsche, *The Antichrist*, trans. R. J. Hollingdale (London: Penguin Books, 1968); Friedrich Nietzsche, *The Will to Power*, ed. and trans. Walter Kaufmann (New York: Random House, 1968); Friedrich Nietzsche, *Ecce Homo*, trans. R. J. Hollingdale (London: Penguin Books, 1979); Friedrich Nietzsche, *Beyond Good and Evil: A Prelude to a Philosophy of the Future*, trans. Walter Kaufmann (New York: Vintage Books, 1989); Friedrich Nietzsche, *Philosophy and Truth: Selections from Nietzsche's Notebooks of the Early 1870's*, trans. Daniel Breazeale (London: Humanities Press International, 1979); Friedrich Nietzsche, "The Greek State" and "Homer's Contest," in *On the Genealogy of Morals,* trans C. Diethe, ed. Keith Ansell-Pearson (Cambridge: Cambridge University Press, 1994); Friedrich Nietzsche, "Truth and Lies in an Extra-Moral Sense," in *The Birth of Tragedy*, trans. R. Speirs (Cambridge: Cambridge University Press, 1999); and Friedrich Nietzsche,

"The Philosopher. Reflections on the Struggle between Art and Knowledge," in *Philosophy and Truth: Selections from Nietzsche's Notebooks of the Early 1870's*, trans. Daniel Breazeale (London: Humanities Press International, 1979). The translations of the *Nachlass* are my own. Where I believe it is helpful I quote the German in brackets. I use the following edition on Nietzsche: Friedrich Nietzsche, *Kritische Studienausgabe in 15 Bänden*, ed. Giorgio Colli and Mazzino Montinari (Berlin: De Gruyter, 1988).

7. For the notion of physiology in Nietzsche, see Volker Gerhardt, "Von der ästhetischen Metaphysik zur Physiologie der Kunst," *Nietzsche-Studien* 13 (1984): 374–93; and Helmut Pfotenhauer, "Physiologie der Kunst als Kunst der Physiologie?" *Nietzsche-Studien* 13 (1984): 399–411.

8. "All organic life is coordinated *as a visible movement* [*als sichtbare Bewegung*] in a *spiritual history* [*geistigen Geschehen*]. An organic being is the visible expression of a *spirit* [*eines Geistes*]" (*KSA* 11:26[35]).

9. For a recent example of the identification of will to power with memory, see Stiegler, *Nietzsche et la biologie*, 50–66.

10. See also *KSA* 11:34[167], where Nietzsche claims that the entire history of organic life is active in every judgment of the senses.

11. Stiegler argues correctly, in my view, that life is directed toward openness, toward what advenes, because the enhancement of its proper internal power is inherently dependent upon the encounter of another power, even if this encounter brings the risk of death and suffering. See Stiegler, *Nietzsche et la biologie*, 73.

12. For a discussion of the similarities and dissimilarities between Nietzsche and Darwin, see Werner Stegmaier, "Darwin, Darwinismus, Nietzsche: Zum Problem der Evolution," *Nietzsche-Studien* 16 (1987): 264–87; Norris, *Beasts of Modern Imagination*, 1–53; Keith Ansell-Pearson, *Viroid Life* (London: Routledge, 1997), 85–122; and recently, Stiegler, *Nietzsche et la biologie*, 45ff.

13. "Continual transition forbids us to speak of 'individuals,' etc.; the 'number' of beings is itself in flux" (*WP* 520; see also the notion of "Seelen-continuum" in *KSA* 11:40[34]). Given the interrelatedness of all forms of life, Nietzsche also rejects the division between the inorganic and the organic worlds as prejudice: "The will to power also rules in the inorganic world, or rather there is no inorganic world. The 'effect of distance' cannot be abolished: *something attracts* [*heranziehen*] *something else, something else feels attracted* [*gezogen*]" (*KSA* 11:34[247]). See also, in comparison, *WP* 655, *GS* 109, and *KSA* 12:9[144].97.

14. What distinguishes the organic from the inorganic is its capacity "*to collect experiences* [*Erfahrungen aufsammelt*]" and that it is "never identical to itself in its processes [*und niemals sich selber gleich ist, in seinem Prozesse*]" (*KSA* 10:12[31]).

15. "That the world is not striving toward a stable condition is the only thing that has been proved. Consequently, one must conceive its climatic conditions in such a way that it is not a condition of equilibrium" (*WP* 639).

16. For an extensive discussion of Nietzsche's notion of life as a struggle toward pluralization and singularization, see Wolfgang Müller-Lauter, "Der Organismus als innerer Kampf," in *Über Werden und Wille zur Macht: Nietzsche-Interpretationen I* (Berlin: De Gruyter, 1999), 97–140.

17. Nietzsche contests the existence of something like the development of humankind, instead he is interested in cultivating plurality within the human being (*KSA* 11:34[179]).

18. Norris describes this challenge as follows: "But the bio-centricity of this tradition—its valuation of the body, its celebration of unmediated experience—renders its writings at war with themselves, hostile to art, impervious to representation, inimitable" (Norris, *Beasts of Modern Imagination*, 3). And further down, "[o]f course, the paradox implicit in this caveat, of producing an art *within* culture, that is, not *of* culture, is only imperfectly resolvable in practice" (ibid., 15). See also Shapiro, who identifies the question of how to bring forth forms of culture that are full of life as a question explicit in Nietzsche's *Untimely Considerations*: "How can meaningful stories be told that escape the encroachments of the 'university culture machine' and that offer a significant alternative to the debilitating forms of historical consciousness that the same culture machine was celebrating as the highest manifestations of Western tradition?" (Gary Shapiro, *Nietzschean Narratives* [Bloomington: Indiana University Press, 1989], 21).

19. Sigmund Freud, *Civilization and Its Discontents*, (London: W. W. Norton, 1961). For a comprehensive discussion of the relationship between Nietzsche and Freud, see Johann Figl, ed., *Von Nietzsche zu Freud: Übereinstimmungen und Differenzen von Denkmotiven* (Vienna: WUV-Universitätsverlag, 1996); and Günter Gödde, "Wandelungen des Menschenbildes durch Nietzsche und Freud: Eine vergleichende Interpretation aus philosophiegeschichtlicher Perspektive," *Jahrbuch der Psychoanalyse* (1993): 119–66, as well as, by the same author, "Eine neue Interpretation von Freuds Verhältnis zu Nietzsche," *Nietzsche-Studien* 27 (1998): 463–80.

20. For the view that the overhuman in Nietzsche embodies an idea of the self as autonomous and self-sufficient, see Giuliano Campioni, *Les lectures françaises de Nietzsche* (Paris: PUF, 2001), 51–107.

21. Norris also interprets the overhuman in Nietzsche as a recuperated animal, "an animal 'recovered' in both related senses of the word: as a human creature cured of its pathogenic culture and vitally reclaimed by its instinctual nature" (Norris, *Beasts of Modern Imagination*, 79).

22. Michel Foucault, *The History of Sexuality*, vol. 1 (New York: Vintage Books, 1990), 133–59.

23. On the notion of following the animal, see Jacques Derrida, *The Animal That Therefore I Am*, trans. David Wills (New York: Fordham University Press, 2008).

24. I borrow the term "becoming-animal" from Gilles Deleuze and Felix Guattari, *A Thousand Plateaus: Capitalism and Schizophrenia* (Minneapolis: University of Minnesota Press, 1987), 232–309.

25. Keith Ansell-Pearson, "On the Miscarriage of Life and the Future of the Human: Thinking Beyond the Human Condition with Nietzsche," *Nietzsche-Studien* 29 (2000): 153–77. From the perspective of becoming, the English term "human being" is a contradiction in terms because humans never "are" but always become. I have therefore tried to avoid this term as much as possible to

remain faithful to Nietzsche's conception of human life as something in becoming.

26. For Nietzsche, human life not only incorporates the whole past chain of life (*KSA* 10:12[31]) but also prefigures the future of the chain of life: "We are more than the individual: we are the whole chain as well, with the task of all the future of the chain" (*WP* 687).

27. Foucault, *The History of Sexuality*, 133–59.

28. On the notion of an "affirmative biopolitics," see Roberto Esposito, *Bios: Biopolitics and Philosophy*, trans. Timothy Campbell (Minneapolis: University of Minnesota Press, 2008), 191–94.

1. Culture and Civilization

1. For a theory of modernity based on theories of culture, see Agnes Heller, *A Theory of Modernity* (Malden, Mass.: Blackwell, 1999).

2. For example, Patrick Wotling's *Nietzsche et le problème de la civilisation* (Paris: PUF, 1995) identifies culture with civilization; and Eric Blondel's *Nietzsche: The Body and Culture*, trans. Séan Hand (Stanford: Stanford University Press, 1991) identifies civilization with culture. Both miss the antagonistic relationship that is constitutive of both terms. I agree with Wotling that Nietzsche rethinks the opposition between the German notions of *Kultur* and *Zivilization*. Whereas *Kultur* denotes the intellectual and spiritual realm of the life of a society, *Zivilization* denotes its material and practical conditions. However, I disagree with Wotling's assertion that the novelty of Nietzsche's discourse is that it overcomes the dichotomy between a theoretical (cultural) and a practical (civilizational) understanding of the life of a society in favor of a genealogical investigation of the relationship between the will to power of a particular society and the kinds of cultural types it produces. From the perspective of genealogy, Wotling argues that civilization simply turns out to be a particular kind of culture: "la *Civilisation* devient ainsi un cas spécifique de *Cultur*" (*Nietzsche et le problème de la civilisation*, 29). Wotling investigates the Nietzschean problem of culture ("*le problème de la culture*") as a problem of civilization ("*le problème de la civilisation*") because he holds that the French term "*civilisation*," which designates the entire condition of human existence, more accurately reflects the Nietzschean notion of culture than does the French term "*culture*," which primarily constitutes the realm of theoretical knowledge (ibid.). Wotling translates the German *Kultur* into the French *Civilisation*, and thereby fails, in my view, to give an account of their inherent antagonism. Wotling's *Nietzsche et le problème de la civilisation* is interesting, however, because it provides a critique of Blondel's *Nietzsche: Le corps et la culture*, which investigates the problem of culture as a problem of "*culture*." According to Blondel's reading of Nietzsche, there is a tragic gap within nature that separates human culture from nature. He claims that "a culture is properly the way in which the problem of the *gap* is tackled by such and such a society or age or civilization" (*Nietzsche: The Body and Culture*, 49). In my view, culture in Nietzsche is not a tragic distancing of the human

from nature and the animal, but rather stands for a radical exposure of the human to the otherness of nature and the animal. Culture does not designate a given way of life and/or thought, but an openness that allows for the overcoming of a certain way of life and thought (civilization). Culture is, in this sense, pure hospitality (*WP* 939) or, in the words of Jacques Derrida, "hospitality is culture itself" (Jacques Derrida, *On Cosmopolitanism and Forgiveness* [London: Routledge, 2001], 16). Sarah Kofman does not distinguish explicitly between culture and civilization, but identifies two different notions of culture, one that corresponds to what I refer to as "civilization" and the other to what I refer to as "culture." See Sarah Kofman, *Nietzsche et la scène philosophique* (Paris: Editions Galilée, 1979), 289–318. She does not, however, discuss the relationship between these two conceptions of culture as antagonistic. A distinction between culture and civilization in Nietzsche's early work is also missing in Quentin P. Taylor's monograph *The Republic of Genius: A Reconstruction of Nietzsche's Early Thought.* Taylor answers the question of "What is *Kultur* for Nietzsche?" by saying that "in the broadest sense, *Kultur* for Nietzsche is similar to, if less inclusive than, 'civilization'" (Quentin P. Taylor, *The Republic of Genius: A Reconstruction of Nietzsche's Early Thought* [Rochester, N.Y.: Rochester University Press, 1997], 66). The reason for this might be related to the fact that Taylor "aims at a 'reconstruction' of Nietzsche's early thought, with an emphasis on his positive doctrines and value theory" (ibid.). Taylor recognizes that Nietzsche's *constructive* philosophy emerges out of a radical *critique* of modern civilization, but since his focus is on the former at the expense of the latter, he fails to distinguish the antagonism of culture and civilization as constitutive of Nietzsche's "positive" conception of culture. For a reading of Nietzsche's philosophy that is sensitive to the distinction between culture and civilization, see Tracy B. Strong, *Friedrich Nietzsche and the Politics of Transfiguration* (Berkeley and Los Angeles: University of California Press, 1975).

3. My interpretation of culture in Nietzsche departs from the current reading of Nietzsche's philosophy as an example of moral perfectionism, defined as "an emphasis on each person's obligation to cultivate her (higher) self" (James Conant, "Nietzsche's Perfectionism," in *Nietzsche's Postmoralism: Essays on Nietzsche's Prelude to Philosophy's Future*, ed. Richard Schacht [Cambridge: Cambridge University Press, 2001], 181–257, here 219). Conant, for example, identifies culture as "a longing to overcome one's animality . . . as a desire for the genius in oneself" and claims that this is what Nietzsche identifies as "the root of all culture" (ibid., 224–25). Another example of a perfectionist interpretation of Nietzsche is found in Daniel W. Conway's *Nietzsche and the Political* (Florence, Ky.: Routledge, 1997), 28–42. Conway holds that perfection occurs when the transition from "natural animal" to "human being" is completed (ibid., 13–17) and, furthermore, that this transition "will be completed only when humankind is able to produce sovereign individuals as a matter of design" (ibid., 19). But, in Nietzsche, the idea of improvement attained through civilization is inseparable from mastery and domination over life. Since I take culture to be concerned with

Culture here:

the overcoming of domination over life and over the animal, culture cannot be understood in terms of a moral perfectionism. I further discuss these issues in "Is Nietzsche a Perfectionist?: Rawls, Cavell and the Politics of Culture in Nietzsche's *Schopenhauer as Educator," Journal of Nietzsche Studies* 34 (2007): 5–27.

4. Although Nietzsche primarily speaks of the antagonism between culture and civilization in his late work, I show that this antagonism is also very useful in an analysis of his earlier views on culture and civilization.

5. The political significance of the "memory of the will" in *On the Genealogy of Morals* is further discussed in Chapter 2.

6. For earlier and later versions of this thesis, see *SE* 1 and *TI* "Morality" and "Improvers."

7. I borrow the term "counter-memory" from Michel Foucault, "Nietzsche, la généalogie, l'histoire," in *Hommage à Jean Hyppolite* (Paris: PUF, 1971), 145–72.

8. From the perspective of the animals, morality has jeopardized the human animal's mental health: *"Animals' criticism.*—I fear that the animals see the human being as a being like them who in a most dangerous manner has lost its animal common sense—as the insane animal, as the laughing animal, the weeping animal, the miserable animal" (*GS* 224).

9. In *The Birth of Tragedy*, Nietzsche contrasts the Dionysian pessimism of the Greek tragedy with the Socratic optimism of Greek philosophy and puts forth the hypothesis that pessimism is a sign of health, and optimism a sign of weakness and decline. The health of the Dionysian pessimist arises from a fruitful relationship with animality. It does not need animality to be veiled and sublimated by an illusion of morality, but affirms animality as an opponent worth competing with. Dionysian pessimism represents a preference for the difficult and dangerous, a preference for the effort and challenges involved in human becoming and self-overcoming.

10. I borrow the term "crossing" from John Sallis, *Crossings* (Chicago: University of Chicago Press, 1991). See also *PTA* 5.

11. The citation continues: "Now the slave is a free man, now all the rigid, hostile barriers, which necessity, caprice, or 'impudent fashion' have established between human beings break asunder" (*BT* 1).

12. "Without myth, however, all cultures lose their healthy, creative, natural energy; only a horizon surrounded by myth encloses and unifies a cultural movement. Only by myth can all the energies of fantasy and Apollonian dream be saved from aimless meandering . . . even the state knows of no more powerful unwritten laws than the mythical fundament" (*BT* 3).

13. Taylor, in his reconstruction of Nietzsche's early thought, gives a different interpretation of this passage. He claims that greatness in the Greeks is related to their instinctive recognition of "the unity of the natural and the human" and to their not seeking to "eliminate the all-too-human aspect of man's animal being" (*The Republic of Genius,* 53). In this account the Greeks are "overhuman," i.e.,

great, because they preserve their "all-too-human" nature. In contrast, I argue, first, that the "inhuman" and "terrible" aspect of human nature refers to the human's animality and that, therefore, what gives rise to greatness is not the "fertile soil" of the "all-too-human" but the "fertile soil" of animality; and, second, that what distinguishes the "all-too-human," in contrast to the animal, is its lack of "inhuman" and "terrible" forces.

14. Nietzsche even goes so far as to compare the pleasure derived from the sight of the wholeness and simplicity reflected in the higher ethical nature of the Greek to the pleasure derived from the sight of animals (*KSA* 8:6[36]).

15. On the imitation of what is inimitable, see Philippe Lacoue-Labarthe, *L'imitations des Modernes* (Paris: Editions Galilée, 1986).

16. A forgetting of the origin (i.e., a forgetting of the genealogy of morality, for example) inherently defines the project of civilization: "A morality, a mode of living tried and proved by long experience and testing, at length enters consciousness as a law, as dominating—And therewith the entire group of related values and states enters into it: it becomes venerable, unassailable, holy, true; it is part of its development that its origin should be forgotten—That is a sign it has become master—Exactly the same thing could have happened with the categories of reason: they could have prevailed, after much groping and fumbling, through their relative utility—There came a point where one collected them together, raised them to consciousness as a whole—and when one commanded them, i.e. when they had the effect of a command—From then on, they counted as a priori, as beyond experience, as irrefutable. And yet perhaps they represent nothing more than the expediency of a certain race and species—their utility alone is their 'truth'" (*WP* 514). See in comparison, "How scarcely moral the world would seem without forgetfulness! A poet could say God has placed forgetfulness as a doorkeeper on the threshold to the temple of human dignity" (*HH* 92).

17. See in comparison: "The domestication (the 'culture') of the human being does not go deep—where it does it at once becomes degeneration (type: Christian). The 'savage' (or, in moral terms, the evil one) is a 'return to nature'—and in a certain sense its recovery, its *cure* from 'culture'" (*WP* 684).

18. It should be noted, however, that Nietzsche concedes that civilization contributes to the rise of culture only indirectly: not by virtue of its "higher" reason and "higher" morality but because of its inherent stupidity. Civilization is "this tyranny, this caprice, this rigorous and grandiose stupidity" that has *educated* the spirit (*BGE* 188). Nietzsche speculates whether the stupidity of civilization may, in fact, be a secret tool employed by nature to foster culture.

19. In *Twilight of the Idols,* Nietzsche distinguishes between a "morality of taming" and a "morality of breeding" (*TI* "Improvers" 1–5). Both pursue a project of moral improvement and, therefore, have to be understood within the larger project of civilization. Nietzsche is particularly critical of "moralities of taming" represented primarily by Western Christianity because, as Conway writes, it "imposes upon all forms of life a single ideal, with respect to which the higher, more exotic type must be broken down" (*Nietzsche and the Political,* 35). Conway

holds that, instead, Nietzsche embraces a "morality of breeding," represented by Manu, because it "encourages the simultaneous flourishing of a plurality of forms of life" (ibid.). I agree with this view insofar as Nietzsche explicitly favors the project of Manu over that of Western Christianity, but his reason is simply that whereas the first breeds three types of human beings (and not a plurality of forms of life as Conway claims), the second only produces one type (the herd type). Manu is "more gentle and rational" than Christianity, but, nonetheless, Nietzsche rejects Manu for being just another "improver of the humankind" (*TI* "Improvers" 3), an example of the kind of morality that fails to cultivate a genuine plurality of life forms.

20. See this translation in Margot Norris, *Beasts of Modern Imagination: Darwin, Nietzsche, Kafka, Ernst, and Lawrence* (Baltimore: Johns Hopkins University Press, 1985), 9. Consider also *TI* "Improvers" 2, "Morality" 1–2, and the following passage from *Beyond Good and Evil:* "Almost everything we call 'higher culture' is based on the spiritualization of *cruelty*, on its becoming more profound: this is my proposition. That 'savage animal' has not really been 'mortified'; it lives and flourishes, it has merely become—divine" (*BGE* 229).

21. The noble soul "does not like to look 'up'—but either *ahead*, horizontally and slowly, or down: *it knows itself to be at a height*" (*BGE* 265). For the importance of the horizontal perspective in Nietzsche's conception of nobility, see my article "Nietzsches Vision einer 'neuen Aristokratie,'" *Deutsche Zeitschrift für Philosophie* 56 (2008): 365–83.

22. For Nietzsche's new conception of hierarchy, see also Barbara Stiegler, *Nietzsche et la biologie* (Paris: PUF, 2001), 55–56.

23. Norris also argues that aggression in the overhuman is "a pure discharge of vitality and power, which does not have as its aim the domination of the minds and souls of others" (*Beasts of Modern Imagination*, 4).

24. For the overhuman as an affirmation of becoming, that is, of "self-overcoming, transformation, and change rather than conservation, repetition and stability," see Alan D. Schrift, "Rethinking the Subject: Or How One Becomes-Other Than What One Is," in *Nietzsche's Postmoralism: Essays on Nietzsche's Prelude to Philosophy's Future*, ed. Richard Schacht (Cambridge: Cambridge University Press, 2001), 55.

25. On self-overcoming as a becoming untruthful to oneself, see Jean-Luc Nancy, "'Notre Probité' sur la vérité au sens moral chez Nietzsche," in *L'impératif Catégorique* (Paris: Flammarion, 1983), 61–86. This text is also available in English as "'Our Probity!' On Truth in the Moral Sense in Nietzsche," in *Looking after Nietzsche*, ed. Laurence A. Rickels (Albany: State University of New York Press, 1990), 67–87.

26. Ansell-Pearson argues that in Nietzsche "the human is from the beginning of its formation and deformation implicated in an overhuman becoming, and that this is a becoming that is dependent upon non-human forces of life, both organic and inorganic" (Keith Ansell-Pearson, "On the Miscarriage of Life and the Future of the Human: Thinking Beyond the Human Condition with Nietzsche," *Nietzsche-Studien* 29 [2000]: 177). He names this condition of human life,

(i.e., its implication in becoming) its "transhuman condition." In his *Viroid Life* (London: Routledge, 1997), Ansell-Pearson argues that one of the main differences between Darwin and Nietzsche is that, for Darwin, the evolution of the human species is a matter of natural selection and, for Nietzsche, it is a matter not of natural, but of cultural selection, i.e., the result of unnatural (i.e., cultural) self-experimentation of the human species on itself. Accordingly, humanity understood as a process of self-experimentation is, to use a Nietzschean metaphor, like a bridge, always already beyond itself, leading toward something other than itself. Ansell-Pearson holds the view that nature is always already culture, or, as Kofman puts it, that nature is always already an interpretation of culture. But while Kofman insists on the poetic aspect of culture as an art of interpretation, Ansell-Pearson insists on the technological aspect of culture as a technique of self-experimentation. The significance Ansell-Pearson attributes to technology (*techné*) over interpretation (*poiesis*) might explain why he generally assigns a greater role to memory than to forgetfulness in the becomings of human life (ibid., 9–55, 85–122, and 151–89).

27. "What the Greek saw in his satyr was nature, as yet untouched by knowledge, with the bolts of culture still closed, but he did not for this reason equate the satyr with the monkey" (*BT* 8).

28. Zarathustra affirms that he has adopted the idea of the overhuman among humans: "It is among the humans that Zarathustra claims to have picked up the word 'overhuman' by the way and that the human being is something that must be overcome" (*Z* 3 "On Old and New Tablets"), indicating that the idea of the overhuman inherently belongs to the human.

29. See Kofman, *Nietzsche et la scène philosophique*, 289–318.

30. The notion of the dream in what follows is not reduced to the notion of the Apollonian dream as Nietzsche discusses it in *The Birth of Tragedy*. For the notion of dream and dream narratives in Nietzsche, see Gary Shapiro, *Nietzschean Narratives* (Bloomington: Indiana University Press, 1989), 24–26; and also by the same author, "'This Not a Christ,'" in *Why Nietzsche Still?* ed. Alan D. Schrift (Berkeley and Los Angeles: University of California Press, 2000), 79–98.

31. "How wonderful and new and yet how fearful and ironic my new insight makes me feel towards all existence! I have discovered for myself that the ancient humanity and animality, indeed the whole pre-history and past of all sentient being, continues within me to fabulate, to love, to hate, and to infer—I suddenly awoke in the middle of this dream, but only to the consciousness that I am dreaming and that I *must* go on dreaming lest I perish—as the sleepwalker has to go on dreaming in order to avoid falling down" (*GS* 54). This aphorism from *The Gay Science* was of particular interest to Freud, who quotes Nietzsche in order to show that dream analysis can lead to knowledge of an archaic heritage innate to everyone. See Sigmund Freud, *Interpretation of Dreams* (New York: Avon Books, 1965), 588.

32. "All organic life insofar as it 'judges [*urteilt*]' acts like an artist" (*KSA* 11:25[333]).

33. On dream as a primordial form of human life, see also Foucault: "In the dream, everything says 'I,' even the things and the animals, even objects distant and strange which populate the phantasmagoria. . . . To dream is not another way of experiencing another world, it is for the dreaming subject the radical way of experiencing its own world" (Ludwig Binswanger and Michel Foucault, "Dream, Imagination, and Existence," in *Dream and Existence*, ed. Keith Hoeller [Atlantic Highlands, N.J.: Humanities Press International, 1993], 59). The notions of a dream and dream images in Nietzsche are further discussed in Chapter 6.

27. "*The Logic of dream.* . . . In dream this piece of primeval humanity continues to exercise itself, for it is the basis upon which higher rationality evolved and continues to evolve in every human being: the dream takes us back again to remote stages of human culture and provides us with a means of understanding them better" (*HH* 13). Shapiro holds that passages such as these do not, in spite of appearances, betray a progressive view of human rational development. He correctly emphasizes, in my view, that Nietzsche's notion of dream cannot be identified with an Enlightenment perspective. "It is clear that he sees the dream as much more than a residue of an earlier state or as a tolerable interruption of a more rational life; and he also suggests that it is not only the mundane narratives of savage life that are analogous to the dream but also those waking narratives that we relate about ourselves as well as the culturally central narratives of history, religion and philosophy" (Shapiro, *Nietzschean Narratives*, 25–26).

35. On the relationship between returning ghosts and creativity see Jean Starobinski, *Portrait de l'artiste en saltimbanque* (Paris: Flammarion, 1970).

36. On the dream state as the dissolution of civilization, see Sigmund Freud, *Civilization and Its Discontents* (New York: W. W. Norton, 1961); also Freud, *Le délire et les rêves dans la gradiva de Jensen* (Paris: Gallimard, 1986), 137–249.

37. "*Dream and Culture.* —The function of the brain that sleep encroaches upon most is the memory: not that it ceases altogether —but it is reduced to a condition of imperfection such as in the primeval ages of humankind may have been normal by day and in waking" (*HH* 12).

38. Nietzsche's conception of forgetfulness and of memory in "On the Use and Disadvantage of History for Life" is discussed at length in Chapter 5.

39. Conversely, the forgetfulness of culture, that is, the forgetting of the memory of civilization, should not be confused with the voluntary act of forgetting: "It has not yet been proved that there is any such thing as forgetting; all we know is that the act of recollection does not lie within our power. We have provisionally set into this gap in our power that word 'forgetting,' as if it were one more addition to our faculties. But what, after all, does lie within our power!—if that word stands in a gap in our power, ought the other words not to stand in a gap in our *knowledge of our power?*" (*D* 126).

40. On the art of grasping the moment (*kairos*), see Jean Paul Vernant and Marcel Detienne, *Les ruses de l'intelligence* (Paris: Flammarion, 1974).

41. For an interpretation of genius as our life insofar as life does not belong to us, see Giorgio Agamben, *Profanierungen* (Frankfurt: Suhrkamp, 2005), 7–17;

and Jean-Luc Nancy, "Praesens," in *The Gift: Generous Offerings Threatening Hospitality* (Milan: Edizioni Charta, 2001), 191–99.

42. "[The genius of culture] flows out, he overflows, he uses himself up, he does not spare himself—with inevitability, fatefully, involuntarily, as a river's bursting of its banks is involuntary. But because one owes a great deal to such explosive beings one has bestowed a great deal upon them in return, for example a kind of *higher morality*. . . . For that is the nature of human gratitude: it *misunderstands* its benefactors" (*TI* "Skirmishes" 44).

43. The Subverting ones reverse all of the evaluations that have been turned "on their heads" by the rule of civilization and Christianity: "Stand all evaluations *on their head—that* is what they had to do! And break the strong sickly o'er great hopes, cast suspicion on the joy in beauty, bend everything haughtily, manly, conquering, domineering, all the instincts characteristic of the highest and best-turned-out type of 'human being,' into security, agony of conscience, self-destruction—indeed, invert all love of the earthly and of dominion over the earth into hatred of the earth and the earthly—that is the task the church posed for itself and had to pose, until in its estimation 'becoming unworldly,' 'non-sensual,' and 'higher human being' were fused into a single feeling" (*BGE* 62).

44. "One could conceive of the delight and power of self-determination, a *freedom* of the will in which the spirit takes leave of faith and every wish for certainty, practiced as it is in maintaining itself on light ropes and possibilities and dancing even beside abysses. Such a spirit would be the *free spirit* par excellence" (*GS* 347).

45. "*The instinct*—When the house burns one forgets even lunch.—Yes, but one eats it later in the ashes" (*BGE* 83).

2. Politics and Promise

1. For a recent interpretation of Nietzsche as a precursor to totalitarian and authoritarian ideologies, see Don Dombowsky, *Nietzsche's Machiavellian Politics* (London: Palgrave Macmillan, 2004); and Domenico Losurdo, *Nietzsche, Il ribelle aristocratico: Biografia bilancio critico* (Turin: Bollati Boringhieri, 2002). For a discussion of whether Nietzsche's political thought is a precursor to totalitarian and authoritarian ideologies, see my article, "Nietzsches Vision einer 'Neuen Aristokratie'," *Deutsche Zeitschrift für Philosophie* 56 (2008): 365–83. The most influential reading of Nietzsche's philosophy as nonpolitical is found in Walter Kaufmann's *Nietzsche: Philosopher, Psychologist, Antichrist* (Princeton, N.J.: Princeton University Press, 1974), 158–67 and 412–18. He holds that Nietzsche is not proto-Nazi and that his philosophy is inherently nonpolitical. Contrary to popular misconceptions concerning Nietzsche's views on race and German nationalism, Kaufmann emphasizes Nietzsche's distinctiveness as a moral rather than a political philosopher. For a more recent interpretation of Nietzsche's philosophy as nonpolitical, see also Thomas H. Brobjer, "The Absence of Political Ideas in Nietzsche's Writings: The Case of the Law of Manu and the Associated Caste Society," *Nietzsche-Studien* 27 (1998): 300–18. Not unlike Kaufmann's

reading, Stanley Cavell's reading of Nietzsche as a moral perfectionist emphasizes the moral value of Nietzsche's philosophy. In contrast to Kaufmann, however, the overall aim pursued by Cavell's reading of Nietzsche is to reconcile the latter with a liberal theory of justice. See Stanley Cavell, *Conditions Handsome and Unhandsome: The Constitution of Emersonian Perfectionism* (Chicago: University of Chicago Press, 1990), 33–63. For a discussion of whether Nietzsche's political thought can be understood in terms of moral perfectionism, see my article, "Is Nietzsche a Perfectionist?: Rawls, Cavell and the Politics of Culture in Nietzsche's *Schopenhauer as Educator*," *Journal of Nietzsche Studies* 34 (2007): 5–27. For an excellent review of the recent literature on Nietzsche's political philosophy, see Herman W. Siemens, "Nietzsche's Political Philosophy: A Review of the Recent Literature," *Nietzsche-Studien* 30 (2001): 499–526.

2. "For the fear of wild animals [*wildes Gethier*], that was bred [*angezüchtet*] in the human being longest of all—including the animal [*their*] it harbors itself and fears: Zarathustra calls it 'the inner beast [*Vieh*]'" (*Z* "On Science").

3. See Thomas Hobbes, *The Leviathan* (Cambridge: Cambridge University Press, 1996). The question of whether social and political organization is inseparable from power over animal life and, therefore, inevitably biopolitical, has been pursued by authors such as Max Horkheimer and Theodor W. Adorno, *Dialektik der Aufklärung: Philosophische Fragmente* (Frankfurt: Suhrkamp, 1981); Michel Foucault, *Sécurité, territoire, population: Cours au Collège de France 1977–1978* (Paris: Seuil/Gallimard, 2004); as well as Giorgio Agamben, *Homo Sacer: Sovereign Power and Bare Life*, trans. Daniel Heller-Roazen (Stanford: Stanford University Press, 1998).

4. On the recovery of responsibility in Nietzsche, see Bonnie Honig, *Political Theory and the Displacement of Politics* (Ithaca, N.Y.: Cornell University Press, 1993), 42–75. For a different view, see Christa D. Acampora, "On Sovereignty and Overhumanity: Why It Matters How We Read Nietzsche's Genealogy II:2," *International Studies in Philosophy* 36:3 (2004): 127–45.

5. It is partly due to this agonistic spirit that several authors have tried to attribute to Nietzsche an agonistic conception of democracy. For recent examples of this approach, see Lawrence Hatab, *A Nietzschean Defense of Democracy: An Experiment in Postmodern Politics* (Chicago: Open Court, 1995); Dana Villa, "Democratizing the Agon: Nietzsche, Arendt and the Agonistic Tendency in Recent Political Theory," in *Why Nietzsche Still?* ed. Alan D. Schrift (Berkeley: University of California Press, 2000), 224–46; Herman W. Siemens, "Agonal Communities of Taste: Law and Community in Nietzsche's Philosophy of Transvaluation," *Journal of Nietzsche Studies* 24 (2002): 83–112; and Christa D. Acampora, "Demos Agonistes Redux: Reflections on the Streit of Political Agonism," *Nietzsche-Studien* 32 (2003): 374–90.

6. This life-preserving aspect of the memory of civilization is comparable to that of antiquarian history (*HL* 2). Both preserve the continuity between the past and the future by conserving the traditions, habits, and costumes of any given society.

7. For the interdependence between human memory and society, see also Paul S. Loeb, "Finding the Übermensch in Nietzsche's *Genalogy of Morality*," *Journal of Nietzsche Studies* 30 (2005): 75–77.

8. "Intellect and morality—One has to have a good memory if one is to keep a promise. One has to have a powerful imagination if one is to feel sympathy. So closely is morality tied to the quality of the intellect" (*HH* 59). Apart from memory, Nietzsche repeatedly insists on language and consciousness as indispensable tools for the formation of society and the state. He notes, for example, that "consciousness is present only to the extent that it is useful" to society and the state (*KSA* 12:2[95]; *WP* 505). I return to the interrelation among consciousness, language, and society in Chapter 6.

9. In an earlier text, Nietzsche already underlines that "the state enforces the process of civilization" (*GSt*).

10. On violence and the origin of the state in Machiavelli, see Niccolo Machiavelli, *The Prince* (Chicago: University of Chicago Press, 1998), chaps. VI–IX; and Niccolo Machiavelli, *Florentine Histories* (Princeton, N.J.: Princeton University Press, 1988), 122–24. In an early text, Nietzsche writes: "Power [*Gewalt*] gives the first *right*, and there is no right which is not fundamentally presumption, usurpation and violence" (*GSt*). In accordance with his view that the foundation of political power is inherently violent and illegitimate, Nietzsche does not develop a conception of legitimate domination. Whereas Esposito sees, in this absence, a strength in Nietzsche's political thought (Roberto Esposito, *Bios: Biopolitica e filosofia* [Turin: Biblioteca Einaudi, 2004], 81), Ansell-Pearson sees in it one of its greatest weaknesses (Keith Ansell-Pearson, *An Introduction to Nietzsche as Political Thinker* [Cambridge: Cambridge University Press, 1994], 41, 139–40, and 154).

11. It is interesting to compare the figure of the ascetic priest in Nietzsche to the figure of the Grand Inquisitor in Dostoevsky's *The Brothers Karamazov*. Both are figures of political terror, moral dogmatism, and irresponsibility (Fyodor Dostoevsky, *The Grand Inquisitor, with Related Chapters from the Brothers Karamazov*, ed. Charles B. Guignon, trans. Constance Garnett [Indianapolis: Hackett, 1993]). They stand in opposition to the figure of the Prince in Machiavelli, who employs violence responsibly. It is this opposition between Machiavellian and Nietzschean ideas of the responsible use of violence that informs Max Weber's famous essay, "The Vocation of Politics." In this essay, Weber sets an ethics of responsibility against one of conviction, and shows why and on what grounds the latter's use of violence tends to escape responsibility and degenerate into terror, while the former's use of violence is based on the affirmation of responsibility as an essential component of legitimate political power. See, in particular, the following passage: "It seems that the ethics of conviction is bound to founder hopelessly on this problem of how the end is to sanctify the means. Indeed the only position it can logically take is to *reject any* action which employs morally dangerous means. Logically, in the real world, admittedly, we repeatedly see the

proponent of the 'ethics of conviction' suddenly turning into a chiliastic prophet. Those who have been preaching 'love against force' one minute, for example, issue a call to force the next; they call for one *last* act of force to create the situation in which *all* violence will have been destroyed forever, just like our military leaders who said to the soldiers before every attack that this would be the last, that it would bring victory and then peace. The man who espouses an ethic of conviction cannot bear the ethical irrationality of the world. He is a cosmic-ethical 'rationalist.' Those of you who know their Dostoevsky will recall the scene with the Grand Inquisitor, where the problem is dissected very acutely" (Max Weber, *Political Writings* [Cambridge: Cambridge University Press, 1994], 361). On Nietzsche's influence on Weber, see also Wilhelm Hennis, "Die Spuren Nietzsches im Werk Max Webers," *Nietzsche-Studien* 16 (1987): 382–404.

12. In an early text Nietzsche writes: "If we now see how, in no time at all, the subjected hardly bother about the dreadful origin of the state, so that basically history informs us less well about the way those sudden, violent, bloody and at least in *one* aspect inexplicable usurpations came about than about any other kind of event" (*GSt*). For the need of forgetfulness for the stability of rule, see Machiavelli, *The Prince*, chaps. IV and V. Machiavelli writes about the Romans' difficulty stabilizing their rule over Spain, France, and Greece because of the numerous principalities that existed in those states: "As long as their memory lasted, the Romans were always uncertain of their possession, but when their memory was eliminated with the power and long duration of the empire, the Romans became secure possessors of them" (ibid., 19). Interestingly, Machiavelli argues that the most stable form of rule is a republican one because the memory of freedom can never be forgotten: "And whoever becomes the patron of a city accustomed to living free and does not destroy it, should expect to be destroyed by it; for it always has as a refuge in rebellion the name of liberty and its own ancient orders which were never forgotten either through length of time or because of benefits received" (ibid., 21).

13. Chapter 5 discusses Nietzsche's notion of critical history as a form of memory that undoes the forgetfulness of civilization and brings back the memory of the violence and injustice committed in the past with the aim of overthrowing a form of rule that no longer acts in the service of life.

14. The coincidence of civilization and morality is not only reflected in the figure of the ascetic priest but also in the modern state seeking to become a new church: "It wants men to render it the same idolatry they formally rendered the church" (*SE* 4).

15. In a fragment from the *Nachlass*, Nietzsche opposes the egoism of the animal (*Raubthiere*) to the altruism of human animals who live in society with others and notes that animals (*Raubthiere*) are more individual (*individueller*) than humans (*KSA* 10: 8[11]).

16. In *The Present Age*, Kierkegaard, like Nietzsche in *On the Genealogy of Morals* (*GM* I), identifies resentment at the root of the leveling process: "The

resentment which results from want of character can never understand that eminent distinction really is distinction. Neither does it understand itself by recognizing distinction negatively (as in the case of ostracism) but wants to drag it down, wants to belittle it so that it really ceases to be distinguished. And *resentment* not only defends itself against all *existing* forms of distinction but against that which is still *to come*. The *resentment* which is *establishing itself* is the process of leveling, and while a passionate age storms ahead setting up new things and tearing down old, raising and demolishing as it goes, a reflective and passionless age does exactly the contrary: it *hinders and stifles* all action; it levels" (Søren Kierkegaard, *The Present Age* [New York: Harper and Row, 1962], 51).

17. Adorno and Horkheimer show that this process of identification reflects the "course of European civilization." It inherently belongs to what Adorno and Horkheimer refer to as the dialectic of enlightenment: "What was different is equalized. That is the verdict which critically determines the limits of possible experience. The identity of everything with everything else is paid for in that nothing may at the same time be identical with itself. Enlightenment dissolves the injustice of the old inequality—unmediated lordship and mastery—but at the same time perpetuates it in universal mediation, in the relation of any one existent to any other. It does what Kierkegaard praises his Protestant ethic for, and what in the Heraclitean epic cycle is one of the primal images of mythic power; it excises the incommensurable. Not only are qualities dissolved in thought, but men are brought to actual conformity" (Max Horkheimer and Theodor W. Adorno, *Dialectic of Enlightenment,* trans. John Cumming [New York: Continuum, 2002], 12). Nietzsche, like Adorno and Horkheimer after him, rejects the politics of identity inherent to the process of civilization. For a discussion of Nietzsche as a proponent of a politics of identity, see Don Dombowsky, "A Response to Alan Schrift's 'Nietzsche for Democracy?,'" *Nietzsche-Studien* 29 (2000): 278–90; and Alan D. Schrift, "Response to Don Dombowsky," *Nietzsche-Studien* 29 (2000): 291–97.

18. For a recent discussion of the figure of the criminal in Nietzsche's politics, see Friedrich Balke, "die Figuren Des Verbrechers in Nietzsches Biopolitik," *Nietzsche-Studien* 32 (2003): 171–205.

19. See in comparison in *Thus Spoke Zarathustra*: "No Shepherd and one herd! Everybody wants the same, everybody is the same: whoever feels different goes voluntarily into a madhouse" (*Z:* 5 "Prologue").

20. A critique of morality as the enemy of singularity is a common theme of nineteenth-century philosophy found not only in the liberal tradition—for example, in John Stuart Mill's *On Liberty* (Indianapolis: Hackett, 1978) and in Ralph Waldo Emerson's *Self-Reliance,* in *Selected Writings* (New York: Penguin Books, 1965), 262–85; but also in that of its critics, such as Kierkegaard, *The Present Age,* and Dostoevsky, *The Grand Inquisitor.*

21. For an example of the connection between voluntary servitude and responsibility, see Michel Foucault's notion of pastoral power in *Sécurité, territoire, population,* 119–93.

22. Just like every form of civilization produces a form of counterculture, every form of history produces a form of counterhistory. On monumental, antiquarian, and critical history as forms of counterhistory, see Chapter 4.

23. "Great men, like great epochs, are explosive material in whom tremendous energy has been accumulated; their prerequisite has always been, historically and physiologically, that a protracted assembling, accumulating, economizing and preserving has preceded them—that there has been no explosion for a long time. If the tension in the mass has grown too great the merest accidental stimulus suffices to call the 'genius,' the 'deed,' the 'great destiny' into the world" (*TI* "Skirmishes" 44).

24. Also, Kierkegaard holds that the normalizing process of civilization ends up taking away the individual's responsibility (Kierkegaard, *The Present Age*, 53). Nietzsche, moreover, points out that disciplining the animal and making it obedient does not contribute to its cultivation, but rather to its barbarization (*DS* 1).

25. On the value of forgetfulness and memory in the Greek polis, see Nicole Loraux, *La cité divisée: L'oublie et la mémoire d'Athène* (Paris: Payot, 1997), who shows that, in the polis, the oath serves as a means against discord only insofar as it is tied to forgetfulness as that force which dissolves the memory of misdeeds and hatred. According to Loraux, the oath (promise) safeguards the stability and harmony of the Greek polis because it reflects a commitment to forget rather than to remember.

26. "Every philosophy which believes that the problem of existence is touched on, not to say solved, by a political event is a joke and pseudo-philosophy" (*SE* 4). When it comes to the question of how to bring forth an animal that truly deserves the privilege of promising, what is required above all is freedom from politics. This freedom from politics is also one of the conditions for bringing forth a philosophical genius: "These then are some of the conditions under which the philosophical genius can at any rate come into existence in our time despite the forces working against it: free manliness of character, early knowledge of humankind [*Menschenkenntnis*], no scholarly education, no narrow patriotism, no necessity [*Zwang*] for bread-winning, no ties with the state—in short, freedom and again freedom; that wonderful and perilous element in which the Greek philosophers were able to grow up" (*SE* 8).

27. "Would that you were as perfect as animal at least! But animals have innocence. Do I counsel you to slay your senses? I counsel the innocence of the senses" (*Z* "On Chastity").

28. On the need for forgetfulness, see Alan D. Schrift, "Rethinking the Subject: Or How One Becomes-Other Than What One Is," in *Nietzsche's Postmoralism: Essays on Nietzsche's Prelude to Philosophy's Future*, ed. Richard Schacht (Cambridge: Cambridge University Press, 2001), 47–62. Schrift argues that in the opening of the second essay of the *Genealogy of Morals* what is at stake is the active forgetting of the sovereign individual who has earned the right to make promises: "It is only in the case of this 'emancipated individual' [*Freigewordene*]—this 'master of the free will' [*Herr des Freien Willens*] (*GM* II: 2) who is

capable of becoming other than he was by forgetting what he was—that promising becomes a praiseworthy act of responsibility" (Schrift, "Rethinking the Subject," 59).

29. On the notion of probity, see Jean-Luc Nancy, "'Notre probibité'! sur la vérité au sense moral chez Nietzsche," in *L'impératif catégorique* (Paris: Flammarion, 1983), 61–86. Nietzsche's notion of the promise of the sovereign individual is, in this sense, comparable to the promise of Abraham in Kierkegaard. In *Fear and Trembling*, the figure of Abraham exemplifies the idea that true freedom is possible only on the basis of a fundamental disagreement between an individual and the ethical community. True freedom in Kierkegaard can therefore never be achieved through politics or through agreement and consensus within an ethical community, but only through an experience of faith. Faith in Kierkegaard is the carrier of genuine freedom, where freedom stands for the strength to break with the ethical community in the name of one's singular responsibility. The virtues Kierkegaard attributes to Abraham are similar to those that Nietzsche attributes to the sovereign individual: both "suspend the ethical," that is, the power of the group, in the name of individual self-responsibility. See Søren Kierkegaard, *Fear and Trembling* (London: Penguin Books, 1985), Problema II and III.

30. "What does your conscience say?—'You shall become who you are'" (*GS* 270); and "If we train [*dressiert*] our conscience, it kisses us while it hurts [*beisst*] us" (*BGE* 98).

31. Emmanuel Lévinas, *Totalité et infini* (La Haye: Nijhoff, 1961).

32. For examples of readings of sovereignty in Nietzsche as a form of power over others, see Hannah Arendt, *The Human Condition* (Chicago: University of Chicago Press, 1958), 241ff; and Alasdair MacIntyre, *After Virtue* (Notre Dame, Ind.: Notre Dame University Press, 1984). For a discussion of Arendt's reading of the promise in Nietzsche, see my article "Memory and Promise in Arendt and Nietzsche," *Revista de Ciencia Politica* 26, no. 2 (2006): 161–74. On sovereignty in Nietzsche as an overcoming of domination, see Alex McIntyre, *The Sovereignty of Joy: Nietzsche's Vision of Great Politics* (Toronto: University of Toronto Press, 1997), 3–21; and Michel Haar, *Nietzsche and Metaphysics*, trans. Michael Gendre (Albany: State University of New York Press, 1996), 25.

33. For the idea that the promise of responsibility is unlimited, consider Zarathustra's comment: "I love him who casts golden words before his deeds and always does even more than he promises: for he wants to go under" (*Z:* 4 "Prologue"). In *Thus Spoke Zarathustra*, gold is a metaphor for the gift-giving virtue. The use of the gold metaphor in the above citation suggests that the promise, as Nietzsche imagines it, is intimately related to gift-giving.

34. The notion of gift-giving in Nietzsche has affinities with Bataille's notion of unproductive expenditure. In both authors, "wealth appears as an acquisition to the extent that power is acquired by a rich man, but it is entirely directed towards loss in the sense that this power is characterized as power to lose. It is only through loss that glory and honor are linked to wealth" (Georges Bataille, "The Notion of Expenditure," in *Visions of Excess, Selected Writings 1927–1939*, ed. Allan Stoekl [Minneapolis: University of Minnesota Press, 1985], 122).

35. As such, both the figure of the tragic hero and the figure of the sovereign individual reveal an aspect of Nietzsche's conception of life: "Life is not a 'substance' rather it is something that thrives towards augmentation [*Verstärkung*] and that wants to 'preserve' itself only indirectly (it wants to surpass itself [*sich überbieten*])" (*KSA* 12:9[98]). See also *KSA* 11:27[3].

36. See in comparison Hatab, who objects to the view that the sovereign individual foreshadows Nietzsche's creator type. According to him, "such a connection is quite problematic because of the meaning of 'sovereignty,' its textual association with morality, and Nietzsche's critique of modernist freedom" (Hatab, *A Nietzschean Defense of Democracy*, 38).

37. Nietzsche believed his conceptions of freedom and virtue (virtuosity) were anticipated by Machiavelli's notions of *fortuna* and *virtù*. See also "Overcome yourself even in your neighbor: and a right that you can rob, you should not let it be given to you" (*Z*: 4 "Of Old and New Tablets").

38. On the relationship between agon and the need for strong institutions, see Strong, *Friedrich Nietzsche and the Politics of Transfiguration*, 194–204.

39. Nietzsche saw his ideal of an agonistic relationship between the individual and the state realized in the Greek city-state. Unlike the modern state, the Greek city-state is: "not a supervisor, regulator, and watchman, but a vigorous and muscular companion and friend" (*FEI* 3), that is, an enemy worth competing with.

40. Brown argues that "permanent resistance to the state that both limits and ensures the democratic form becomes a means of sustaining democracy insofar as it is the state form that dissolves democracy. Only through the state are the people constituted as a people; only in resistance to the state do the people remain a people" (Wendy Brown, "Nietzsche for Politics," in *Why Nietzsche Still?*, ed. Alan D. Schrift [Berkeley and Los Angeles: University of California Press, 2000], 205–23).

41. For an extended discussion of Nietzsche's relationship to modern political ideologies, see Henning Ottmann, *Philosophie und Politik bei Nietzsche* (Berlin: De Gruyter, 1987).

42. Nietzsche fears that, under the dogmatic rule of herd morality, a rule that tolerates no other morality, no other form of life, will be allowed alongside it: " 'Equality of rights' could all too easily be changed into equality in violating rights [*Gleichheit der Unrechte*]—I mean, into a common war on all that is rare, strange, privileged [*Bevorrechtigten*], the higher human being, the higher soul, the higher duty, the higher responsibility, and the abundance of creative power that entails being noble, wanting to be by oneself, being able to be different, standing alone and having to live independently" (*BGE* 212). Contrary to the dogmatism of herd morality, and in the aim of preserving antagonism, Nietzsche holds that herd morality is "merely one type of human morality besides which, before which, and after which many other types, above all higher moralities, are, or ought to be, possible" (*BGE* 202). In contrast to the dogmatism of herd morality, he suggests that greatness is found in someone's "range [*Umfänglichkeit*] and multiplicity [*Vielfältigkeit*], in one's wholeness [*Ganzheit*] in manifoldness [*Vielen*]" (*BGE* 212).

43. The struggle against rule always brings with it the risk of overthrowing and altering rule. Acampora explicitly articulates this inherent risk of agon: "a political order modeled on Nietzsche's ideas about the agon, would have to allow for a kind of thorough-going critique that none of the most extensive accounts of agonistic democracy seem to be able to accommodate, and which I doubt any political order (in so far as it remains an ordering) could sustain" (Acampora, "Demos Agonistes Redux: Reflections on the Streit of Political Agonism," 390).

44. On a future that is already past, a "past future," Caning writes: "The fantasy works (effects) like a promise that remembers itself even—and especially—in the absence of the subject's conscious recall. It promises—it is bound—to recur, to come back in variations both of its psychic representation of itself, and in the personal- and world-historical event. It always remembers the future" (Peter Canning, "How the Fable Becomes a World," in *Looking after Nietzsche*, ed. Laurence A. Rickels [Albany: State University of New York Press, 1990], 186). Deleuze also distinguishes between two kinds of memories in Nietzsche. One is the memory specific to the "man of resentment," i.e., a memory of the will that cannot forget, and the other is an active memory that is no longer a function of the past, but of the future. Deleuze identifies the latter kind of memory as a "memory of the future itself" which is exemplified by the promise of the overhuman. Gilles Deleuze, *Nietzsche et la philosophie* (Paris: PUF, 1962), 131–33 and 153–55.

45. The temporality of the promise in Nietzsche has affinities with the temporality of the signature in Derrida. The structure of the signature reflects the ambivalence between the performative and the constative aspects of the signature. Every signature, just like every promise, corresponds to a stable "I." It fixes and stabilizes itself for an indefinite period of time. This is the constative aspect of the signature. Its constative aspect assures, recollects, and unifies a past, and establishes the continuity of the signature. Through this unification, the signature promises to assure the continuity in question: it stops time, equalizing the present, the future, and the past. The signature becomes that trace that seems true to itself and to those who put trust in it. Like the promise (the memory of the will) in Nietzsche, the signature is a form of memory that conserves time as well as one's relationship to the self and others. It implies all the risks of that monumentality which Nietzsche contests in his *Untimely Considerations*. However, the truth of the constative aspect of the signature exists only for a moment, not forever. Instead of being stable and continuous, it is provisional. The forces of life and thought are accumulated in light of future spending, which overcomes, destabilizes, and destroys what was previously accumulated and fixed. The latter describes the performative aspect of the signature, the overcoming of the fixed and stabilized "I" in light of future life to come. In its performative aspect, the signature expresses the promise and the desire of the one who signs to become who he or she is, that is, precisely, who he or she is not yet. The signature then becomes that trace which designates an abyss between the past and the present and between the present and the future. It reflects the promise that, in signing,

one makes a promise to oneself and to others to become who he or she was not in the past and is not yet in the present, but who he or she will be in the future. As such, the signature reflects a vision, a projected aim emerging on the horizon of the future, a project whose realization remains open, very much like Nietzsche's vision (promise) of the overhuman. Derrida claims that, properly speaking, the one who signs does not exist. He or she does not exist before the act of signing. Whether he or she is able to become who he or she is depends on the act of his or her signature. As such, the signature invents the one who signs. It becomes the producer and the guarantor of the one who signs. The act of signing becomes fiction, and this fiction leaves a trace only because of the inequality, the nonidentity, which exists within the self. Derrida argues that every signature requires the effacing of another signature, the dissolving of the relations of paternity or maternity which are foregone in it. The future calls out for the destruction of the past, just as every new life stands on past life. In this sense, the signature reflects the ongoing struggle between the one who signs and the one who signed, or who will sign. Jacques Derrida, *Otobiographies: L'enseignement de Nietzsche et la politique du nom propre* (Paris: Galilée, 1984).

46. For an analogous conception of spectrality, see Jacques Derrida's reading of Marx in *Specters of Marx* (London: Routledge, 2006).

47. In other roughly contemporary texts, Sartre's notion of responsibility has a distinctly humanistic meaning (see, for example, Jean-Paul Sartre, *Existentialism and Humanism* [New York: Philosophical Library, 1984], 20, 30, 44–47, 54–61), inspired by the Kantian notion of practical freedom as expressed in the universal duty of treating the other like another self. In contrast, Nietzsche treats the other as inaccessible for it is only as radically other that the singularity of the other can be preserved. For Nietzsche, the other always remains at an infinite distance, nontransparent, secret, and inherently different. The freedom of the other is never identical to the freedom of the self and, hence, cannot be approached from a universal point of view. Responsibility and freedom exceed the limit of the self, de-centering rather then centering the ego and, hence, are antihumanistic rather than humanistic. In the texts concerned with the problem of writing, for example, "Writing for One's Age" and "*Introducing* Les Temps modernes," Sartre defines responsibility in what are arguably anti- or nonhumanistic terms, i.e., responsibility as the becoming other of the self. This is why the latter can be compared to a Nietzschean (and maybe even Lévinasian) conception of responsibility. See Jean-Paul Sartre, *"What Is Literature?" and Other Essays* (Cambridge, Mass.: Harvard University Press, 1988), 239–67. For another reading of Sartre along these lines, see Jacques Derrida, "'*Il courait mort*': *Salut, salut. Notes pour un courrier aux* Temps Modernes," *Les Temps Modernes* 587 (Mars–Avril–Mai 1996): 7–54. Neither Sartre nor Derrida see the affinity between the myth of the Marathon Messenger and Nietzsche's life as a writer. The first to draw this analogy, as far as I am aware, is Stefan Zweig: "Même le plus lucide génie du siècle n'a pas été assez clair pour que son temps ait pu le comprendre: comme le coureur de Marathon qui, après avoir accompli tout haletant la longue distance

qui le séparait d'Athènes, ne put annoncer la défaite des Perses que par un su-prême cri d'extase (après quoi il fut pris d'une hémorragie mortelle), Nietzsche sut prédire l'effroyable catastrophe de notre culture mais ne put l'empêcher. Il jeta simplement à son époque un formidable et inoubliable cri d'extase: ensuite l'esprit se brisa en lui" (Stefan Zweig, *Nietzsche: Le combat avec le démon* [Paris: Editions Stock, 1993], 143).

48. Jacques Derrida, "*'Il courait mort'*: *Salut, salut. Notes pour un courrier aux Temps Modernes*," *Les Temps Modernes* 587 (Mars–Avril–Mai 1996): 7–54.

49. "For what is freedom! That one has the will to self-responsibility. That one preserves the distance which divides us. That one has become more indiffer-ent to hardship, toil, privation, even to life. That one is ready to sacrifice human beings to one's cause oneself not excepted" (*TI* "Skirmishes" 38).

50. See in comparison, Jacques Derrida, *Aufzeichnungen eines Blinden* (Pader-born, Germany: Wilhelm Fink Verlag, 1997).

51. On the nomadic character of Nietzsche's thought, see Gilles Deleuze, "Pensée Nomade," in *Nietzsche Aujourd'hui?* (Paris: Union Générale d'Éditions, 1973), 158–74. See also Michel Foucault, *La pensée du dehors* (Paris: Fata Mor-gana, 1986).

52. For an illustration and discussion of André Masson's *Acéphale*, see Georges Bataille, *Visions of Excess*, 178–81.

53. See in comparison Schrift, who argues that Nietzsche's commitment to a philosophy of becoming, as well as his view of life as a process of continuous self-overcoming, "make it impossible for any actual subject to be an *Übermensch*" (Schrift, "Response to Don Dombovsky," 292).

3. Culture and Economy

1. For instance, Ansell-Pearson identifies Nietzsche's aristocratism as a "po-litical programme of a new aristocratic legislation" where "the aim is to gain con-trol of the forces of history and produce through a conjunction of philosophical legislation and political power ('great politics') a new humanity" (Keith Ansell-Pearson, *An Introduction to Nietzsche as Political Thinker* (Cambridge: Cambridge University Press, 1994), 42–43 and 148).

2. On the priority of culture over politics, see Tracy B. Strong, *Friedrich Nietzsche and the Politics of Transfiguration* (Berkeley and Los Angeles: University of California Press, 1975), 94–95 and 201–2.

3. Conway draws a useful distinction between what he calls "the macro-political (or institutional) and micro-political (or infra-institutional)—incarnations of his [Nietzsche's] perfectionism" (Daniel D. Conway, *Nietzsche and the Political* [Florence, Ky.: Routledge, 1997], 48). Leaving the question of Nietzsche's perfectionism aside, one could say that the politics of civilization, as I use the term, is always primarily a form of "macro-politics" concerned with the institution of social and political forms, while the politics of culture, as I use the term, is primarily a form of "micro-politics" operating outside, beneath, and, most importantly, against the institutional framework of civilization. The only

disadvantage I see with the phrase "micro-politics" is that it does not capture Nietzsche's understanding of the politics of culture as a "great politics." "Great politics" is micro-political in the sense that it transcends institutions, but macro-political in the sense that it seeks to effect a transformation of institutions. I return to the notion of "great politics" at the end of this book.

4. For a discussion of Nietzsche's vision of a future aristocratic society, see my article, "Nietzsches Vision einer 'Neuen Aristokratie,'" *Deutsche Zeitschrift für Philosophie* 56 (2008): 365–83.

5. In an earlier text, Nietzsche already identifies "as a cruel-sounding truth the fact that *slavery belongs to the essence of culture*" (*GSt*). In the Greek polis, the relationship between slavery and culture takes the following form: "Culture [*Bildung*], which is first and foremost a real hunger for art, rests on one terrible premise: but this reveals itself in the nascent feeling of shame. In order for there to be a broad, deep, fertile soil for the development of art, the overwhelming majority has to be slavishly subjected to life's necessity in the service of the minority, *beyond* the measure that is necessary for the individual. At their expense, through their extra work, that privileged class is to be removed from the struggle for existence, in order to produce and satisfy a new world of necessities" (*GSt*). The Greek model of slavery is not, however, a model for the "new type of enslavement" Nietzsche refers to when he explains his notion of a "higher aristocracy" of the future (*GS* 377).

6. "The tremendous machine of the state overpowers the individual . . . everything a human being does in the service of the state is contrary to its nature" (*WP* 717).

7. Nietzsche is pessimistic concerning the problem of slavery because he believes that the need to provide for the necessities of life cannot be abolished (*BT* 18). He therefore rejects the idea of a final emancipation from need in a future (communist) state. In this sense, Nietzsche anticipates Arendt's critique of Marx's conception of freedom as a freedom from need. Like Nietzsche, Arendt questions the possibility of a final emancipation from need and, instead, holds that genuine freedom must reflect an overcoming of domination. See Hannah Arendt, *The Human Condition* (Chicago: University of Chicago Press, 1958), 79–135.

8. One may ask whether, at an even deeper level, slavery is not an expression of the fact that life "is only a means to something, it is the expression of forms of growth of power" (*WP* 706). If life as will to power reflects a radical logic of means and not ends, that is, if everything is a means (meaningful) to another means, and so forth, if everything lives off everything else, then slavery in an extra-moral sense, like will to power, could be interpreted as that which links all forms of life to each other.

9. For an interpretation of culture as a transcendence of animality, see Walter Kaufmann, *Nietzsche: Philosopher, Psychologist, Antichrist* (Princeton, N.J.: Princeton University Press, 1974), 152; and James Conant, "Nietzsche's Perfectionism," in *Nietzsche's Postmoralism: Essays on Nietzsche's Prelude to Philosophy's Future*, ed. Richard Schacht (Cambridge: Cambridge University Press, 2001), 224–25.

10. In "Schopenhauer as Educator," Nietzsche uses the metaphor of fragments of a sculpture that need to be assembled for a complete sculpture of the
higher human being to appear (*SE* 6). In the *Nachlass,* he uses the metaphor of
the fragments of a play, of human beings as "preludes and rehearsals" of a higher
"synthetic human being" (*WP* 881) as well as the metaphor of the fragments of
an image, possibly a puzzle, that needs to be completed, piece by piece, for the
whole image of the higher human being to become visible (ibid.). Finally, he
speaks of the human being as incomplete and fragmentary under the rule of civilization (society) and as complete and whole under the rule of culture (*WP* 997;
719).

11. For an extensive discussion of the relation between completeness and
economy in Nietzsche, see Wolfgang Müller-Lauter, *Über Freiheit und Chaos:
Nietzsche-Interpretationen II* (Berlin: De Gruyter, 1999), 173–226.

12. Nietzsche distinguishes his notion of human animal becoming, elevation,
and advancement from the modern idea of progress: "Humanity [*Menschheit*]
does *not* represent the development of the better or the stronger or the higher in
the way that is believed today. 'Progress' is merely a modern idea, that is to say a
false idea. The European of today is of far less value than the European of the
Renaissance; onward development is not by *any* means, by any necessity the same
thing as elevation, advance, strengthening" (*A* 4). On the difference between becoming and evolution, see also Alan Schrift, "Rethinking the Subject: Or How
One Becomes-Other Than What One Is," in *Nietzsche's Postmoralism: Essays on
Nietzsche's Prelude to Philosophy's Future,* ed. Richard Schacht (Cambridge: Cambridge University Press, 2001), 47–62.

13. In my view, Nietzsche does not invent a grand narrative of the economy
of life/nature to justify, legitimize, and sanctify a conception of "higher culture"
or the authoritarian politics of domination needed to attain it. His narrative on
culture as an economic problem persists throughout his work and keeps returning
in different forms. This indicates that his conception of the economy of life
should not be thought of as something exterior to his conception of culture and
politics, as something added in order to justify a so-called politics of domination,
but rather as a constitutive part of his conception of culture and politics.

14. See, in comparison, "Economy of goodness [*Güte*].—Goodness [*Güte*]
and love as the most salutary medicine in traffic between human beings are such
precious inventions one could well wish they might be employed as economically
as possible: but this is impossible. Economy of goodness [*Güte*] is the dream of
the boldest utopian" (*HH* 48).

15. Nietzsche's distinction between the economies of civilization and culture
clearly influenced Bataille's distinction between the productive and unproductive
activities of human beings. Bataille argues that "human activity is not entirely
reducible to processes of production and conservation, and consumption must
be divided into two distinct parts. The first, reducible part is represented by the
use of the minimum necessary for the conservation of life and the continuation
of individuals' productive activity in a given society; it is therefore a question

simply of the fundamental condition of productive activity. The second part is represented by so-called unproductive expenditures: luxury, mourning, war, cults, the construction of sumptuary monuments, games, spectacles, arts, perverse sexual activities (i.e., deflected from genital finality)—all these represent activities which, at least in primitive circumstances, have no end beyond themselves" (George Bataille, "The Notion of Expenditure," in *Visions of Excess: Selected Writings 1927–1939,* ed. Allan Stoekl [Minneapolis: University of Minnesota Press, 1985], 116–29: 118).

16. The theme of redeeming stupidity is typical of the nineteenth century (as, for example, in Dostoevsky's *The Idiot*). It reflects a critique of the Enlightenment ideal put forth in Kant's essay *What Is Enlightenment?*, which favors the public use of reason over the private (that is, stupid) use of reason. See Immanuel Kant, "What Is Enlightenment?" in *What Is Enlightenment? Eighteenth-Century Answers and Twentieth Century Questions,* ed. James Schmidt (Berkeley and Los Angeles: University of California Press, 1996), 58–63. On the redemption of stupidity in Nietzsche, see also *GS* 3.

17. For an example of this kind of exploitation, see Foucault's notion of disciplinary power. Michel Foucault, *Discipline and Punish* (New York: Vintage Books, 1995), 170–228.

18. These symptoms are particularly dominant in the liberal ideal: "One knows, indeed, *what* they bring about: they undermine the will to power, they are the leveling of mountain and valley exalted to a moral principle, they make small, cowardly and smug—it is the herd animal which triumphs with them every time. Liberalism: in plain words, *reduction to the herd animal* [*Heerden-Verthierung*] . . ." (*TI* "Skirmish" 38).

19. These aspects of Nietzsche's critique of modern economic and political ideologies have been pursued at great length in Georges Bataille, *The Accursed Share: An Essay on General Economy,* trans. Robert Hurley, vols. 2 and 3 (New York: Zone Books, 1991). In the original, Georges Bataille, "Le sens de l'économie générale," in *La Part Maudit* (Paris: Les éditions de Minuit, 1970), 57–80.

20. Bataille, "The Notion of Expenditure," 129.

21. On the attempt to link the aristocratic and democratic aspects of Nietzsche's political thought together, see Wendy Brown, "Nietzsche for Politics," in *Why Nietzsche Still?* ed. Alan D. Schrift (Berkeley and Los Angeles: University of California Press, 2000), 205–23. Hatab distinguishes between "the aristocracy-democracy encounter in the cultural sphere" and "the aristocracy-democracy encounter in the political sphere" (Lawrence Hatab, "Prospects for a Democratic Agon: Why We Can Still Be Nietzscheans," *Journal of Nietzsche Studies* 24 (2002): 132–47). Whereas the first encounter pertains to "matters of creativity and normalcy, excellence and mediocrity," the latter pertains to "the formation of institutions, actual political practices, the justification of coercion, and the extent of sovereignty" (ibid., 141). Hatab maintains that "Nietzsche's aristocratism is defensible regarding the first encounter but not so regarding the second encounter" and hypothesizes whether one could perhaps "argue for a coexistence

of a Nietzschean cultural elite and a democratic egalitarian politics" (ibid.). In my view, this coexistence could be conceived as an agonistic relationship that, on the one hand, democratizes culture and, on the other hand, cultivates democracy.

22. "If one had made the rise of the great and rare men dependent upon the approval of the many . . .—well, there would have never been a single significant man!" (*WP* 885).

23. A noble type of person (a solitary personality) "can maintain and develop himself most easily in a democratic society: namely, when the coarser means of defense are no longer necessary and habits of order, honesty, justice and trust are part of the usual conditions" (*WP* 887).

24. Arendt's vision of public action is, in this sense, comparable to Nietzsche's vision of public life under the rule of culture. For a comparison between Nietzsche and Arendt that brings out the affinity between both authors, see Herman W. Siemens's "Action, Performance and Freedom in Hannah Arendt and Friedrich Nietzsche," *International Studies in Philosophy* 37, no. 3 (2006): 107–26.

25. In a passage in his posthumous work, Nietzsche raises the "wicked and seductive" question of whether or not it is time "to make the experiment of a fundamental, artificial and conscious breeding of the opposite [higher] type and of its virtues" (*WP* 954). Such a proposal stands in harsh contrast to the insight that the cultivation of a higher type of human being is not predictable, controllable, or conscious. Therefore, I suggest that the "experiment of a fundamental, artificial and conscious breeding" of a higher overhuman type could possibly be embraced by a future civilization and morality, but not by a future aristocratic society and culture. For when culture comes to rule, it does so by a stroke of luck rather than by conscious social planning.

26. See in comparison *KSA* 13:14(182).

27. The interdependence of culture and civilization, that is, between freedom and morality (*Zwang*), rests on their antagonistic relationship. According to Siemens and Gerhardt, what is crucial in this antagonism is that it generates ethical laws (Herman W. Siemens, "Agonal Communities of Taste: Law and Community in Nietzsche's Philosophy of Transvaluation," *Journal of Nietzsche Studies* 24 [2002]: 83–112; Volker Gerhardt, "Prinzip des Gleichgewichts," *Nietzsche-Studien* 12 [1983]: 111–33. For both authors, the role of the genius is to give ethical laws to the community. The latter is possible under the condition that the antagonistic relationship between the genius and the community is measured and in equilibrium. On the importance of measure, see Paul von Tongeren, "Nietzsche's Greek Measure," *Journal of Nietzsche Studies* 24 (2002): 5–24. I agree with the above authors on the point that genius considered from the perspective of civilization is not only the inspiration of "new moralities," but also that the aim of agon is to achieve "an equilibrium of tyrannical forces" as a condition of possibility for the application of "new moralities" (Herman W. Siemens, "Agonal Communities of Taste: Law and Community in Nietzsche's Philosophy

of Transvaluation," *Journal of Nietzsche Studies* 24 [2002]: 106). From the perspective of culture, however, the genius is not only a source of ethical laws, but, primarily, a source of freedom. The genius is a liberator who breaks ethical laws, who outbalances "the equilibrium of tyrannical forces" that defines the rule of civilization in view of a new more just equilibrium of forces to come.

4. Giving and Forgiving

1. John Rawls, *A Theory of Justice* (Cambridge, Mass.: Harvard University Press, 1999), 23–24.

2. Nietzsche's conception of gift-giving shares this aspect with the proponents of the theory of the gift from Marcel Mauss to Alain Caillé and Jacques T. Godbout. In my view, what distinguishes Nietzsche's notion of gift-giving from theirs is that it provides an alternative to biopolitical practices that reflect forms of power over life and, in particular, over the animality of the human being. For a brief discussion of the affinity between Nietzsche's notion of gift-giving and Mauss's theory of the gift, see Gary Shapiro, *Alcyone: Nietzsche on Gift, Noise and Women* (Albany: State University of New York Press, 1991), 18–20 and 35.

3. On the double meaning of gift as gift and poison, see Emile Benveniste, *Problème de linguistique générale*, vol. 1 (Paris: Gallimard, 1966), 315–26.

4. On the gift-giving virtue in Nietzsche see also Shapiro, *Alcyone: Nietzsche on Gift, Noise and Women*; Alan D. Schrift, "Rethinking Exchange: Logics of the Gift in Cixous and Nietzsche," *Philosophy Today* (1996): 197–205; and Alan D. Schrift, *Nietzsche's French Legacy: A Genealogy of Poststructuralism* (New York and London: Routledge, 1995), 82–102; Rosalyn Diprose, *Corporeal Generosity: On Giving with Nietzsche, Merleau-Ponty, and Lévinas* (Albany: State University of New York Press, 2002). It is noteworthy that Schrift, in his reading of gift-giving, also emphasizes the importance of forgetfulness. He does not, however, identify the forgetfulness associated with gift-giving as a force that is derived from the animal. His overall concern is with the question of whether gift-giving is "masculine," as he sees exemplified in Nietzsche, or whether it is "feminine," as he sees exemplified in Cixous (Schrift, "Rethinking Exchange: Logics of the Gift in Cixous and Nietzsche," 197–205). In contrast, Shapiro, in his reading of gift-giving, hints at the possibility that a specific relationship to animals and animality could be central to an understanding of gift-giving in Nietzsche: "Could a philosophical bestiary play some role in articulating the space between animal and *Übermensch*, the space in which the higher men move and in which the question of friendship becomes acute?" (Shapiro, *Alcyone: Nietzsche on Gift, Noise and Women*, 52).

5. On giving and forgiving in Derrida, see Jacques Derrida, *The Gift of Death* (Chicago: University of Chicago Press, 1995); Jacques Derrida, *Given Time: 1. Counterfeit Money* (Chicago: University of Chicago Press, 1992); Jacques Derrida, *On Cosmopolitanism and Forgiveness* (London: Routledge, 2001); and Jacques Derrida, *Pardonner: l'impardonnable et l'imprescriptible* (Paris: L'Herne, 2005).

6. In the current debate on the social and political value of gift-giving in archaic and contemporary societies, Derrida's deconstruction of Mauss's conception of the gift has been criticized on two main grounds (Marcel Mauss, "Essai sur le don," in *Sociologie et anthropologie* [Paris: PUF, 1950], 145–284). First, it has been accused of missing the social and political aspect of the gift, due to a shift toward the ethical question of whether the gift is interested, disinterested or economic. According to this critique, Derrida's defense of a pure, disinterested, and noneconomic gift undermines the social and political dimension of Mauss's conception of the gift understood as the triple social obligation of giving, receiving, and returning gifts. Second, Derrida's deconstruction of the Maussian notion of the gift has been accused of reducing the latter to "purely religious thought (Jewish and Christian) about the gift which identifies the gift, charity and gratuity" and, hence, dismisses Mauss's discovery that the gift is "not a charitable gift," "not unselfish, but agonistic" (Alain Caillé, "Notes on the Paradigm of the Gift," in *The Gift* [Milan: Edizioni Charta, 2001], 247–69 and 253). I contest both of the above views on the basis of my comparison between Nietzsche and Derrida on giving and forgiving. I argue, first, that Derrida's conception of the gift makes a significant contribution to the current debate on the social and political value of the gift. Secondly, his notion of the gift is not identified with the Judeo-Christian tradition but rather subverts it.

7. Arendt, *The Human Condition* (Chicago: University of Chicago Press, 1958), 236–43.

8. Derrida, *On Cosmopolitanism and Forgiveness*, 59.

9. Ibid., 36; see also 43 and 59.

10. Ibid., 238.

11. Ibid., 236–37.

12. Ibid., 241.

13. Interestingly, Derrida detects a similar tension within the Judeo-Christian tradition of forgiveness. He distinguishes between an "unconditional, gracious, infinite, aneconomic forgiveness granted to the guilty as guilty, without counterpart, even to those who do not repent or ask for forgiveness" and "a conditional forgiveness proportionate to the recognition of the fault, to repentance, to the transformation of the sinner who then explicitly asks for forgiveness" (Derrida, *On Cosmopolitanism and Forgiveness*, 35). Derrida holds that although the idea of forgiveness falls into ruin as soon as it is deprived of its unconditional purity, it remains nonetheless inseparable from what is heterogeneous to it, namely, the order of conditions, repentance, and transformation. The reason for this is that "if one wants . . . forgiveness to become effective, concrete, historic, if one wants it to arrive, to happen by changing things, it is necessary that this purity engages itself in a series of conditions (psychological, sociological, political)" (ibid., 45). According to Derrida, it is between these two irreconcilable but related poles, the unconditional and the conditional, the ethical and the political, that "decisions and responsibilities are taken" (ibid.).

14. On the prohibition to judge as a precondition for the becoming of justice, see also Dostoevsky, "Conversations and Exhortations of Father Zossima," in

Fyodor Dostoevsky, *The Grand Inquisitor, with Related Chapters from the Brothers Karamazov*, trans. Constance Garnett and ed. Charles B. Guignon (Indianapolis: Hackett, 1993), 77–78. See also "Pour en finir avec le jugement," in Gilles Deleuze, *Critique et clinique* (Paris: Editions de Minuit, 1993), 158–69.

15. For a later version of this idea, see also in comparison: "No *one* is accountable for existing at all, or for being constituted as he is, or for living in the circumstances and surroundings in which he lives" (*TI* "Errors" 8).

16. Nietzsche's criticism is directed against Kant in particular, since he links virtue to an abstract and universal "feeling" of respect, rather than to the instinct of life. Nietzsche identifies Kant as a "nihilist with Christian-dogmatic bowels" who "understands joy (*Lust*) as an *objection*" (*A* 11). In the *Nachlass*, Nietzsche counts among "the great crimes in psychology" the fact that "all strong feelings of pleasure . . . have been branded as sinful, as a seduction, as suspicious," that, conversely, "all displeasure, all misfortune has been falsified with the idea of wrong (guilt)," and that "pain has been robbed of innocence" (*WP* 296).

17. For the view that forgetfulness is indispensable to the overcoming of revenge, see also Schrift, "Rethinking Exchange: Logics of the Gift in Cixous and Nietzsche," 199.

18. On the relation between forgetfulness and rebeginning, see also: "Bad memory.—The advantage of a bad memory is that one can enjoy the same good things for the first time *several* times" (*HH* 580).

19. See also, "I walk among humans as among fragments of the future—that future which I envisage. And this is all my creating and striving, that I create and carry together into One what is fragment and riddle and dreadful accident" (*Z* "On Redemption").

20. Derrida, *On Cosmopolitanism and Forgiveness*, 39.

21. Arendt, *The Human Condition*, 240 and ff.

22. See Bonnie Honig, *Political Theory and the Displacement of Politics* (Ithaca, N.Y.: Cornell University Press, 1993), 84–87.

23. For a more comprehensive discussion of memory and promise in Arendt and Nietzsche, see my article "Memory and Promise in Arendt and Nietzsche," *Revista de Ciencia Politica* 26, no. 2 (2006): 161–74.

24. Derrida, *Given Time: I. Counterfeit Money*, 16 and ff.

25. For an earlier version of this analysis, see Vanessa Lemm, "Justice and Gift-Giving in *Thus Spoke Zarathustra*," in *Before Sunrise: Essays on Thus Spoke Zarathustra*, ed. James Luchte (London: Continuum International Publishers, 2009), 165–81.

26. Derrida, *On Cosmopolitanism and Forgiveness*, 29.

27. Ibid., 44.

28. Ibid., 28, 41, 54, and 57.

29. "All contact [*Umgang*] is bad contact except with one's equals" (*BGE* 26).

30. See, in comparison, "A friend should be a master at guessing [*im Errathen*] and keeping silent [*Stillschweigen*]: you must not want to see everything. Your dream should betray to you what your friend does while awake" (*Z* "On the

Friend"). In Nietzsche, the relationship to the other is not based on knowledge of the other. What one "knows" of the other are the transformations he or she provokes in oneself: "What is our neighbor? We understand nothing of him except the *changes in us* [*Veränderungen an uns*] of which he is the cause—our knowledge of him is like hollow space which has been shaped [*unser Wissen von ihm gleicht einem hohlen geformten Raume*]" (*D* 118).

31. See also, "[a]s soon as a third party intervenes, one can again speak of amnesty, reconciliation, reparation, etc. but certainly not of pure forgiveness in the strict sense" (Derrida, *On Cosmopolitanism and Forgiveness*, 42–43; and Derrida, *Pardonner*, 78). "The anonymous body of the State or of a public institution cannot forgive. It has neither the right nor the power to do so; and besides, that would have no meaning. The representative of the State can judge, but forgiveness has precisely nothing to do with judgment. Or even with the public or political sphere" (Derrida, *On Cosmopolitanism and Forgiveness*, 43).

32. Derrida, *Pardonner*, 62–63.

33. Derrida, *The Politics of Friendship*, 52.

34. G. W. F. Hegel, *Phänomenologie des Geistes* (Frankfurt: Suhrkamp, 1970), 464–94.

35. Arendt, *The Human Condition*, 241.

36. Ibid., 243.

37. Derrida, *Pardonner*, 82–84.

38. Ibid.

39. Derrida's objection to the reduction of forgiveness to a verbal, human, "all-too-human" virtue is directed against Arendt. For Arendt, forgiveness constitutes a human possibility that is reflected in the human ability to forgive. She claims that forgiveness is ordinary and normative, an "everyday occurrence which is in the very nature of action's constant establishment of new relationships within a web of relation" (Arendt, *The Human Condition*, 240), a "constant mutual release" that exemplifies the human being's "constant willingness to change their minds and start again" (ibid.). Since Arendt identifies forgiving with the human, she believes that it concerns trespassing as an "everyday occurrence," rather than "crime and willed evil" (ibid.). Derrida disagrees with Arendt on two points: first, he contests the idea that forgiveness belongs only to humans. In agreement with Nietzsche, he holds that genuine forgiveness occurs through an (animal) otherness that cannot be reduced to the human, that it is always more than the human, pointing beyond the human. Second, he contests the idea that forgiveness is a "structural element of the domain of the human," and hence something that will no longer have meaning when a crime has become "out of proportion to all human measure" (Derrida, *On Cosmopolitanism and Forgiveness*, 37). Unlike Arendt, Derrida holds that forgiveness is only meaningful in relation to that which does not stand in any proportion and, hence, cannot be normalized. For Derrida, forgiveness should not be "normal, normative and normalizing," but must remain, like the gift, "exceptional and extraordinary, in the face of the impossible" (ibid., 31–32).

40. In "The Honey Sacrifice," Zarathustra asks his animals to see to it that he will have honey at hand to offer for the honey sacrifice. Once Zarathustra has spent all the honey, his animal friends gather new honey for him (Z "The Cry of Distress"). Later, in "The Welcome," Zarathustra offers his hospitality, his realm (*Reich*) and dominion (*Herrschaft*), by saying that his guest will be served by his animals.

41. On the metaphor of gold, see, in comparison, Shapiro, *Nietzschean Narratives*, 53–59; and Shapiro, *Alcyone: Nietzsche on Gift, Noise and Women*, 68–69. In *Nietzschean Narratives*, Shapiro shows only an indirect interest in the metaphor of gold. He discusses the analogy between the gift-giving virtue and gold in order to give a general account of Nietzsche's use of metaphors. In *Alcyone*, Shapiro briefly discusses the metaphor of gold in opposition to the gold standard, the fetishizing of that which Marx was describing in order to emphasize the antiutilitarian aspect of Nietzsche's conception of the gift. The relationship between the gold metaphor and the gift-giving virtue does not seem to be of central importance to either Gooding-Williams's or Laurence Lampert's readings of *Thus Spoke Zarathustra*. See Laurence Lampert, *Nietzsche's Teaching* (New Haven, Conn. and London: Yale University Press, 1986); and Robert Gooding-Williams, *Zarathustra's Dionysian Modernism* (Stanford: Stanford University Press, 2001).

42. Derrida, *Given Time: I. Counterfeit Money*, 138.

43. For a different reading, see Lampert, who argues that the gift-giving virtue is a "measure giver" (Lampert, *Nietzsche's Teaching*, 75).

44. For different but complementary views on the gift-giving virtue as the "unnameable" virtue, see Lampert (ibid., 194–95); Gooding-Williams, *Zarathustra's Dionysian Modernism*, 125, n. 80; and Shapiro, *Alcyone: Nietzsche on Gift, Noise and Women*, 18 and ff.

45. On the antiutilitarian aspect of gift-giving, see Lampert, *Nietzsche's Teaching*, 74; and Shapiro, *Alcyone*, 18–19, 35–36.

46. The noble's understanding of life in Nietzsche resonates with Derrida's interpretation of "Counterfeit Money." According to Derrida's reading, the narrator in "Counterfeit Money" cannot forgive his friend because "he has failed to honor the contract binding him naturally to nature; he has acquitted himself of his debt—of a natural debt, thus a debt without debt or an infinite *debt*" (Derrida, *Given Time: 1. Counterfeit Money*, 169).

47. If by reason one means calculating in terms of costs and benefits, then gift-giving is "not very accessible to reason" (*WP* 317). Rather, gift-giving, like justice, obeys the logic of passion, the logic of a "gift-giving love" (*Z*: 2 "On the Gift-Giving Virtue"), which contains a grain of madness, for "there is always some madness in love" (*Z*: 5 "Prologue"). This madness, however, is in the words of Derrida "perhaps not so mad" (*On Cosmopolitanism and Forgiveness*, 60) for "there is also always some reason in madness" (*Z*: 5 "Prologue"). Like Nietzsche, Derrida compares giving and forgiving to reason: "In giving the reasons for giving, in saying the reason of the gift, it signs the end of the gift" (*Given Time: 1.*

Counterfeit Money, 156). According to Derrida, the gift confronts us with a decision between the gift and justice, on the one hand, and reason and morality, on the other. This decision is crucial insofar as the possibility of entering into a relationship with the other which is free, like the gift, "not bound in its purity, not even binding, obligatory or obliging," depends on it (ibid., 137).

48. See in comparison, "*Gratefulness*—One grain of gratitude [*dankkbaren Sinnes*] and piety too much—and one suffers from it as from a vice [*Laster*] and, for all one's honesty [*Redlichkeit*] and independence [*Selbstständigkeit*] falls prey to a bad conscience [*böse Gewissen*]" (*D* 293). For Nietzsche, giving and forgiving begins with the question of whether the one who receives owes thanks to the one who gives or, instead, whether the one who gives owes thanks to the one who receives in return for accepting the other's gifts: "Oh my soul, I gave you all, and I have emptied all my hands to you; and now—now you say to me smiling and full of melancholy, 'Which of us has to be thankful? Should not the giver be thankful that the receiver received? Is not giving a need? Is not receiving a mercy?'" (*Z* "On the Great Longing"). In Derrida, this reflection reveals the excessiveness of both giving and forgiving: the one who gives is always already in need of being forgiven for not being grateful enough toward those who have received and, conversely, the one who forgives always already stands in need of asking forgiveness for not having given enough: "A priori one must, therefore ask forgiveness for the gift itself, one must be forgiven for the gift, the sovereignty, or the desire of sovereignty which always haunts the gift. And, pushing this matter to its limit, one would even have to ask this forgiveness to be forgiven, for it itself also contains the risk of being a carrier of an unavoidable equivocation of an affirmation of sovereignty and even of mastery" (Derrida, *Pardonner*, 9–10).

49. Whereas I see in the gift-giving virtue an alternative conception of the individual's relationship with others, Gooding-Williams sees in the gift-giving virtue a resurrection of the body. In his account, the gift-giving virtue primarily concerns a relationship of the self to itself and, in particular, to its bodily passions: "the gift-giving virtue is the virtue of finding a place within one's body for passions that one hitherto willed to exterminate" (Gooding-Williams, *Zarathustra's Dionysian Modernism*, 125). He, furthermore, argues that "in order to resurrect one's body, one must go-under to a passional chaos that the last man cannot experience. More exactly, one must surrender one's ascetic will to annihilate one's passions (that is, to master them and render them functional *by* annihilating them) and *then* go-under into passional chaos" (ibid.). As such, acquiring the gift-giving virtue leads to a transformation of the self and the body by incorporating some previously repressed passions (ibid., 67). Both interpretations may complement each other insofar as a "going-under" of the self, in Gooding-Williams's sense, may be conceived as a condition for a "going-over" to the other, in my sense of the term. For a contrary view, see Alexander Nehamas, "For Whom the Sun Shines: A Reading of *Also sprach Zarathustra*," ed. Volker Gerhardt (Berlin: Academie Verlag, 2000), 165–90.

50. I agree with Gooding-Williams that Zarathustra's descent is not motivated by the belief that the human being is in some way deficient and is therefore

in need of being given Zarathustra's gifts. On the contrary, Gooding-Williams correctly holds that the human being is important to Zarathustra not for what it is (perfect or imperfect), but for what else it could become (Gooding-Williams, *Zarathustra's Dionysian Modernism*, 62).

51. Nietzsche overcomes the myth of the self-sufficient solitary one, without being trapped by the naive belief that a relationship to the other is self-evident. On the contrary, a relationship to the other is possible only after the long purification of solitude. Friendship is, in this sense, essentially a relationship among those who have gone through the experience of solitude because solitude constitutes the first and inevitable step toward a relationship to the other that is not cannibalistic (*AOM* 348) or parasitic, as Shapiro argues. See Shapiro, *Alcyone: Nietzsche on Gift, Noise and Women*, 53–107.

52. Later, in "The Honey Sacrifice," the animals describe Zarathustra as "one having overmuch of the good," as someone who is "becoming ever yellower and darker." Zarathustra confirms: "It is the *honey* in my veins that makes my blood thicker and my soul calmer."

53. See, in comparison, Derrida, who claims that "there where there is subject and object, the gift would be excluded (*Given Time: 1. Counterfeit Money*, 24).

54. See, in comparison: "I love those who do not first seek behind the stars for a reason to go under and be a sacrifice, but who sacrifice themselves for the earth, that the earth may some day become the overhuman's" (*Z*: 4 "Prologue").

55. On the difference between gift-giving and the Christian idea of self-sacrifice, see Lampert, *Nietzsche's Teaching*, 78–79.

56. Derrida, *Given Time: I. Counterfeit Money*, 101–2.

57. The friends' practice of gratefulness and revenge, in contrast to those in whom virtue makes small, exemplifies this idea: "Gratitude and revenge. The reason the powerful [*der Mächtige*] is grateful is this. His benefactor [*Wohltäter*] has, through the help he has given him [*durch seine Wohltat*], as it were laid hands on the sphere of the powerful and intruded into it: now by way of requital [*Vergeltung*], the powerful in turn lays hands on the sphere of his benefactor [*Wohltäters*] through the act of gratitude [*Act der Dankbarkeit*]. It is a milder form of revenge [*Rache*]. If he did not have the compensation [*Genugthung*] of gratitude, the powerful would have appeared unpowerful and thenceforth counted as such. That is why every community of the good, that is to say originally the powerful, places gratitude among its first duties [*Pflichten*]" (*HH* 44).

58. Consider also Nietzsche's view that an author's writings, her gifts to her readers, should not reflect a victory over them, but always only over herself: "Writing ought always to advertise a victory . . . an overcoming [*Überwindung*] of *oneself* which has to be communicated for the benefit of others; but there are dyspeptic authors who write only when they cannot digest something . . . they involuntarily [*unwillkürlich*] seek to transfer [*Verdruss zu machen*] their annoyance [*Ärger*] to the reader and in this way exercise power over him: that it so say, they too desire victory but over others" (*AOM* 152).

59. "A good friendship originates when one party has a great respect for the other, more indeed than for himself, when one party likewise loves the other,

though not so much as he loves himself, and when finally, one party knows how to facilitate the association [*Verkehrs*] by adding to it a delicate *tinge* of intimacy while at the same time prudently withholding actual and genuine intimacy and the confounding of I and Thou" (*AOM* 241).

60. "Love and Duality [*Zweiheit*].—What is love but understanding and rejoicing at the fact that another lives, feels and acts in a way different from and opposite to ours? If love is to bridge theses antitheses [*Gegensätze*] it may not deny [*aufheben*] or seek to abolish [*leugnen*] them.—Even self-love presupposes an unblendable duality (or multiplicity) [*Vielheit*] in one person" (*AOM* 75).

61. "In parting [*Scheiden*].—It is not in how one soul approaches another but in how it distances itself from it that I recognize their affinity [*Verwandschaft*] and relatedness [*Zusammengehörigkeit*]" (*AOM* 251).

62. For a discussion of the significance of the meaning of the earth in Nietzsche's philosophy, see Gary Shapiro, "Beyond Peoples and Fatherlands: Nietzsche's Geophilosophy and the Direction of the Earth," *Journal of Nietzsche Studies* 35 (2008): 9–27; and Adrian del Caro, *Grounding the Nietzsche Rhetoric of the Earth* (Berlin: De Gruyter, 2004).

63. The same holds true for the one who has been done ill and who seeks justice in return. Through the speeches of Zarathustra, Nietzsche recommends that "if you have an enemy, do not requite him evil with good, for that would put him to shame. Rather prove him that he did you some good. And rather be angry than put to shame. And if you are cursed, I do not like it that you want to bless. Rather join a little in the cursing" (*Z* "On the Adder's Bite").

64. Derrida, *Given Time: I. Counterfeit Money*, 13–14.

65. Ibid.

66. Ibid., 101–102.

67. Ibid., 119.

5. Animality, Creativity, and Historicity

1. I hold that the importance Nietzsche attributes to animality and animal forgetfulness in "On the Use and Disadvantage of History for Life" is neither exclusive to this text nor to the early period of his writing, but prepares and stands in continuity with his later works, in particular *On the Genealogy of Morals*. An earlier version of this chapter was published as "Animality, Creativity and Historicity: A Reading of Friedrich Nietzsche's *Vom Nutzen und Nachtheil der Historie für das Leben*," *Nietzsche-Studien* 36 (2007): 169–200. I thank Dr. Gertrud Grünkorn for the permission to reproduce the article in this book.

2. Examples of the second approach include: Catherine Zuckert, "Nature, History and the Self: Nietzsche's Untimely Considerations," *Nietzsche-Studien* 5 (1976): 55–82; T. J. Reed, "Nietzsche's Animals: Idea, Image and Influence," in *Nietzsche: Imaginary and Thought*, ed. Malcolm Pasley (Berkeley and Los Angeles: University of California Press, 1978), 159–219; Gilles Deleuze and Felix Guattari, *A Thousand Plateaus: Capitalism and Schizophrenia* (Minneapolis: University of Minnesota Press, 1987), 232–309; Philippe Lacoue-Labarthe, "History and

Mimesis," in *Looking after Nietzsche*, ed. Laurence Rickels (Albany: State University of New York Press, 1990), 209–31; Achim Geisenhanslücke, "Der Mensch als Eintagswesen: Nietzsches Kritische Anthropologie in der Zweiten Unzeitgemässen Betrachtung," *Nietzsche-Studien* 28 (1999): 125–40. The following could be read as examples of the first approach: Martin Heidegger, *Zur Auslegung Von Nietzsche's Zweiter Unzeitgemässen Betrachtung*, vol. 46, *Gesamtausgabe* (Frankfurt: Vittorio Klostermann, 2003); Jörg Salaquarda, "Studien zur Zweiten Unzeitgemässen Betrachtung," *Nietzsche-Studien* 13 (1984): 1–45; Volker Gerhardt, *Pathos und Distanz* (Stuttgart: Reclam, 1988), 133–62; Herman W. Siemens, "Agonal Configurations in the *Unzeitgemässe Betrachtungen*: Identity, Mimesis and the Übertragung of Cultures in Nietzsche's Early Thought," *Nietzsche-Studien* 30 (2001): 80–106.

3. Claude Lévi-Strauss claims, in accordance with the Nietzschean view that memory arises from forgetfulness, that "twenty years of forgetfulness were required before I could establish communion with my earlier experience, which I had sought the world over without understanding its significance or appreciating its essence" (Claude Lévi-Strauss, *Triste Tropiques* [New York: Penguin Books, 1992], 44).

4. I share Brobjer's view of the value that historical studies and methods have in Nietzsche's work, although I disagree with his reading of "On the Use and Disadvantage of History for Life." Whereas he claims the second *Untimely Consideration* is only a "severe and hostile critique of historical studies," I argue that the second *Untimely Consideration* features a new conception of history and historiography. See Thomas H. Brobjer, "Nietzsche's View of the Value of Historical Studies and Methods," *Journal of the History of Ideas* (2004): 301–22; and, recently, Thomas H. Brobjer, "Nietzsche's Relation to Historical Methods and Nineteenth-Century German Historiography," *History and Theory* 46 (March 2007): 155–79.

5. For the notion of "effective history [*wirkliche Historie*]" in Nietzsche, see Michel Foucault, "Nietzsche, la généalogie, l'histoire," in *Hommage à Jean Hyppolite* (Paris: PUF, 1971), 145–72.

6. For a contemporary example of such an approach to animal life, see J. M. Coetzee, *The Lives of Animals* (Princeton, N.J.: Princeton University Press, 1999).

7. "Betrachte die Heerde, die an dir vorüberweidet: sie weiss nicht was Gestern, was Heute ist springt umher, frisst, ruht, verdaut, springt wieder, und so vom Morgen bis zur Nacht und von Tage zu Tage, kurz angebunden mit ihrer Lust und Unlust, nämlich an den Pflock des Augenblicks und deshalb weder schwermüthig noch überdrüssig" (*HL* 1). In comparison Giacomo Leopardi: "O meine Heerde, die du ruhst, ich preise / Dich glücklich, dass erspart dir bleibt, zu erkennen / Dein Elend. Ach, wie muss ich dich beneiden! / . . . / Verständest Du zu sprechen, würd'ich fragen: / Sag mir, warum in Ruhe, / In müssigem Behagen / Das Thier sich freut, *mich* aber / Befällt der Überdruss, sobald ich ruhe?" (Giacomo Leopardi, 1866) as cited in Gerhardt, *Pathos und Distanz*, 91–95.

8. "That is why it affects him like a vision of a lost paradise to see the herds grazing or, in closer proximity to him, a child which, having as yet nothing of the past to shake off, plays in blissful blindness between the hedges of past and future" (*HL* 1).

9. For a later version of this view in Nietzsche, see *TI* "Skirmishes" 48.

10. For the notion of bad conscience in Nietzsche, see the second essay of *On the Genealogy of Morals*, as well as its interpretation by Judith Butler, "Circuits of Bad Conscience: Nietzsche and Freud," in *Why Nietzsche Still?* ed. Alan D. Schrift (Berkeley and Los Angeles: University of California Press, 2000), 121–35.

11. As discussed in the previous chapter, in *Thus Spoke Zarathustra*, Nietzsche refers to such a reversal of time as "the redemption of the past" (*Z* "On Redemption"; *Z*: 3 and 12 "Of Old and New Tablets"; *Z*: 4 "Prologue"; see also *WP* 593). The past is redeemed when every "it was" has been formed and transformed into a "thus shall it be."

12. Nietzsche's position on forgetfulness is not open to the charge that it allows for historical revisionism, since he believes that a truly responsible relationship to the past is possible only through the overcoming of a moral perspective on the past. For Nietzsche, genuine responsibility does not begin with feelings of resentment, guilt, and revenge, but, as discussed in the previous chapter, with the affirmation that "everything is innocence" (*HH* 107).

13. Forgetfulness and memory are like light and dark, both indispensable to the growth and health of life: "Forgetting is essential to action of any kind, just as not only light but darkness too is essential for the life of everything organic" (*HL* 1).

14. For a discussion of the relationship between the suprahistorical and the metaphysical perspective on life and its consequences for the study of history, see Foucault, "Nietzsche, la généalogie, l'histoire," 159.

15. Rejecting the suprahistorical position, in a note from 1885, Nietzsche affirms: "We believe in becoming also in the matters of the spirit, we are historical through and through" (*KSA* 11:34[73]).

16. "It is true that only by imposing limits on this unhistorical element, by thinking, reflecting [*überdenkend*], comparing, distinguishing [*trennend*], drawing conclusions [*zusammenschliessend*], only through the emergence within that encompassing cloud of a vivid flash of light—thus only through the power of employing the past for the purposes of life and of again introducing into history that which has been done and is gone—did the human being [*Mensch*] become human [*Mensch*]: but with an excess [*Übermasse*] of history the human being again ceases to exist, and without that envelope of the unhistorical he would never have begun or dare to begin" (*HL* 1).

17. "An individual who wanted to feel historical through and through would be like one forcibly deprived of sleep or an animal that had to live only by rumination and ever repeated rumination" (*HL* 1). Nietzsche uses the example of the ruminant to illustrate the impossibility of life living off the past and only the past. Compare, also, Nietzsche's reflections on the *Unzeitgemässen Betrachtungen*

in *Ecce Homo*: Nietzsche depreciatingly distinguishes the philosopher as "fearful explosive material" from "the academic 'ruminants' and other professors of philosophy" (*EH* "Books" UB: 3). In contrast, in the preface to *On the Genealogy of Morals*, he uses the example of the ruminant to show that the process of interpretation and philology requires returning to the past, and going on and on about it in order to produce new meanings and new readings (*GM* "Preface" 8). Nietzsche praises the ruminant as the ideal reader, slowly and carefully reading and rereading and repeatedly returning to the text.

18. Nietzsche's arguments in favor of forgetfulness and animality in "On the Use and Disadvantage of History for Life" are comparable to the position he defends in "Homer's Contest." In "Homer's Contest," as discussed in Chapter 1, he hypothesizes that it is the human being's animality that is responsible for the greatness of human culture.

19. For a later version of this idea see Zarathustra, who praises the therapeutic power of forgetfulness after his convalescence: "O, how lovely it is that we forget" (*Z*: 2 "The Convalescent").

20. Nietzsche cites Luther, who also claims that, at the beginning, was forgetfulness: "Luther himself once opined that the world existed only through a piece of forgetful negligence on God's part" (*HL* 3).

21. See also: "The One condition of all historical happening: the blindness and injustice in the soul of the actor [*Handelnden*]" (*HL* 1).

22. "It is the same with all great things, 'which never succeed without some frenzy [*Wahn*]' as Hans Sachs says in the Meistersinger" (*HL* 7).

23. The view that animality is a source of nobility is also found in an aphorism in *The Gay Science*: "Noble [*edel*] and Common [*gemein*]. . . . Compared to them [common natures], the higher type [*höhere Natur*] is more *unreasonable*, for those who are noble [*Edle*], magnanimous [*Grossmüthigen*], and self-sacrificial do succumb to their instincts [*Trieben*], and when they are at their best [*seinen besten Augenblicken*], their reason *pauses*. An animal that protects its young at the risk of its life, or that during the mating period follows the female even into death, does not think of danger and death; its reason also pauses, because the pleasure [*Lust*] in its young or in the female and the fear of being deprived of this pleasure [*Lust*] dominate [*beherrscht*] it totally; the animal becomes more stupid than usual—just like those who are noble [*Edlen*] and magnanimous [*Grossmüthigen*]" (*GS* 3).

24. The account that Nietzsche gives in "On the Use and Disadvantage of History for Life" of perishing in the pursuit of one's highest aims is comparable to the account he gives of the heroic in "Homer's Contest" and in "Schopenhauer as Educator": the hero's highest aim is to go under in competition against a great enemy. For the hero, victory is not achieved over others; rather, the hero sees victory in her own going-under (*Untergang*) as the going-over (*Übergang*) to something greater than herself. To perish in *Selbstvergessenheit* and not become the measure of all things is what she strives for (*SE* 4). With respect to self-forgetfulness, as discussed previously, the figure of the hero resembles that of the genius

of culture who overflows to the other because she creates in complete self-forget-fulness (*TI* "Skirmishes" 44; *AOM* 407).

25. Similarly, Nietzsche claims that in order to be able to keep on creating truth, one has to believe in truth. Accordingly, although truth is an illusion and not a reality, one must think of truth as something one discovers in order to go on creating it in one's dreams. For this aspect of truth in Nietzsche, see also Alexander Nehamas, *Nietzsche: Life as Literature* (Cambridge, Mass.: Harvard University Press), 1985, 42–73.

26. See also "Bad memory.—The advantage of a bad memory is that one can enjoy the same good things for the first time *several* times" (*HH* 580). For the relationship between forgetfulness and rebeginning in Nietzsche, see also Peter Canning, "How the Fable Becomes a World," in *Looking after Nietzsche*, ed. Laurence A. Rickels (Albany: State University of New York Press, 1990), 190.

27. See also "Disturbance while thinking" (*WS* 342).

28. See Nietzsche to Meta von Salis auf Marschlins, August 22, 1988, Nr. 1094, S. 396, KSB 8; and Nietzsche to Heinrich Köselitz, December 9, 1988, Nr. 1181, S. 513, KSB 8. For the relevance of these letters in an interpretation of Nietzsche's second *Untimely Consideration*, see also Jörg Salaquarda, "Studien Zur Zweiten Unzeitgemässen Betrachtung," *Nietzsche-Studien* 13 (1984): 4.

29. Nietzsche reemphasizes, as discussed in Chapter 2, the active involvement of forgetfulness in memory in his genealogical investigation of the breeding of animals that are able to make promises (*GM* II: 1).

30. "[T]hat knowledge of the past [*Vergangenheit*] has at all times been desired only in the service of the future and the present and not for the weakening of the present or for depriving a vigorous future of its roots" (*HL* 4).

31. Nietzsche's early conception of history as a counter-memory can be read as a precursor to Nietzsche's later notion of genealogy. Foucault is the first to use the term "counter-memory" to name this new notion of history in Nietzsche: "De toute façon, il s'agit de faire de l'histoire un usage qui l'affranchisse à jamais du modèle, à la fois métaphysique et anthropologique, de la mémoire. Il s'agit de faire de l'histoire une contre-mémoire—et d'y déployer par conséquent une toute autre forme du temps" (Foucault, "Nietzsche, la généalogie, l'histoire," 160).

32. For a later version of this idea, see *Thus Spoke Zarathustra:* "To redeem what is past in the human being and to re-create all 'it was' until the will says 'Thus I willed it! Thus I shall will it'" (*Z:* 3 "On Old and New Tablets").

33. For the affirmation of human animal life as artistic and creative, not rational and moral, see *GS* 107.

34. For history, imitation, and *mimesis,* see Lacoue-Labarthe, "History and Mimesis," 209–31; and also Siemens, "Agonal Configurations in the *Unzeitgemässe Betrachtungen*. Identity, Mimesis and the Übertragung of Cultures in Nietzsche's Early Thought," *Nietzsche-Studien* 30 (2001): 80–106.

35. For a later argument in favor of the idea that all perspectives are perspectives of life and that a perspective outside of life is impossible, see *TI* "Improvers" 1.

36. See in comparison: "Le sens historique, tel que Nietzsche l'entend, se sait perspective, et ne refuse pas le système de sa propre injustice" (Foucault, "Nietzsche, la généalogie, l'histoire," 163).

37. "Each of the three forms of history which exist belongs to a certain soil and a certain climate and only to that: in any other it grows into a devastating weed" (*HL* 2).

38. For the relationship between life and history, see also *GM* "Preface" 2. For the historicity of truth and its relation to life, see Werner Stegmaier, "Nietzsches Neubestimmungen der Wahrheit," *Nietzsche-Studien* 14 (1985): 69–95.

39. "That the great moments in the struggle of the human individual constitute a chain, that this chain unites humankind across the millennia like a range of human mountain peaks, that the summit of such a long ago moment shall be for me still living, bright and great—this is the fundamental idea of the faith in humanity which finds expression in the demand for a *monumental* history" (*HL* 2).

40. "There have been ages, indeed, which were quite incapable of distinguishing between a monumentalized past and a mythical fiction" (*HL* 2). On the notion of monumental history as fabulation see also Gilles Deleuze and Felix Guattari, *A Thousand Plateaus: Capitalism and Schizophrenia*, 232–309.

41. The value of antiquarian history stands in direct opposition to a morality that believes that great actions are always transgressions of piety: "To whom one is rarely just.—Many people cannot become enthusiastic for something great and good without doing a great injustice to something else: this is *their* kind of morality" (*D* 404).

42. See in comparison, "[E]very moment devours the moment preceding it, every birth is the death of a countless number of beings, to generate life and to kill it is one and the same" (*GSt*).

43. When life calls out for the destruction of life, it provokes a dangerous state of exception, "because it is so hard to know the limit to denial of the past and because second natures are usually weaker than first" (*HL* 3).

44. "It is not justice which sits here in judgment; it is even less mercy which pronounces the verdict: it is life alone, that dark, driving power that insatiably thirsts for itself [*sich selbst begehrende Macht*]" (*HL* 3).

45. "For those who employ critical history for the sake of life, there is even a noteworthy [*merkwürdigen*] consolation: that of knowing that this first nature was once a second nature and that every victorious second nature will become a first" (*HL* 3).

46. Nietzsche diagnoses the modern's desire for ever greater knowledge of the past as a sickness and fever that has befallen his contemporaries (*HL* "Preface"; *HL* 10).

47. "Insofar as history stands in the service of life, history stands in the service of an unhistorical power, and, thus subordinate, it can and should never become a pure science such as, for instance, mathematics is (*HL* 1)." In comparison, see also *D* 307: "*Facta! Yes, Facta ficta!*—A historian has to do, not with what actually [*wirklich*] happened, but only with events supposed [*vermeintlichen Ereignissen*]

to have happened: for only the latter have *produced an effect*. . . . All historians speak of things which have never existed except in imagination."

48. "For it [science] likewise lives in a profound antagonism toward the eternalizing powers of art and religion, for it hates forgetting, which is the death of knowledge, and seeks to abolish all limitations of horizon and launch mankind upon an infinite and unbounded sea of light whose light is knowledge of all becoming . . . so life itself caves in and grows weak and fearful when the *concept-quake* caused by science robs the human being of the foundation of all its rest and security, its belief in the enduring and eternal" (*HL* 10).

49. In "Truth and Lies in an Extra-Moral Sense," this forgetfulness not only enables the belief in a scientific and rational world but also the belief in the moral nature of the human agent. It is because the human being forgets itself as animal and as amoral that it comes to understand itself as human and as moral.

50. Nietzsche claims to have been greatly inspired by Machiavelli's notion of *virtù* and confirms the latter's influence on his own conception of freedom (*TI* "Skirmishes" 38). For an analysis of *virtù* and historical consciousness in Machiavelli that has affinities with this reading of Nietzsche, see Miguel Vatter, *Between Form and Event: Machiavelli's Theory of Political Freedom* (Dordrecht: Kluwer Academic Publishers, 2000), 154–93.

51. "*If you are to venture to interpret the past you can do so only out of the fullest exertion of the vigor of the present*: only when you put forth your noblest qualities in all their strength will you divine what is worth knowing and preserving in the past. . . . When the past speaks it is always as an oracle: only if you are an architect of the future and know the present will you understand it" (*HL* 6).

52. Nietzsche considers the *wissenschaftliche Gelehrte* (philistine and scientist) to be an essentially impotent being who manifests a natural aversion against the genius of culture: "the scholar is by nature *unfruitful* . . . he harbors a certain hatred for the fruitful human being; which is why genius and scholar have at all times been at odds with one another. For the latter want to kill, dissect and understand nature, while the former want to augment nature with new living nature; and so there exists a conflict of activities and intentions" (*SE* 6).

53. On the relation between knowledge, life, and action, see also the preface to "On the Use and Disadvantage of History for Life," where Nietzsche approvingly cites Goethe: "In any case, I hate everything that merely instructs me without augmenting or directly invigorating my activity" (*HL* "Preface").

54. In *Ecce Homo*, Nietzsche retrospectively confirms this idea: "The *second* untimely essay (1874) brings to light what is dangerous, what gnaws at and poisons life, in our way of carrying on science [*Wissenschafts-Betriebs*] —: life *sick* with this inhuman [*entmenschten*] clockwork and mechanism. . . . The *goal* [*Zweck*] gets lost, culture—the means, the modern way of carrying on science [*Wissenschafts-Betriebs*], *barbarizes* [*barbarisiert*]. . . . In this essay 'the historical sense' of which this century is so proud is recognized [*erkannt*] for the first time as a sickness, as a typical sign of decay [*Verfalls*]" (*EH* "Books" UB: 1).

55. "The origin of historical culture—its quite radical conflict with the spirit of any 'new age,' any 'modern awareness'—this origin *must* itself be known historically, history *must* itself resolve the problem of history, knowledge *must* turn its sting against itself—this threefold *must* is the imperative of the 'new age,' supposing this age does contain anything new, powerful, original and promising more life" (*HL* 8).

56. In comparison, see also *The Gay Science*, where Nietzsche returns to the artistic culture of the Greeks in order to transform a philosophy saturated with knowledge into one bursting with creativity: "There are a few things we now know too well, we knowing ones [*Wissenden*]: oh, how we now learn to forget well and to be good at *not* knowing [*nicht-zu-wissen*], as artists!" (*GS* "Preface" 4).

57. Nietzsche's critique of the scientific scholar (*Gelehrte*) in the *Untimely Consideration*, and, in particular, in "On the Use and Disadvantage of History for Life" and "Schopenhauer as Educator," can be read as a direct response to Kant's essay "*What Is Enlightenment?*" Contrary to Kant's notion of enlightenment as the exit of humanity from immaturity by means of knowledge and reason, Nietzsche accuses Kantian enlightenment of being responsible for keeping the human animal weak and in a state of immaturity. Whereas Kant sees the scholar as the carrier of future life, Nietzsche sees in Kant's naïve optimism a symptom of declining life: "There is, indeed, rejoicing that now 'science is beginning to dominate life': that condition may, possibly, be attained; but life thus dominated is not of much value because it is far less *living* and guarantees far less life for the future than did a former life dominated not by knowledge but by instinct and powerful illusion [*kräftige Wahnbilder*]" (*HL* 7). For Nietzsche, not the scientific scholar, but the artistic historian promises future enlightenment. On Nietzsche's challenging of Kantian enlightenment, see also David Owen, "The Contest of Enlightenment," *Journal of Nietzsche Studies* 25 (2003): 35–57.

58. Nietzsche defines the Greek's "plastic power [*Kraft*]" as follows: "I mean by plastic power [*Kraft*] the capacity to develop out of oneself in one's own way, to transform and incorporate into oneself what is past and foreign to heal wounds, to replace what has been lost, to recreate broken moulds" (*HL* 1). The affinity between the notion of "plastic power" and Nietzsche's later concept of "will to power" has been commented on by many Nietzsche scholars.

59. Nietzsche claims that strength is measured by how much history one can bear: "*History can be borne only by strong personalities, weak ones are utterly extinguished by it*" (*HL* 5). Nietzsche identifies the Greeks as having the strongest natures with the greatest memory: they transform all that is past into future life and forget all that they cannot appropriate.

60. "There is a parable for each one of us: . . . His honesty, the strength and truthfulness of his character must at some time or other rebel against a state of things in which he only repeats what he has learned, learns what is already known, imitates what already exists; he will then begin to grasp that culture can be something other than a *decoration of life*, that is to say at bottom no more than dissimulation and disguise; for all adornment conceals that which is adorned.

Thus the Greek conception of culture will be unveiled to him—in antithesis to the Roman—the conception of culture as a new and improved *physis*, without inner and outer, without dissimulation and convention, culture as an unanimity of life, thought, appearance and will" (*HL* 10).

61. On the preface as a literary genre, see Jean Genette, *Seuils* (Paris: Seuil, 1987). On the preface as a philosophical genre, see Jacques Derrida, *La Dissemination* (Paris: Seuil, 1972), 8–67.

62. This does not mean that Nietzsche simply projects onto his early work views he only developed in his later work. For a reading of "An Attempt at Self-Criticism," which argues that Nietzsche's retrospective claims shed considerable light on *The Birth of Tragedy*, see Daniel Came, "Nietzsche's Attempt at Self-Criticism: Art and Morality in The Birth of Tragedy," *Nietzsche-Studien* 33 (2004): 37–67.

63. Another image Nietzsche uses to illustrate a backward movement that is oriented toward the future is that of the spiral. In response to the Conservatives of his time, Nietzsche claims that "a reversion, a turning back in any sense and to any degree, is quite impossible" (*TI* "Skirmishes" 43). The only thing one can do to overcome decadence is to retard it, that is, to wind up decadence against itself and thus provoke its future overcoming. All three images—the spiral, the bow, and the jump—point to movements of overcoming constituted by a return to the past that is oriented toward the future.

64. For the theme of rebirth in Nietzsche's prefaces, see also Daniel D. Conway, "Annunciation and Rebirth: The Prefaces of 1886," in *Nietzsche's Futures*, ed. John Lippitt (London: Macmillan, 1999), 30–47.

65. For the theme of the death of the authors, see Roland Barthes, "The Death of the Author," in *Image-Music-Text* (New York: Noonday Press, 1988), 142– 48; Michel Foucault, "What Is an Author?" in *Aesthetics, Method, and Epistemology: Essential Works of Foucault, 1954–1984*, vol. 2 (New York: New Press, 1998), 205–22; Giorgio Agamben, "Der Autor als Geste," in *Profanierungen* (Frankfurt: Suhrkamp, 2005), 57–69. On the relation between (animal) life and authorship, see Jacques Derrida, *Otobiographies: L'enseignement de Nietzsche et la politique du nom propre* (Paris: Galilée, 1984), 33–114; and, now, Jacques Derrida, *L'animal que donc je suis* (Paris: Galilée, 2006). See also, in comparison, Marie-Louise Mallet, *L'animal autobiographique*, ed. Marie-Louise Mallet (Paris: Galilée, 1999).

66. Sarah Kofman, *Nietzsche et la scène philosophique* (Paris: Editions Galilée, 1979), 289–318.

67. Ibid., 293–94. On reading, writing, and interpretation see also Sarah Kofman, *Nietzsche et la métaphore* (Paris: Editions Galilée, 1983), 147–71 and 173–206.

68. In her investigation of Nietzsche as an author who belongs to a "biocentric" tradition of writers, philosophers, artists, and poets who write with their animality speaking, Norris sees Nietzsche's *Ecce Homo* as a work that is particularly revealing in this respect (Margot Norris, *Beasts of Modern Imagination: Darwin, Nietzsche, Kafka, Ernst, and Lawrence* [Baltimore: Johns Hopkins University

Press, 1985], 73–100). According to her, "'becoming what one is' requires a series of animal acts, that, for the writer, include such literary (or perhaps anti-literary) strategies as 'forgetting' the figurative meanings of metaphors, allegories and parables, and restoring to them their repressed, literal, or bodily sense and their exuberant dithyrambic affect" (ibid., 79).

69. See Derrida, *Otobiographies: L'enseignement de Nietzsche et la politique du nom propre*, 35–114.

70. For this aspect of becoming what one is, see also Alan D. Schrift, "Re-thinking the Subject: Or How One Becomes-Other Than What One Is," in *Nietzsche's Postmoralism: Essays on Nietzsche's Prelude to Philosophy's Future*, ed. Richard Schacht (Cambridge: Cambridge University Press, 2001), 47–62.

71. In contrast, Norris argues that Nietzsche's preface to *Ecce Homo* is "motivated more by the pleasure of the activity than by any hermeneutical necessity" (Norris, *Beasts of Modern Imagination*, 82).

72. See, in comparison, *EH* "Books" GM, where Nietzsche claims that "the three essays of which this Genealogy consists are in regard to expression, intention and art of surprise perhaps the uncanniest [*Unheimlichste*] things that have ever been written."

73. Foucault, "Nietzsche, la généalogie et l'histoire," 149. See in comparison *PTA* 1.

74. In comparison, see also *EH* "Books" D: 1, where Nietzsche recalls that also *Dawn* ends with a question.

75. For the idea that Nietzsche's prefaces provide examples of how Nietzsche envisages the meaning and practice of philosophy as a prelude, see also Richard Schacht, *Making Sense of Nietzsche* (Urbana and Chicago: University of Illinois Press, 1995), 243–66.

6. Animality, Language, and Truth

1. For this expression, see Maudemarie Clark, *Nietzsche on Truth and Philosophy* (Cambridge: Cambridge University Press, 1990), 1–4.

2. Both of these claims are discussed and refuted in Martin Heidegger, "Der Wille zur Macht als Erkenntnis," in *Nietzsche* (Stuttgart: Verlag Günter Neske, 1998), vol. I, 445–64. At the same time, Heidegger argues that Nietzsche's doctrine of truth as "evaluation [*Wertschätzung*]" fits within the margins of the traditional understanding of truth as correctness and correspondence to facts. This, however, is not the place to discuss Heidegger's interpretation of Nietzsche in detail.

3. See Eugen Fink, *La philosophie de Nietzsche* (Paris: Les Éditions de Minuit, 1965), 204–16, where he speaks of Nietzsche's "negative ontology of the thing." This does not mean, however, that there is a lack of becoming. Rather, for Nietzsche, the world is chaos, flow of becoming, plenitude of forces. For Nietzsche's later conception of the world as chaos, see also Heidegger, *Nietzsche*, vol. I, 506–13; and Wolfgang Müller-Lauter, *Über Freiheit und Chaos: Nietzsche-Interpretationen II* (Berlin: De Gruyter, 1999), 139–73.

4. Here I am using "metaphysical" as it is used in Martin Heidegger, *The Fundamental Concepts of Metaphysics: World, Finitude, Solitude,* trans. William McNeill and Nicholas Walker (Bloomington: Indiana University Press, 1995), 37–57. See also the relation between the one and the many that Jürgen Habermas designates as "metaphysical" in *Nachmetaphysisches Denken* (Frankfurt: Suhrkamp, 1988), 36–42.

5. I borrow this expression from the homonymous title of Richard Rorty's essay, "The World Well Lost," in *Consequences of Pragmatism* (New York: Harvester Wheatsheaf, 1991), 3–18.

6. The notion of *Anschauungsmetapher* has frequently been overlooked, especially in the Anglo-American reception of Nietzsche, with the exception of Anthony K. Jensen, "The Centrality and Development of *Anschauung* in Nietzsche's Epistemology," *International Studies in Philosophy* (2007): n.p. The reason for this might be related to the translation of this term. It is sometimes translated as "intuited metaphor," other times as "sensuous perception," but most often simply as "metaphor," which makes it impossible to distinguish between Nietzsche's use of the term *Anschauungsmetapher* and his use of the term *Metapher* in "On Truth and Lies in an Extra-Moral Sense."

7. For examples of this view, see Martin Heidegger, *Nietzsche Seminare 1937–1944* (Frankfurt: Vittorio Klostermann, 2004), 235–38; Clark, *Nietzsche on Truth and Philosophy,* 1; Alexander Nehamas, *Nietzsche: Life as Literature* (Cambridge, Mass.: Harvard University Press, 1985), 41–44; Robert B. Pippin, "Truth and Lies in the Early Nietzsche," in *Idealism as Modernity: Hegelian Variations* (Cambridge: Cambridge University Press, 1997), 311–29; Bernard Williams, *Truth and Truthfulness: An Essay in Genealogy* (Princeton, N.J.: Princeton University Press, 2002), 17.

8. Examples of this perspective are mainly found in the French reception of Nietzsche, for example in the work of Michel Haar, *Nietzsche and Metaphysics,* trans. Michael Gendre (Albany: State University of New York Press, 1996), 69ff; see also, Peter Bornedal, "A Silent World: Nietzsche's Radical Realism: World, Sensation, Language," *Nietzsche-Studien* 34 (2005): 1–47. Bornedal rejects the discontinuity thesis (ibid., 7–11), although his general argument centers on the middle and late Nietzsche. According to yet another reception of "On Truth and Lies in an Extra-Moral Sense," this text has been rejected on the grounds that it "copies" from Gustav Gerber's "*Sprache als Kunst.*" See Philippe Lacoue-Labarthe, "Le détour (Nietzsche et la rhétorique)," *Poétique* 2 (1971): 53–76; and Philippe Lacoue-Labarthe and Jean-Luc Nancy, "Friedrich Nietzsche: Rhétorique et langage, textes traduits, présentés et annotés," *Poétique* 2 (1971); 99–143. In opposition to this view, Schrift defends the originality of "On Truth and Lies in an Extra-Moral Sense" as being "located in Nietzsche's application of theses rhetorical insights to a deconstruction of certain philosophical 'errors'" (Alan D. Schrift, "Language, Metaphor, Rhetoric: Nietzsche's Deconstruction of Epistemology," *Journal of the History of Philosophy* 23 [1985]: 379). See also Anthonie

Meyers, "Gustav Gerber und Friedrich Nietzsche: Zum historischen Hintergrund der sprachphilosophischen Auffassungen des frühen Nietzsche," *Nietzsche-Studien* 17 (1988): 367–90. I am grateful to Tracy Strong for having alerted me to this literature.

9. For a recent discussion of the notion of pictorial thinking (*Bilderdenken*) in Nietzsche's early work, see Sören Reuter, "Reiz-Bild-Unbewusste Anschauung: Nietzsches Auseinandersetzung mit Hermann Helmholtz's Theorie der unbewussten Schlüsse in *Über Wahrheit und Lüge im Aussermoralischen Sinne*," *Nietzsche-Studien* 33 (2004): 351–72.

10. Tracy Strong has emphasised with particular clarity the importance of this genre of Nietzsche's discourse on truth in his chapter "The Epistemology of Nihilism": "For Nietzsche all life must be rooted in a particular realm of the unquestioned. A foundation must be taken for granted and questions of such a foundation must not exist" (Tracy B. Strong, *Friedrich Nietzsche and the Politics of Transfiguration* [Berkeley and Los Angeles: University of California Press, 1975], 54ff). See also in the same book the connection between language and commonality (ibid., 62ff).

11. Heidegger puts this "traditional determination of truth as correctness" as follows: "Truth is the correctness of a representation of a being. All representing of beings is a predicating about them. . . . The most common form of predication is the assertion, the simple proposition, the *logos*, and therefore the correctness of representation—truth—is to be found there in the most immediate way. Truth has its place and seat in *logos*" (Martin Heidegger, *Basic Questions of Philosophy*, trans. Richard Rojcewicz and André Schuwer [Bloomington: Indiana University Press, 1994], 14–15).

12. See Alasdair MacIntyre's discussion of recent literature that questions this claim: *Dependent Rational Animals: Why Human Beings Need the Virtues* (Chicago: Open Court, 2001), in particular 35ff where he speaks of "an elementary pre-linguistic distinction between truth and falsity" and ascribes it to animals as well as humans.

13. See Aristotle, *Politics*, book I, and *Metaphysics*, book I. For a questioning of these assumptions, see the works of Agamben, in particular Giorgio Agamben, *The Open: Man and Animal* (Stanford: Stanford University Press, 2004), 33–38.

14. This is the basis of the misunderstanding found in Elisabeth de Fontenay's interpretation of animality in Nietzsche. Elisabeth de Fontenay, *Le silence des bêtes: La philosophie à l'épreuve de l'animalité* (Paris: Fayard, 1998), 599–610.

15. Jacques Derrida, *L'animal que donc je suis* (Paris: Galilée, 2006), 48ff and 163ff.

16. For an analysis of the animal's silent glance, see Derrida, ibid.; and Theodor W. Adorno and Max Horkheimer, "Mensch und Tier," in *Dialektik der Aufklärung: Philosophische Fragmente* (Frankfurt: Suhrkamp, 1981), 283–92.

17. On the notion of *Bilderdenken* in Nietzsche, see in comparison, *KSA* 7:19[66]; 19[75]; 19[77–79]; 19[107]; 19[162]); and also *KSA* 11:25[325].

18. Nietzsche later refers to this irreducibly singular experience and vision of the world as an expression of each and every individual's genius, each and every individual's singular truth (*SE* 1).

19. My reading of intuited metaphor as human animal life's primordial contact with the world as becoming or chaos is analogous to Bornedal's recent discussion of the way in which "sensation" simultaneously does and does not falsify and deceive the world: "The task must be to understand, rather, in which sense senses deceive, and in which sense senses don't deceive" (Bornedal, "A Silent World: Nietzsche's Radical Realism: World, Sensation, Language," 12). For Bornedal, nonhuman reality is chaos (what he calls the *Urgrund* of our knowledge of the world), and our senses falsify it by simplifying its multiplicity through the very physiological constitution of our "optics," our sensory apparatus (ibid., 14–15). In a second moment, this first simplification gives us the "human horizon" (ibid., 15) within which we perceive the world, again falsifying it through language and concepts (ibid., 14, n. 28 and 31–40). The first falsification corresponds to what I call pictorial thinking related to intuited metaphors, whereas the second falsification corresponds to what I call conceptual thinking. Where I diverge from Bornedal is that I also account for why senses "don't deceive" more than he does: the senses don't deceive because, as first metaphors, they represent contact with the world as radical multiplicity. This is the way contact is made with becoming, and this contact is truthful and honest (the contact does not, in itself, express that the world is anything other than chaos). Additionally, first metaphors do not deceive because they are the primordial "artistic" and "aesthetic" relationship with the world (rather than representational and epistemic). Intuitive metaphors are truthful because they are artistic, not, as Bornedal asserts, because they are "non-conscious and pure perception," or "self-presence of the present" or an expression of "animal stupidity" (ibid., 17). In fact, Bornedal's reading emphasizes the radical difference between the world as chaotic *Urgrund* and the human world as constituted by falsification and anthropomorphism, while simultaneously deemphasizing the continuity between human and animal life. Bornedal thereby accepts the humanist premises of much of the discourse on Nietzschean perspectivism in the literature (Nehamas, *Nietzsche: Life as Literature*, 64–65), despite having consistently rejected them for always starting too late and being unfaithful to the *Urgrund*. On the other hand, Bornedal does not see that, for Nietzsche, the return to contact with the *Urgrund* is made possible by the denial of the discontinuity between animal and human life.

20. "We are not sufficiently refined to see what is projected in the absolute flow of becoming [*absoluten Fluss des Geschehens*]. Our crude organs only have a capacity for the enduring, and summarize and exhibit a surface that does not exist as such. The tree is in every immediate now [*Augenblick*] something new; but we postulate a form, because we are incapable of perceiving the minute absolute movements [*die feinste absolute Bewegung*]. We expertly add [*legen . . . hinein*] a mathematical average line to the absolute movement. We indeed invent lines and surfaces, because our intellect takes for granted the error: the assumption of

equality and stability; we can only see the stable and only remember the equal" (*KSA* 9:11[293], as cited in Bornedal, "A Silent World: Nietzsche's Radical Realism: World, Sensation, Language," 28.

21. See, in comparison, a note from the *Nachlass* written at the time of *The Gay Science*: "What distinguishes the similar [*das Ähnliche*] from the same [*Gleichen*] is not a matter of degree: rather the similar is something completely different [*völlig Verschiedenes*] from the same" (*KSA* 9:11[166]; see also *KSA* 8:23[2]).

22. See in comparison *Human, All Too Human*, where Nietzsche writes that "[h]e who thinks a great deal, and thinks objectively, can easily forget his own experiences, but not the thoughts these experiences called forth" (*HH* 526).

23. In Freud's reception of Nietzsche, the above intuition seems to be reflected by his axiom that the unconscious works by symbolic displacement of two types: condensation and displacement, metaphor and simile. See also Bornedal, "A Silent World: Nietzsche's Radical Realism: World, Sensation, Language," 37–41.

24. A passage from Nietzsche's later work illustrates that the loss of the singular and the real is also reflected in the vulgarity and meanness of conceptual language: "We no longer have a sufficiently high estimate for ourselves when we communicate. Our true experiences are not garrulous. They could not communicate themselves even if they wanted to: they lack words. We have already grown beyond whatever we have words for. In all talking there lies a grain of contempt. Speech [*Sprache*], it seems, was devised only for the average, medium, communicable. The speaker has already *vulgarized* himself by speaking—From a moral code for deaf-mutes and other philosophers" (*TI* "Skirmish" 26).

25. Nietzsche's critique of metaphysical truth is neither Kantian nor Schopenhauerian: it is not a critique that starts off from a dualism between thing-in-itself and appearance, or will and representation. Clark, on the contrary, claims that in "On Truth and Lies in an Extra-Moral Sense," Nietzsche's conception of truth as metaphor takes off from its adherence to a metaphysical realism: "Nietzsche assumes the existence of things themselves, objects that exist independently of consciousness. He also identifies these objects with the Kantian thing-in-itself. But his mere affirmation of things themselves does not force him into this Kantian identification of reality with the thing-in-itself. Rather, this identification stems from his denial that we have perceptual or linguistic access to things themselves. Nietzsche's representational theory of perception forces him to treat the thing itself (the thing considered as having existence independent of consciousness) as a Kantian thing-in-itself (a thing considered as having qualities independent of human beings). Since the thing itself remains hidden from us (precisely by our representations of it), its nature is also hidden. We can only conceive of this nature as an unknown and unknowable X" (Clark, *Nietzsche on Truth and Philosophy,* 82–83). Clark argues that Nietzsche, in his early writings, cannot remain at the level of "common sense realism," which Clark calls "ontological realism" (ibid., 39–41), because his theory of perception (of Schopenhauerian

descent) forces him to posit the existence of "things in themselves" that are unperceivable, thereby pressuring him into metaphysical realism (see also ibid., 92). In contrast, in his later works, Nietzsche renounces metaphysical realism and can "return" to the common sense idea of truth as correspondence to things themselves, i.e., to ontological realism understood as the idea that the things we speak about exist independently of the way we speak about them. It is Nietzsche's theory of perception, in short, that underlies his theory of truth as only a metaphor (ibid., 78). Contrary to this view, I hold that, Nietzsche from the beginning rejects the Kantian idea of the "mysterious X of the thing-in-itself" in favor of an idea of singular truth concealed in metaphorical thinking. Clark seems to think of Nietzsche's idea of an intuited metaphor as synonymous with the idea that "perception gives us only metaphors of things" because "perception gives us only appearances, not things-in-themselves" (ibid., 78–79). Thus where Clark reads Nietzsche's idea of metaphors by making sense of their possibility via the assumption of a dualism between thing-in-itself and appearance, I read Nietzsche's idea of intuited metaphors as entailing the impossibility of maintaining that Kantian distinction. Analogously, see how Rorty's critique of representational ideas of truth depends on his denial of Kantian dualism ("The World Well Lost," 3–18). Other interpreters who reject the idea that the early Nietzsche was a Kantian (or even Schopenhauerian) are Nehamas, *Nietzsche: Life as Literature*, 45ff; Haar, *Nietzsche and Metaphysics*, 59–81; Paul de Man, *Allegories of Reading: Figural Language in Rousseau, Nietzsche, Rilke and Proust* (New Haven, Conn.: Yale University Press, 1979), 96–101; and Bornedal, "A Silent World: Nietzsche's Radical Realism: World, Sensation, Language," 12 and 30. For a critique of Clark's idea that Nietzsche becomes in his later work a common-sense realist and an empiricist, see Javier A. Ibanez-Noé, "Is Nietzsche a Common Sense Realist?" *International Studies in Philosophy* 37, no. 3 (2006): 91–106. Ibanez-Noé's reading is based on a discussion of Nietzsche's later writings and rejects Clark's assumption that Nietzsche gives up the claim that "the world of ordinary experience is a falsified or illusory world" (ibid., 93). Similarly, see also Bornedal's critique of Clark in Bornedal, "A Silent World: Nietzsche's Radical Realism: World, Sensation, Language," 9–11.

26. A passage from his later notebooks confirms the continuity of Nietzsche's critique of metaphysics: "The world . . . is not factual, instead . . . it is a continuously shifting falsehood which never comes close to truth: because—there is no . . . truth" (*KSA* 8:2[108]).

27. For a later version of this idea, see in comparison: "The human being projects its drive for truth, in a certain sense its 'aim,' outside of itself as an existing world, a metaphysical world, a 'thing in itself,' an already given world. His need as a creator already invents the world, on which he works, presupposes it. This presupposition (this "faith" in truth) is its support. . . . Truth is, therefore, not something that is given and needs to be found or discovered, rather it is something that needs *to be created* and that gives a name to this process, more precisely to this will to overpower which does not come to an end: to put truth

into things as an infinite process, an *active determination*, not a becoming conscious of something that is 'in itself' fixed and determined. It is a name for the 'will to power'" (*KSA* 12:9[91]).

28. As Nietzsche confirms in a later work, the world becomes "infinite" again insofar as one "cannot reject the possibility *that it includes infinite interpretations*" (*GS* 374).

29. See Immanuel Kant, *Kritik der reinen Vernunft* (Frankfurt: Suhrkamp, 1988), B307–8 for the distinction between *noumena* or thing in itself and *phenomena*. In "An Attempt at Self-Criticism," Nietzsche regrets having used Kantian formulas to express ideas that are incommensurable with the Kantian notion of the "thing in itself" and the "world of appearance": "I now regret very much that I did not have the courage (or immodesty?) at that time to permit myself a *language of my very own* for such personal views and acts of daring, laboring instead to express strange and new evaluations in Schopenhauerian and Kantian formulas, things that fundamentally run counter to both the spirit and the taste of Kant and Schopenhauer" ("An Attempt at Self-Criticism"). What Nietzsche seems to be suggesting is that right from the beginning he abolished not only the world behind the world but also the world of appearance (*TI* "World").

30. See Kant, *Die Kritik der reinen Vernunft*, B307–8. In Kant, by contrast, *Vorstellung* names the common genus of representation, whose two species are intuitions and concepts (B81, A56–57, and also B33, 34/A19, 20). On *Vorstellung* in Kant, see also Gilles Deleuze, *La philosophie critique de Kant* (Paris: PUF, 1991), 14.

31. See, in comparison, Bornedal, who speaks of the ways in which different animals have different ways to "open" the chaotic *Urgrund* ("A Silent World: Nietzsche's Radical Realism: World, Sensation, Language," 15); and Ibanez-Noé, who speaks of the difference in Nietzsche between the world of the senses, which does not deceive, and the constructed "empirical world," which does ("Is Nietzsche a Common Sense Realist?," 91–106). Employing my terms, the latter is made possible through *Verstellung*. But the contact that the senses have with the chaotic *Urgrund* cannot be understood in terms of *Vorstellung*. Rather, this contact is the nondeceiving *Verstellung* expressed by intuited metaphors.

32. For a later version of this idea, see, in comparison: "I maintain the phenomenality of the inner world, too: everything of which we become conscious is arranged, simplified, schematized, interpreted through and through—the actual process of 'inner perception,' the causal connection between thoughts, feelings, desires, between subject and object, are absolutely hidden from us—and are perhaps purely imaginary. The 'apparent *inner* world' is governed by just the same forms and procedures as the 'outer' world. We never encounter 'facts': pleasure and displeasure are subsequent and derivative intellectual phenomena—. . . 'Thinking,' as epistemologists conceive it, simply does not occur: it is a quite arbitrary fiction, arrived at by selecting one element from the process and eliminating all the rest, an artificial arrangement for the purpose of intelligibility—" (*WP* 477). The same point is made in Strong's interpretation of perspectivism,

which contrasts sharply with Nehamas's reading of perspectivism (Strong, *Friedrich Nietzsche and the Politics of Transfiguration*, 296–99): "Thus, for Nietzsche there is not only no point of view that is privileged in relation to the outer world (which Nehamas acutely points out is a consequence of immanent perspectivism), but also none privileged in relation to the 'inner self,' in relation to consciousness. Indeed, the whole relation between outer and inner is denied" (ibid., 299). This leads Strong to deny "transcendent perspectivism," that is, first, the idea that Nehamas ascribes to Nietzsche according to which "there is such a thing as a 'human' perspective, understood in the sense of *Gattungswesen*; and second, that Nietzsche thinks this human perspective is incommensurable and radically untranslatable into any other possible species-perspective" (ibid., 297). Strong's position is that "we are inevitably meaningful to and for all creatures we encounter. That we want to deny this is the source of the disease of transcendent perspectivism, of the desire to believe that we are unknowable to others. . . . What Nietzsche is struck by is the fact that we make sense all the time, without having to want to" (ibid., 306). Rorty's takes on Davidson's position, that most of our beliefs are true because they work for us and allow us to be in touch with the world most of the time, is similar to Strong's idea of perspectivism as always having enough meaning (i.e., that everything is meaningful in one way or another). For Rorty on Nietzsche's pragmatic idea of truth, see *Consequences of Pragmatism*, 205. Bornedal's interpretation is faithful to the Nietzschean idea of "two absolutely different spheres," namely, the sphere of chaos and that of the human "empirical world." However, he also contends that the world as chaos (*Urgrund*) is completely indifferent to humans and thus misses Strong's point with respect to the back and forth between the different points of contact (intuitive metaphors, perspectives) with the world as radical multiplicity.

33. See, in comparison, Ibanez-Noé: "The reality exhibited by the senses, Nietzsche tells us, is the reality of difference, change and multiplicity: the reality in which every minute change or difference is given its due. And what about the world of ordinary experience? It is quite clearly the world in which we overlook such small changes. In ordinary experience we hold on to the belief in the existence of relatively permanent spatial objects despite the testimony of the senses" (Ibanez-Noé, "Is Nietzsche a Common Sense Realist?" 10).

34. To will illusion and deception is a painful experience for the philosopher, but in Nietzsche's understanding of tragic feelings, pain "acts as a stimulus": "The psychology of the orgy as an overflowing feeling of life and energy (*Lebens- und Kraftgefühls*) within which even pain acts as a stimulus provided me with the key to the concept of the *tragic* feeling" (*TI* "Ancients" 5).

35. See, in comparison, Adorno's and Horkheimer's *Dialectic of Enlightenment*: "The separation of sign and image is irremediable. Should unconscious self-satisfaction [*ahnungslos selbstzufrieden*] cause it once again to become hypostatized, then each of the two isolated principles tends towards the destruction of truth. In the relationship of intuition (i.e., direct perception) [*Anschauung*] and concept, philosophy already discerned the gulf which opened with that separation, and again tries in vain to close it: philosophy, indeed, is defined by this

very attempt" (*Dialectic of Enlightenment,* 18). In the original, *Die Dialektik der Aufklärung: Philosophische Fragmente* (Frankfurt: Suhrkamp, 2003), 34–35.

36. In the preface to *Beyond Good and Evil,* Nietzsche puts forth the hypothesis that truth is a woman, and that all philosophers, insofar as they are dogmatic, do not know how to approach a woman, how to seduce and be seduced by truth as woman: "Supposing truth is a woman [*Weib*]—what then? Are there not grounds [*gegründet*] for the suspicion that all philosophers, insofar as they were dogmatic, have been very inexpert about women [*sich schlecht auf Weiber verstanden*]? That the gruesome seriousness, the clumsy obtrusiveness with which they have usually approached truth so far have been awkward and very improper methods for winning a woman's heart [*Frauenzimmer*]? What is certain is that she has not allowed herself to be won—and today every kind of dogmatism is left standing dispirited and discouraged" (*BGE* "Preface"). According to Derrida, the idea that truth is a woman designates the infinite distance between truth and the philosopher. It overturns the idea of the philosopher as the one who is in possession of truth. Truth as woman requires the philosopher to maintain distance from truth because the seductive charm of truth works only at a distance. Truth as woman loses its seductive force if its veil is removed. A woman has her reasons (*Gründe*) not to disclose her truth (*Gründe*), or lift her veil. Furthermore, the idea of truth as woman requires adopting the attitude of the warrior who conquers truth. Nietzsche envisages the philosopher of the future as a warrior and seducer and, hence, as the opposite of a dogmatic philosopher who not only lacks the courage of the warrior, but also has bad taste and bad manners. He does not know that one must adore and honor a woman's appearance, her veil of beauty and appearance (*Schein*), but only at a distance. Nietzsche admires the noble ways of the Greeks for they know how to counteract the dogmatic philosopher's insatiable desire to approach everything, to want to know and understand everything, without distinction and at any price. For the Greeks, living wisely requires the courage to stop at the surface, at the fold, adoring appearances, and believing in forms, sounds, and sayings. The Greeks were "superficial by profundity" because they understood how to honor the digression with which truth dissimulates behind enigmas and multicolored uncertainties (*GS* "Preface" 4). See Jacques Derrida, *Éperons: Les styles de Nietzsche* (Paris: Flammarion, 1978); and also Kofman, *Nietzsche et la scène philosophique,* 225–61.

37. On philosophy as an art of interpretation and on the philosopher as an artist, see also Kofman, *Nietzsche et la scène philosophique,* 304; and Taylor, *The Republic of Genius,* 84–85.

38. Clark has a very different idea of the relationship between truth and life in the later Nietzsche. She argues that "it is difficult to see how his commitment to truth [common sense correspondence theory of truth] could conflict with his affirmation of life. One can only affirm life to the extent that one knows the truth about it—otherwise one affirms one's illusions about life, not life itself. The most life-affirming person would therefore be the one who still finds life valuable in the face of the most truth about it. That he takes the affirmation of life as his ideal

would therefore explain why the amount of truth one can endure has become Nietzsche's measure of value" (Clark, *Nietzsche on Truth and Philosophy*, 200). But here it seems that it is the truth (about life) that becomes the measure of the value of life, rather than the opposite, which is Nietzsche's view: life must be the measure of the value of truth. Additionally, Clark seems unaware of Nietzsche's tragic dimension of philosophy, namely, the intuition that, when measured by life, the implacable pursuit of the honest drive to truth leads the philosopher to will illusion in the name of affirming life and freeing herself from the ascetic ideal.

39. On Nietzsche's notion of truth in relation to his conception of the totality of life, see Haar, *Nietzsche and Metaphysics*, 115ff.

40. The citation continues: "Someone could invent a fable like this and yet they would still not have given a satisfactory illustration of just how pitiful [*kläg-lich*], how insubstantial [*schattenhaft*] and transitory [*flüchtig*], how purposeless and arbitrary the human intellect looks within nature; there were eternities during which it did not exist; and when it has disappeared again, nothing will have happened. For this intellect has no further mission that might extend beyond the bounds of human life" (*TL* 1).

41. See also, in comparison, in *On the Genealogy of Morals*, where Nietzsche hypothesizes that "it must have been no different for this semi-animal, happily adapted to the wilderness, war, the wandering life and adventure than it was for sea animals when they were forced to either become land animals or perish—at one go all instincts were devalued and 'suspended.' . . . They did not have their familiar guide any more for this new, unknown world, those regulating impulses which unconsciously lead them to safety—the poor things were reduced to relying on thinking, drawing inferences, calculating, deducing from cause and effect, that is, to relying on their 'consciousness,' that most impoverished and error-prone organ!" (*GM* II: 16). In accordance with this hypothesis, in *The Antichrist*, Nietzsche writes: "Formerly one saw in the consciousness of the human animal, in his 'spirit,' the proof of his higher origin, his divinity; to complete himself the human being was advised to draw his senses back into himself in the manner of the tortoise, to cease to have any traffic with the earthly, to lay aside his mortal frame: then the chief part of him would remain behind, 'pure spirit.' We have thought better of this too: becoming-conscious, 'spirit,' is to us precisely a symptom of a relative imperfection [*Unvollkommenheit*] of the organism as an attempting, fumbling, blundering, as a toiling in which an unnecessarily large amount of nervous energy is expended—we deny that anything can be completed so long as it is still made conscious" (*A* 14).

42. In "On Truth and Lies in an Extra-Moral Sense," Nietzsche even speculates whether nature has given consciousness to humans in order to prevent them from gaining too deep an insight into the functioning of the life of their bodies: "Does not nature remain silent about almost everything, even about our bodies, banishing and enclosing us within a proud, illusory consciousness, far away from the twists and turns of the bowels, the rapid flow of the blood stream and the complicated trembling of the nerve-fibers! Nature has thrown away the key, and

woe betide fateful curiosity should it ever succeed in peering through a crack in the chambers of consciousness, out and down into the depth, and thus gain an intimation of the fact that humanity, in the indifference of its ignorance, rests on the pitiless, the greedy, the insatiable, the murderous—clinging in dreams, as it were, to the back of a tiger" (*TL* 1). See, in comparison, also "On the Pathos of Truth." It is due to an "illusory consciousness" that the human animal can forget its animality and believe it is radically distinct from and superior to all other forms of life.

43. Richard Rorty, *Philosophy and the Mirror of Nature* (Princeton, N.J.: Princeton University Press, 1979).

44. In *Twilight of the Idols*, Nietzsche identifies the tradition of Western philosophy with the history of an error based on a fundamental misunderstanding (i.e., self-misunderstanding) on the part of the human being. This misunderstanding not only concerns the intellect's "capacity" for truth but also its "capacity" for moral virtue (*TI* "Errors").

45. See also, in comparison, a note from the *Nachlass*: "All organic life that 'judges' acts like an artist: it creates out of singular stimuli, stimulations a whole, it leaves many singular details aside and creates a simplification, it sets as equal and affirms its creation as an existing being" (*KSA* 11:25[333]).

46. The citation continues: "As long as something can be called back as a single fact, it is not yet fused together [*eingeschmolzen*]: the most current experiences are still drifting on the surface. Feelings of attractions, repulsions, etc., are symptoms, that unities have already been formed; our so-called 'instincts' are formations [*Bildungen*] of this kind. Thoughts are the most superficial things; value judgments which come up unexpectedly and are there, go deeper, pleasure and pain are effects of complicated value judgments which are regulated by instincts" (*KSA* 11:26[94]).

47. For an analysis of the relation between concept formation and civilizing processes of society formation, see Adorno and Horkheimer, *Dialektik der Aufklärung*, 30.

48. Throughout his writings, Nietzsche maintains that "seeing as equal" and "taking as equal" play a role in the preservation of life. In *The Gay Science*, he puts forth the claim that the struggle for the preservation of life is largely dependent upon finding "equality" (*Gleiche*): "He, for instance, who did not know how to find 'equality' [*Gleiche*] often enough, both with regard to nourishment and to hostile animals—that is, he who subsumed too slowly and was too cautious in subsumption—had a slighter probability of survival than he who in all cases of similarity [*Ähnliche*] immediately guessed that they were equal [*Gleichheit*]. The predominant tendency [*Hang*], however, to treat the similar [*Ähnliche*] as equal [*gleich*], an illogical tendency [*Hang*]—for there is nothing equal [*Gleiches*] as such—is what first supplied all bases [*Grundlage*] for logic" (*GS* 111).

49. See in comparison, a passage from his early work: "one must not understand this need to form concepts, species, forms, purposes, laws ('a world of identical cases') as if we were thereby able to fix the *true* world; but rather as needed

to ready a world for ourselves that makes our existence possible—we create thereby a world that is calculable, simplified, intelligible, etc. for us" (*PW* 17). Citations such as the above have led to what is commonly known as a pragmatist interpretation of truth in Nietzsche. For examples of pragmatist readings of Nietzsche's conception of truth, see Arthur C. Danto, *Nietzsche as Philosopher* (New York: Columbia University Press, 1980), 68–99. For a critique of the pragmatic reading of truth, see Nehamas, *Life as Literature*, 52–53.

50. On the metaphor of the Roman columbarium, see Sarah Kofman, "Metaphoric Architectures," in *Looking After Nietzsche,* ed. Lawrence A. Rieckels (Albany: State University of New York Press), 89–113. See also in Adorno and Horkheimer the idea that the "construction of a pyramidal order based on castes and degrees" reflects a division of labor (*Dialektik der Aufklärung*, 38–39).

51. For a later version of this idea, see "Faith in truth is necessary to the human being. Truth seems to be a social need: . . . The need for truthfulness begins with society. Otherwise the human being lives in eternal dissimulations. The foundation of the state stimulates truthfulness—The drive for knowledge has a *moral* source" (*KSA* 7:19[175]).

52. For a discussion of the relationship between language and consciousness in Nietzsche, see Günter Abel, "Bewußtsein-Sprache-Natur: Nietzsches Philosophie des Geistes," *Nietzsche Studien* 30 (2001):1–43.

53. In *The Gay Science*, Nietzsche also introduces the distinction between conscious and unconscious virtues (*GS* 8). Whereas the former operate in the interest of the group, the latter are a reflection of the irreducible singular truth (genius) of the virtuous one. Accordingly, while "conscious virtues" are shared and communicable in their accessibility to all equally, "unconscious virtues" are singular and incommunicable in their unequal accessibility.

54. On the intimate involvement between freedom and truth, see Stegmaier: "Wahrheiten heisst so wesentlich sich in Freiheit setzten und, da dadurch neue Lebensbedingungen geschaffen werden, neu interpretieren, 'umwerten.' In der Freiheit des Wahrheitens ist Wahrheit *nicht ursprünglich gegeben, sondern geschaffen*, oder: nicht das Gegebene, sondern das Geschaffene ist wahr" ("Nietzsches Neubestimmungen der Wahrheit," 88).

55. "And he has need of protection, for there exist fearful powers [*furchtbare Mächte*] which constantly press in on him and which confront [*entgegenhalten*] scientific truth [*wissenschaftlichen Wahrheit*] with 'truth' of quite another kind, on shield emblazoned with the most multifarious emblems" (*TL* 2).

56. Again Nietzsche's prefaces provide examples of such genuine truthfulness. In the preface of *Human, All Too Human*, Nietzsche explains that at the time of writing this book he was an adherent of positivism, and positivism provided him with an illusion of stability which he needed to cure himself from the frenzy (*Rausch*) induced by Wagner's art and Schopenhauer's philosophy. *The Gay Science* announces Nietzsche's convalescence from the illusions of positivistic science. In "An Attempt at Self-Criticism," Nietzsche claims that the metaphysic of the artist found in *The Birth of Tragedy* was only the beginning of an overcoming of metaphysics. According to his hypothesis, the young Nietzsche had to take

on the Apollonian mask of the German university teacher, whose speech lacks lightness, and of the Wagnerian, whose taste is not subtle and fine, just like the philosopher had to hide behind the mask of the ascetic ideal in order to accumulate greater strength.

57. Nietzsche argues that the reason why imaginary thinking cannot be mastered, just as its animality and animal forgetfulness cannot finally be overpowered, is that humans love nothing more than being tricked and deceived without consequently suffering harm. He recognizes that humans are seduced by those dissimulations (*Verstellungen*) which function as an aid to the foundation and preservation of society because they are comforting and make one feel more secure and protected. However, he claims that what humans love even more than security is to be enchanted and seduced by the dissimulations of art and mythology (culture): "But human beings themselves have an unconquerable urge to let themselves be deceived, and they are as if enchanted with happiness when the bard recites epic fairy-tales as if they were true, or when the actor in a play acts the king more regally than reality shows him to be" (*TL* 2). Essentially, it is due to the human being's "weakness" for the dissimulations of art and mythology (culture) that their artistic animal drives cannot be tamed and defeated.

58. Nietzsche also speaks of "bearing a responsibility for all the coming millennia" (*EH* "Clever" 10).

59. On the notion of great politics, see *KSA* 13:25[1], 25[6], 25[7], 25[11], 25[13]. See also the discussion of "great politics" in Yannis Constantinides, "Nietzsche législateur: Grand politique et réforme du monde," in *Lectures de Nietzsche*, ed. Jean-Francois Balaudé and Patrick Wotling (Paris: Le Livre de Poche, 2000), 208–82.

60. See, in comparison: "There is nothing which is more contrary to the meaning of my noble task than the dammed stirring up of national and racial self-obsession which now passes under the name of 'great politics'; I have no words to express how despicable I find the intellectual level of the German prime minister and of the Prussian officer-attitude of the house of Hohenzollern, this lowest species of human being, who feels called to the task of leading the history of the humankind" (*KSA* 13:25[6]).

61. It is clear that, for Nietzsche, such "degeneration" is linked to the figure of the "ascetic priest": "Let us here leave the possibility open that it is not human kind which is degenerating but only that parasitic species of man the priest, who with the aid of morality has lied himself up to being the determiner of human kind's value" (*EH* "Destiny" 7).

62. See Esposito's reading of Nietzsche's great politics as auto-immunitary in Roberto Esposito, *Bios: Biopolitica e filosofia* (Turin: Biblioteca Einaudi, 2004), 79–114; and *Bios: Biopolitics and Philosophy*, trans. Timothy Campbell (Minneapolis: University of Minnesota Press, 2008), 78–109.

63. Nietzsche says of Plato that he had "the greatest strength any philosopher so far has had at his disposal" (*BGE* 191).

64. On Nietzsche's positive judgment on Plato in relation to his negative judgment on Socrates, see Constantinides, "Nietzsche Législateur," 270–73. On

the overturning of Plato in Nietzsche, see also Sarah Kofman, *Nietzsche et la scène philosophique* (Paris: Galilée, 1986).

65. Nietzsche encourages trust in the body for it is the best advisor in questions of health. Its distinctions are the most reliable: "The body is the best advisor when a distinction between the well brought up and ill-bred needs to be made" (*KSA* 11:25[485]). See, in comparison, Zarathustra who calls his animals the most righteous advisors (*rechte Rathgeber*) (*Z*: 7 "The Ugliest Human Being").

Conclusion: Biopolitics and the Question of Animal Life

1. See Roberto Esposito, *Bios: Biopolitica e filosofia* (Turin: Biblioteca Einaudi, 2004), 79–115, and *Bios: Biopolitics and Philosophy*, trans. Timothy Campbell (Minneapolis: University of Minnesota Press, 2008), 78–109; Friedrich Balke, "Die Figuren des Verbrechers in Nietzsches Biopolitik," *Nietzsche-Studien* 32 (2003): 171–205 (available in English as Friedrich Balke, "From a Biopolitical Point of View: Nietzsche's Philosophy of Crime," *Cardozo Law Review* 24, no. 2 (2003): 705–22.

2. For a more extensive discussion of such an approach, see my article "The Biological Threshold of Modern Politics: Nietzsche, Foucault and the Question of Animal Life," in *Nietzsche, Power and Politics: Rethinking Nietzsche's Legacy for Political Thought*, ed. Herman W. Siemens and Vasti Roodt (Berlin: De Gruyter, 2008), 679–99. In the contemporary debate on the question of animal life, one can distinguish between two different understandings of what this question entails. In the Anglo-American tradition, the question of animal life revolves primarily around the ethical status of nonhuman animals, the question of whether the interests of animals deserve equal consideration with those of humans, and whether, therefore, animals have rights (Peter Singer, Preface in Matthew Calarco and Peter Atterton, *Animal Philosophy*, ed. Peter Atterton and Matthew Calarco [London and New York: Continuum Press, 2004], xv–xxv). By contrast, in the tradition of European Continental philosophy, the question of the animal concerns the status of the animality of the human being, the question of whether the continuity between human and animal life calls for a reconsideration of our "humanist" understanding of life, culture, and politics. My approach to the question of animal life falls within the second tradition. On the question of animal life, see in comparison Cary Wolfe, *Zoontologies: The Question of Animal Life* (Minneapolis: University of Minneapolis Press, 2003).

3. Michel Foucault, *The History of Sexuality*, vol. 1 (New York: Vintage Books, 1990), 142.

4. Ibid.

5. For an example of such an approach, see Volker Gerhardt, *Die angeborene Würde des Menschen* (Berlin: Parerga, 2004). See, in comparison, Thomas Lemke, *Biopolitik zur Einführung* (Hamburg: Junius Verlag, 2007), 34 and 35–46.

6. Foucault, *The History of Sexuality*, 143.

7. On the importance of the distinction between *bios* and *zoe* for an understanding of biopolitics, see Giorgio Agamben, *Homo Sacer: Sovereign Power and*

Bare Life (Stanford: Stanford University Press, 1998), 1–12. See also Balke, who argues that Nietzsche is undoubtedly the philosopher who informs and is informed by the biopolitical paradigm because he no longer grafts the good life (*bios*) onto mere physical existence (*zoe*), but conceptualizes the content of the good life as the result of processes that continuously intervene into mere physical existence, giving it form (Balke, "From a Biopolitical Point of View: Nietzsche's Philosophy of Crime," 705).

8. Foucault, *The History of Sexuality*, 142.

9. Ibid., 146.

10. Foucault, *Sécurité, territoire, population: Cours au Collège de France 1977–1978* (Paris: Seuil/Gallimard, 2004), 119–93; Foucault, "Omnes Et Singulatim: Toward a Critique of Political Reason," in *Power. The Essential Works of Foucault, 1954–1984*, vol. 3 (New York: New Press, 2000), 298–327. For a reading of great politics in Nietzsche as an example and a critique of what Foucault calls pastoral politics, see Balke, who argues that Nietzsche's "great politics" completely changes the role of the political Shepherd. He is no longer considered the first servant of the herd, but the inaugurator of "the experiment of a fundamental, artificial, and conscious breeding of the opposite type" of the "herd animal" ("From a Biopolitical Point of View: Nietzsche's Philosophy of Crime," 719).

11. Foucault, *Sécurité, territoire, population*, 198.

12. Foucault, *The History of Sexuality*, 142.

13. Ibid., 145.

14. Foucault defends the idea of developing "a kind of ethics" which is an "aesthetic of existence" in contraposition to a Sartrian existentialist ethics of authenticity. Foucault acknowledges that, in this sense, his notion of the "aesthetics of existence" is much closer to the Nietzschean project of creating one's life by giving style to it. See Michel Foucault, "On the Genealogy of Ethics," in *Ethics: Subjectivity and Truth. The Essential Works of Foucault, 1954–1984*, vol. 1 (New York: New Press, 1994), 255 and 262.

15. By liberation of animal life, I do not mean that there exists a human nature that has been alienated, repressed, or denied through historical, economical, and social processes and therefore needs to be liberated in order to reconcile the human being with its lost animal nature (on this point, see, in comparison, Foucault, "On the Genealogy of Ethics," 282). Rather, by liberation of animal life I mean liberation from the idea that the human being has a nature in the first place. From the perspective of the continuity between human and animal, organic and inorganic life, the idea of a given, stable, and unalterable origin and beginning of life, whether human, animal, or other, is highly questionable. Accordingly, when Nietzsche prescribes "a return to nature" as a "cure from 'culture,'" i.e., civilization (*WP* 684), he means a "cure" from the belief that the human being is anything always already by nature, for example, moral, rational, or otherwise.

16. Foucault, "On the Genealogy of Ethics," 223–52.

17. Hannah Arendt, *The Origins of Totalitarianism* (New York: Harcourt Brace, 1973), 465.

18. Foucault, *The History of Sexuality*, 137.

Bibliography

Abel, Günter. "Bewußtsein-Sprache-Natur: Nietzsches Philosophie des Geistes." *Nietzsche-Studien* 30 (2001): 1–43.

Acampora, Christa D. "Demos Agonistes Redux: Reflections on the Streit of Political Agonism." *Nietzsche-Studien* 32 (2003): 374–90.

———. "On Sovereignty and Overhumanity: Why It Matters How We Read Nietzsche's Genealogy II:2." *International Studies in Philosophy* 36:3 (2004): 127–45.

Acampora, Christa D., and Ralph Acampora, eds. *A Nietzschean Bestiary: Becoming Animal Beyond Docile and Brutal.* New York: Rowman and Littlefield, 2004.

Adorno, Theodor W., and Max Horkheimer. *Dialectic of Enlightenment.* New York: Continuum, 2002.

———. *Dialektik der Aufklärung: Philosophische Fragmente.* Frankfurt: Suhrkamp, 1981.

Agamben, Giorgio. *Homo Sacer: Sovereign Power and Bare Life.* Trans. Daniel Heller-Roazen. Stanford: Stanford University Press, 1998.

———. *The Open: Man and Animal.* Stanford: Stanford University Press, 2004.

———. *Profanierungen.* Frankfurt: Suhrkamp, 2005.

Ansell-Pearson, Keith. *An Introduction to Nietzsche as Political Thinker.* Cambridge: Cambridge University Press, 1994.

———. "On the Miscarriage of Life and the Future of the Human: Thinking Beyond the Human Condition with Nietzsche." *Nietzsche-Studien* 29 (2000): 153–77.

———. *Viroid Life*. London: Routledge, 1997.

Arendt, Hannah. *The Human Condition*. Chicago: University of Chicago Press, 1958.

———. *The Origins of Totalitarianism*. New York: Harcourt Brace, 1973.

Balke, Friedrich. "Die Figuren des Verbrechers in Nietzsches Biopolitik." *Nietzsche-Studien* 32 (2003): 171–205.

———. "From a Biopolitical Point of View: Nietzsche's Philosophy of Crime." *Cardozo Law Review* 24, no. 2 (2003): 705–22.

Barthes, Roland. "The Death of the Author." In *Image-Music-Text*, 142–48. Trans. Stephan Heath. New York: Noonday Press, 1988.

Bataille, Georges. *The Accursed Share: An Essay on General Economy*. Trans. Robert Hurley. Vols. 2 and 3. New York: Zone Books, 1991.

———. "Le sens de l'économie générale." In *La part maudit.*, 57–80. Paris: Les éditions de Minuit, 1970.

———. "The Notion of Expenditure." In *Visions of Excess: Selected Writings 1927–1939*, ed. Allan Stoekl, 116–29. Minneapolis: University of Minnesota Press, 1985.

———. *Visions of Excess: Selected Writings 1927–1939*, ed. Allan Stoekl. Minneapolis: University of Minnesota Press, 1985.

Benveniste, Emile. *Problème de linguistique générale*. Vol. 1. Paris: Gallimard, 1966.

Blondel, Eric. *Nietzsche: The Body and Culture*. Trans. Séan Hand. Stanford: Stanford University Press, 1991.

Bornedal, Peter. "A Silent World: Nietzsche's Radical Realism: World, Sensation, Language." *Nietzsche-Studien* 34 (2005): 1–47.

Brobjer, Thomas H. "The Absence of Political Ideas in Nietzsche's Writings: The Case of the Law of Manu and the Associated Caste Society." *Nietzsche-Studien* 27 (1998): 300–18.

———. "Nietzsche's Relation to Historical Methods and Nineteenth-Century German Historiography." *History and Theory* 46 (March 2007): 155–79.

———. "Nietzsche's View of the Value of Historical Studies and Methods." *Journal of the History of Ideas* (2004): 301–22.

Brown, Wendy. "Nietzsche for Politics." In *Why Nietzsche Still?* ed. Alan D. Schrift, 205–23. Berkeley and Los Angeles: University of California Press, 2000.

Butler, Judith. "Circuits of Bad Conscience: Nietzsche and Freud." In *Why Nietzsche Still?* ed. Alan D. Schrift, 121–35. Berkeley and Los Angeles: University of California Press, 2000.

Caillé, Alain. "Notes on the Paradigm of the Gift." In *The Gift*, 247–69. Milan: Edizioni Charta, 2001.

Calarco, Matthew, and Peter Atterton, eds. *Animal Philosophy*. London and New York: Continuum Press, 2004.

Came, Daniel. "Nietzsche's Attempt at Self-Criticism: Art and Morality in the Birth of Tragedy." *Nietzsche-Studien* 33 (2004): 37–67.

Campioni, Giuliano. *Les lectures françaises de Nietzsche*. Paris: PUF, 2001.

Canning, Peter. "How the Fable Becomes a World." In *Looking after Nietzsche,* ed. Laurence A. Rickels, 175–93. Albany: State University of New York Press, 1990.

del Caro, Adrian. *Grounding the Nietzsche Rhetoric of the Earth*. Berlin: De Gruyter, 2004.

Cavell, Stanley. *Conditions Handsome and Unhandsome: The Constitution of Emersonian Perfectionism*. Chicago: University of Chicago Press, 1990.

Clark, Maudemarie. *Nietzsche on Truth and Philosophy*. Cambridge: Cambridge University Press, 1990.

Coetzee, J. M. *The Lives of Animals*. Princeton, N.J.: Princeton University Press, 1999. (HV 4708. L57)

Conant, James. "Nietzsche's Perfectionism." In *Nietzsche's Postmoralism: Essays on Nietzsche's Prelude to Philosophy's Future*, ed. Richard Schacht, 181–257. Cambridge: Cambridge University Press, 2001.

Constantinides, Yannis. "Nietzsche Législateur." In *Lectures de Nietzsche*, ed. Jean-Francois Balaudé and Patrick Wotling, 208–82. Paris: Le Livre de Poche, 2000.

Conway, Daniel D. "Annunciation and Rebirth: The Prefaces of 1886." In *Nietzsche's Futures*, ed. John Lippitt, 30–47. London: Macmillan, 1999.

———. *Nietzsche and the Political*. Florence, Ky.: Routledge, 1997.

———. "The Politics of Decadence." *Southern Journal of Philosophy* 37 (1999): 19–33.

Danto, Arthur C. *Nietzsche as Philosopher*. New York: Columbia University Press, 1980.

Deleuze, Gilles. *Critique et clinique*. Paris: Editions de Minuit, 1993.

———. *Nietzsche et la philosophie*. Paris: PUF, 1962.

———. "Pensée Nomade." In *Nietzsche Aujourd'hui?* 158–74. Paris: Union Générale d'Éditions, 1973.

Deleuze, Gilles, and Felix Guattari. *A Thousand Plateaus: Capitalism and Schizophrenia*. Minneapolis: University of Minnesota Press, 1987.

Derrida, Jacques. *The Animal That Therefore I Am*. Trans. David Wills. New York: Fordham University Press, 2008.

————. *Aufzeichnungen eines Blinden.* Paderborn, Germany: Wilhelm Fink Verlag, 1997.

————. *Éperons: Les styles de Nietzsche.* Paris: Flammarion, 1978.

————. *The Gift of Death.* Chicago: University of Chicago Press, 1995.

————. *Given Time: I. Counterfeit Money.* Chicago: University of Chicago Press, 1992.

————. " 'Il courait mort': Salut, salut. Notes pour un courrier aux Temps Modernes." *Les Temps Modernes* 587 (Mars-Avril-Mai 1996): 7–54.

————. *La Dissemination.* Paris: Seuil, 1972.

————. *L'animal que donc je suis.* Paris: Galilée, 2006.

————. *On Cosmopolitanism and Forgiveness.* London: Routledge, 2001.

————. *Otobiographies: L'enseignement de Nietzsche et la politique du nom propre.* Paris: Galilée, 1984.

————. *Pardonner: L'impardonnable et l'imprescriptible.* Paris: L'Herne, 2005.

————. *Specters of Marx.* London: Routledge, 2006.

Detienne, Marcel, and Jean Paul Vernant. *Les ruses de l'intelligence.* Paris: Flammarion, 1974.

Diprose, Rosalyn. *Corporeal Generosity: On Giving with Nietzsche, Merleau-Ponty, and Lévinas.* Albany: State University of New York Press, 2002.

Dombowsky, Don. *Nietzsche's Machiavellian Politics.* London: Palgrave Macmillan, 2004.

————. "A Response to Alan Schrift's 'Nietzsche for Democracy?' " *Nietzsche-Studien* 29 (2000): 278–90.

Dostoevsky, Fyodor. *The Grand Inquisitor, with Related Chapters from the Brothers Karamazov.* Trans. Constance Garnett. Ed. Charles B. Guignon. Indianapolis: Hackett, 1993.

Emerson, Ralph Waldo. *Selected Writings.* New York: Penguin Books, 1965.

Esposito, Roberto. *Bios: Biopolitica e filosofia.* Turin: Biblioteca Einaudi, 2004.

————. *Bios: Biopolitics and Philosophy.* Trans. Timothy Campbell. Minneapolis: University of Minnesota Press, 2008.

Figl, Johann, ed. *Von Nietzsche zu Freud: Übereinstimmungen und Differenzen von Denkmotiven.* Vienna: WUV-Universitätsverlag, 1996.

Fink, Eugen. *La philosophie de Nietzsche.* Paris: Les Éditions de Minuit, 1965.

Fontenay, Elisabeth de. *Le silence des bêtes: La philosophie à l'épreuve de l'animalité.* Paris: Fayard, 1998.

Foucault, Michel. *Discipline and Punish.* New York: Vintage Books, 1995.

——. *Ethics: Subjectivity, and Truth. The Essential Works of Foucault, 1954–1984.* Vol. 1. Ed. Paul Rabinov. New York: New Press, 1994.

——. *The History of Sexuality.* Vol. 1. New York: Vintage Books, 1990.

——. *La pensée du dehors.* Paris: Fata Morgana, 1986.

——. "Nietzsche, la généalogie, l'histoire." In *Hommage à Jean Hyppolite,* 145–72. Paris: PUF, 1971.

——. "Omnes Et Singulatim: Toward a Critique of Political Reason." In *Power. The Essential Works of Foucault, 1954–1984.* Vol. 3. Ed. James D. Faubion. New York: New Press, 2000.

——. *Power. The Essential Works of Foucault 1954–1984.* Vol. 3. Ed. James D. Faubion. New York: New Press, 2000.

——. *Sécurité, territoire, population: Cours au Collège de France 1977–1978.* Paris: Seuil/Gallimard, 2004.

——. "What Is an Author?" In *Aesthetics, Method, and Epistemology. The Essential Works of Foucault, 1954–1984.* Ed. James D. Faubion, 205–22. Vol. 2. New York: New Press, 1998.

Foucault, Michel, and Ludwig Binswanger. "Dream, Imagination, and Existence." In *Dream and Existence,* ed. Keith Hoeller, 31–78. Atlantic Highlands, N.J.: Humanities Press International, 1993.

Freud, Sigmund. *Civilization and Its Discontents.* New York: W. W. Norton, 1961.

——. *Interpretation of Dreams.* New York: Avon Books, 1965.

——. *Le délire et les rêves dans la gradiva de Jensen.* Paris: Gallimard, 1986.

Geisenhanslücke, Achim. "Der Mensch als Eintagswesen: Nietzsches Kritische Anthropologie in der Zweiten Unzeitgemässen Betrachtung." *Nietzsche-Studien* 28 (1999): 125–40.

Genette, Jean. *Seuils.* Paris: Seuil, 1987.

Gerhardt, Volker. *Die angeborene Würde des Menschen.* Berlin: Parega, 2004.

——. *Pathos und Distanz.* Stuttgart: Reclam, 1988.

——. "Prinzip des Gleichgewichts." *Nietzsche-Studien* 12 (1983): 111–33.

——. "Von der Ästhetischen Metaphysik zur Physiologie der Kunst." *Nietzsche-Studien* 13 (1984): 374–93.

Gödde, Günter. "Eine neue Interpretation von Freuds Verhältnis zu Nietzsche." *Nietzsche-Studien* 27 (1998): 463–80.

——. "Wandelungen des Menschenbildes durch Nietzsche und Freud: Eine vergleichende Interpretation aus philosophiegeschichtlicher Perspektive." *Jahrbuch der Psychoanalyse* (1993): 119–66.

Gooding-Williams, Robert. *Zarathustra's Dionysian Modernism*. Stanford: Stanford University Press, 2001.

Haar, Michel. "Du symbolisme animal en général, et notamment du serpent." *Alter: Revue de Phénoménologie*, no. 3 (1995): 319–43.

———. *Nietzsche and Metaphysics*. Trans. Michael Gendre. Albany: State University of New York Press, 1996.

Ham, Jennifer. "Taming the Beast: Animality in Wedekind and Nietzsche." In *Animal Acts*, ed. Jennifer Ham and Matthew Senior, 145–63. London and New York: Routledge, 1997.

Hatab, Lawrence. *A Nietzschean Defense of Democracy: An Experiment in Postmodern Politics*. Chicago: Open Court, 1995.

———. "Prospects for a Democratic Agon: Why We Can Still Be Nietzscheans." *Journal of Nietzsche Studies* 24 (2002): 132–47.

———. "Time-Sharing in the Bestiary: On Daniel Conway's 'Politics of Decadence.'" *Southern Journal of Philosophy* 37 (1999): 35–41.

Hegel, G. W. F. *Phänomenologie des Geistes*. Frankfurt: Suhrkamp, 1970.

Heidegger, Martin. *Basic Questions of Philosophy*. Bloomington: Indiana University Press, 1994.

———. *Die Grundbegriffe der Metaphysik: Welt-Endlichkeit-Einsamkeit*. Frankfurt: Vittorio Klostermann, 1992.

———. *Nietzsche*. Vols. 1 and 2. Stuttgart: Verlag Günter Neske, 1998.

———. *Nietzsche Seminare 1937–1944*. Frankfurt: Vittorio Klostermann, 2004.

———. *Zur Auslegung Von Nietzsche's Zweiter Unzeitgemässen Betrachtung*. Vol. 46, *Gesamtausgabe*. Frankfurt: Vittorio Klostermann, 2003.

Heller, Agnes. *A Theory of Modernity*. Malden, Mass.: Blackwell, 1999.

Hennis, Wilhelm. "Die Spuren Nietzsches im Werk Max Webers." *Nietzsche-Studien* 16 (1987): 382–404.

Hobbes, Thomas. *The Leviathan*. Cambridge: Cambridge University Press, 1996.

Honig, Bonnie. *Political Theory and the Displacement of Politics*. Ithaca, N.Y.: Cornell University Press, 1993.

Ibanez-Noé, Javier A. "Is Nietzsche a Common-Sense Realist?" *International Studies in Philosophy* 37, no. 3 (2006): 91–106.

Jensen, Anthony K. "The Centrality and Development of *Anschauung* in Nietzsche's Epistemology." *International Studies in Philosophy* (2007): n.p.

Kant, Immanuel. "What Is Enlightenment?" In *What Is Enlightenment? Eighteenth-Century Answers and Twentieth-Century Questions*, ed. James Schmidt, 58–63. Berkeley and Los Angeles: University of California Press, 1996.

Kaufmann, Walter. *Nietzsche: Philosopher, Psychologist, Antichrist*. Princeton, N.J.: Princeton University Press, 1974.

Kierkegaard, Søren. *Fear and Trembling*. London: Penguin Books, 1985.

———. *The Present Age*. New York: Harper and Row, 1962.

Kofman, Sarah. *Nietzsche et la métaphore*. Paris: Editions Galilée, 1983.

———. *Nietzsche et la scène philosophique*. Paris: Editions Galilée, 1979.

Lacoue-Labarthe, Philippe. "History and Mimesis." In *Looking after Nietzsche*, ed. Laurence Rickels, 209–31. Albany: State University of New York Press, 1990. (Kofman : ' Metaphoric Architecture)

———. "Le détour (Nietzsche et la rhétorique)." *Poétique* 2 (1971): 53–76.

———. *L'imitations des Modernes*. Paris: Editions Galilée, 1986.

Lampert, Laurence. *Nietzsche's Teaching*. New Haven, Conn. and London: Yale University Press, 1986.

Langer, Monika. "The Role and the Status of the Animals in Nietzsche's Philosophy." In *Animal Others: On Ethics, Ontology, and Animal Life*, ed. Peter Steeves. New York: State University of New York Press, 1999.

Lemke, Thomas. *Biopolitik zur Einführung*. Hamburg: Junius Verlag, 2007.

Lemm, Vanessa. "Animality, Creativity and Historicity: A Reading of Friedrich Nietzsche's *Vom Nutzen und Nachtheil der Historie für das Leben*." *Nietzsche-Studien* 36 (2007): 169–200.

———. "The Biological Threshold of Modern Politics: Nietzsche, Foucault and the Question of Animal Life." In *Nietzsche, Power and Politics: Rethinking Nietzsche's Legacy for Political Thought*. Ed. Herman W. Siemens and Vasti Rodt, 679–99. Berlin: De Gruyter, 2008.

———. "Is Nietzsche a Perfectionist? Rawls, Cavell and the Politics of Culture in Nietzsche's *Schopenhauer as Educator*." *Journal of Nietzsche Studies*, no. 34 (2007): 5–27.

———. "Justice and Gift-Giving in *Thus Spoke Zarathustra*." In *Before Sunrise:, Essays on Thus Spoke Zarathustra*. Ed. James Luchte, 165–81. London: Continuum International Publishers, 2009.

———. "Memory and Promise in Arendt and Nietzsche." *Revista de Ciencia Politica* 26, no. 2 (2006): 161–74.

———. "Nietzsches Vision einer 'Neuen Aristokratie.'" *Deutsche Zeitschrift für Philosophie* 56 (2008): 365–83.

Lévinas, Emmanuel. *Totalité et infini*. La Haye, Netherlands: Nijhoff, 1961.

Lévi-Strauss, Claude. *Triste Tropiques*. New York: Penguin Books, 1992.

Lippit, Akira Mizuta. *Electric Animal*. Minneapolis: University of Minnesota Press, 2000.

Loeb, Paul S. "Finding the Übermensch in Nietzsche's *Genealogy of Morality.*" *Journal of Nietzsche Studies* 30 (2005): 70–101.

Loraux, Nicole. *La cité divisée: L'oublie et la mémoire d'Athène.* Paris: Payot, 1997.

Losurdo, Domenico. *Nietzsche, Il ribelle aristocratico: Biografia bilancio critico.* Turin: Bollati Boringhieri, 2002.

Machiavelli, Niccolo. *Florentine Histories.* Princeton, N.J.: Princeton University Press, 1988.

———. *The Prince.* Chicago: University of Chicago Press, 1998.

MacIntyre, Alasdair. *After Virtue.* Notre Dame, Ind.: Notre Dame University Press, 1984.

———. *Dependent Rational Animals: Why Human Beings Need the Virtues.* Chicago: Open Court, 2001.

Mallet, Marie-Louise. *L'animal autobiographique.* Ed. Marie-Louise Mallet. Paris: Galilée, 1999.

Man, Paul de. *Allegories of Reading: Figural Language in Rousseau, Nietzsche, Rilke and Proust.* New Haven, Conn.: Yale University Press, 1979.

Mauss, Marcel. *The Gift.* New York and London: W. W. Norton, 2000.

———. *Sociologie et anthropologie.* Paris: PUF, 1950.

McIntyre, Alex. *The Sovereignty of Joy: Nietzsche's Vision of Great Politics.* Toronto: University of Toronto Press, 1997.

Meyers, Anthonie. "Gustav Gerber und Friedrich Nietzsche: Zum Historischen Hintergrund der Sprachphilosophischen Auffassungen des Frühen Nietzsche." *Nietzsche-Studien* 17 (1988): 368–90.

Mill, John Stuart. *On Liberty.* Indianapolis: Hackett, 1978.

Moore, Gregory. *Nietzsche: Biology and Metaphor.* Cambridge, Mass.: Harvard University Press, 2002.

Müller-Lauter, Wolfgang. *Über Freiheit und Chaos: Nietzsche-Interpretationen II.* Berlin: De Gruyter, 1999.

———. *Über Werden und Wille zur Macht: Nietzsche-Interpretationen I.* Berlin: De Gruyter, 1999.

Nancy, Jean-Luc. "'Notre Probité' sur la vérité au sens moral chez Nietzsche." In *L'impératif catégorique,* 61–86. Paris: Flammarion, 1983.

———. "'Our Probity!' On Truth in the Moral Sense in Nietzsche." In *Looking after Nietzsche,* ed. Laurence A. Rickels, 67–87. Albany: State University of New York Press, 1990.

———. "Praesens." In *The Gift: Generous Offerings Threatening Hospitality,* 191–99. Milan: Edizioni Charta, 2001.

Nancy, Jean-Luc, and Philippe Lacoue-Labarthe. "Friedrich Nietzsche: Rhétorique et langage, textes traduits, présentés et annotés." *Poétique* 2 (1971): 99–143.

Nehamas, Alexander. "For Whom the Sun Shines: A Reading of *Also Sprach Zarathustra*." In *Also Sprach Zarathrustra*. Ed. Volker Gerhardt, 165–90. Berlin: Akademie Verlag, 2000.

———. *Nietzsche: Life as Literature*. Cambridge, Mass.: Harvard University Press, 1985.

Nietzsche, Friedrich. *The Antichrist*. Trans. R. J. Hollingdale. London: Penguin Books, 1968.

———. "An Attempt at Self-Criticism." Preface to *The Birth of Tragedy*. Trans. R. Speirs. Cambridge: Cambridge University Press, 1999.

———. *Beyond Good and Evil: Prelude to a Philosophy of the Future*. Trans. Walter Kaufmann. New York: Vintage Books, 1989.

———. *The Birth of Tragedy*. Trans. R. Speirs. Cambridge: Cambridge University Press, 1999.

———. *The Case of Wagner*. Trans. Walter Kaufmann. Toronto: Random House, 1967.

———. *Daybreak*. Trans. R. J. Hollingdale. Cambridge: Cambridge University Press, 1997.

———. *Ecce Homo*. Trans. R. J. Hollingdale. London: Penguin Books, 1979.

———. *The Gay Science*. Trans. J. Nauckoff. Cambridge: Cambridge University Press, 2001.

———. "The Greek State." In *On the Genealogy of Morals*. Trans C. Diethe. Ed. Keith Ansell-Pearson. Cambridge: Cambridge University Press, 1994.

———. "Homer's Contest." In *On the Genealogy of Morals*. Trans C. Diethe. Ed. Keith Ansell-Pearson. Cambridge: Cambridge University Press, 1994.

———. *Human, All Too Human*. Trans. R. J. Hollingdale. Cambridge: Cambridge University Press, 1986.

———. *Kritische Studienausgabe in 15 Bänden*. Ed. Giorgio Colli and Mazzino Montinari. Berlin: De Gruyter, 1988.

———. *On the Genealogy of Morals*. Trans. C. Diethe. Ed. Keith Ansell-Pearson. Cambridge: Cambridge University Press, 1994.

———. "The Philosopher. Reflections on the Struggle between Art and Knowledge." In *Philosophy and Truth: Selections from Nietzsche's Notebooks of the Early 1870's*. Trans. Daniel Breazeale. London: Humanities Press International, 1979.

———. *Philosophy and Truth: Selections from Nietzsche's Notebooks of the Early 1870's*. Trans. Daniel Breazeale. London: Humanities Press International, 1979.

————. *Sämtliche Briefe, Kritische Studienausgabe in 8 Bänden*. Berlin: De Gruyter, 1986.

————. *Thus Spoke Zarathustra*. Trans. Walter Kaufmann. New York: Modern Library, 1995.

————. "Truth and Lies in an Extra-Moral Sense." In *The Birth of Tragedy*. Trans. R. Speirs. Cambridge: Cambridge University Press, 1999.

————. *Twilight of the Idols*. Trans. R. J. Hollingdale. London: Penguin Books, 1968.

————. *Untimely Meditations*. Translated by R. J. Hollingdale. Cambridge: Cambridge University Press, 1997.

————. *The Will to Power*. Trans. and ed. Walter Kaufmann. New York: Random House, 1968.

Norris, Margot. *Beasts of Modern Imagination: Darwin, Nietzsche, Kafka, Ernst, and Lawrence*. Baltimore: Johns Hopkins University Press, 1985.

Ottmann, Henning. *Philosophie und Politik bei Nietzsche*. Berlin: De Gruyter, 1987.

Owen, David. "The Contest of Enlightenment." *Journal of Nietzsche Studies* 25 (2003): 35–57.

————. "Equality, Democracy and Self-Respect: Reflections on Nietzsche's Agonal Perfectionism." *Journal of Nietzsche Studies* 24 (2002): 113–31.

Pfotenhauer, Helmut. "Physiologie der Kunst als Kunst der Physiologie?" *Nietzsche-Studien* 13 (1984): 399–411.

Pippin, Robert B. "Truth and Lies in the Early Nietzsche." In *Idealism as Modernity: Hegelian Variations*, 311–29. Cambridge: Cambridge University Press, 1997.

Rawls, John. *A Theory of Justice*. Cambridge, Mass.: Harvard University Press, 1999.

Reed, T. J. "Nietzsche's Animals: Idea, Image, and Influence." In *Nietzsche: Imaginary and Thought*, ed. Malcolm Pasley, 159–219. Berkeley and Los Angeles: University of California Press, 1978.

Reuter, Sören. "Reiz-Bild-Unbewusste Anschauung: Nietzsches Auseinandersetzung mit Hermann Helmholtz's Theorie des Unbewussten Schlüsse in Über Wahrheit und Lüge im aussermoralischen Sinne." *Nietzsche-Studien* 33 (2004): 351–72.

Rorty, Richard. *Philosophy and the Mirror of Nature*. Princeton, N.J.: Princeton University Press, 1979.

————. "The World Well Lost." In *Consequences of Pragmatism*, 3–18. New York: Harvester Wheatsheaf, 1991.

Salaquarda, Jörg. "Studien zur Zweiten Unzeitgemässen Betrachtung." *Nietzsche-Studien* 13 (1984): 1–45.

Sallis, John. *Crossings*. Chicago: University of Chicago Press, 1991.

Sartre, Jean-Paul. *Existentialism and Humanism*. New York: Philosophical Library, 1984.

———. "*Introducing* Les temps modernes." In *"What Is Literature?" and Other Essays*, 246–67. Trans. Jeffrey Mehlman. Cambridge, Mass.: Harvard University Press, 1988.

———. *"What Is Literature?" and Other Essays*. Cambridge, Mass.: Harvard University Press, 1988.

———. "Writing for One's Age." In *"What Is Literature?" and Other Essays*, 239–45. Trans. Bernard Frechtman. Cambridge, Mass.: Harvard University Press, 1988.

Schacht, Richard. *Making Sense of Nietzsche*. Urbana and Chicago: University of Illinois Press, 1995.

Schrift, Alan D. "Language, Metaphor, Rhetoric: Nietzsche's Deconstruction of Epistemology." *Journal of the History of Philosophy* 23 (1985): 371–95.

———. *The Logic of the Gift*. Ed. Alan D. Schrift. New York and London: Routledge, 1997.

———. *Nietzsche's French Legacy: A Genealogy of Poststructuralism*. New York and London: Routledge, 1995.

———. "Response to Don Dombovsky." *Nietzsche-Studien* 29 (2000): 291–97.

———. "Rethinking Exchange: Logics of the Gift in Cixous and Nietzsche." *Philosophy Today* (1996): 197–205.

———. "Rethinking the Subject: Or How One Becomes-Other Than What One Is." In *Nietzsche's Postmoralism: Essays on Nietzsche's Prelude to Philosophy's Future*, ed. Richard Schacht, 47–62. Cambridge: Cambridge University Press, 2001.

Shapiro, Gary. *Alcyone: Nietzsche on Gift, Noise and Women*. Albany: State University of New York Press, 1991.

———. *Archaeologies of Vision: Foucault and Nietzsche on Seeing and Saying*. Chicago: University of Chicago Press, 2003.

———. *Nietzschean Narratives*. Bloomington: Indiana University Press, 1989.

———. "Beyond Peoples and Fatherlands: Nietzsche's Geophilosophy and the Direction of the Earth." *Journal of Nietzsche Studies* 35 (2008): 9–27.

———. "This Is Not a Christ." In *Why Nietzsche Still?* ed. Alan D. Schrift. Berkeley and Los Angeles: University of California Press, 2000.

Siemens, Herman W. "Action, Performance and Freedom in Hannah Arendt and Friedrich Nietzsche." *International Studies in Philosophy* 37, no. 3 (2006): 107–26.

————. "Agonal Communities of Taste: Law and Community in Nietzsche's Philosophy of Transvaluation." *Journal of Nietzsche Studies* 24
(2002): 83–112.

————. "Agonal Configurations in the Unzeitgemässe Betrachtungen:
Identity, Mimesis and the Übertragung of Cultures in Nietzsche's
Early Thought." *Nietzsche-Studien* 30 (2001): 80–106.

————. "Nietzsche's Political Philosophy: A Review of the Recent Literature." *Nietzsche-Studien* 30 (2001): 509–26.

Siemens, Herman W., and Vasti Roodt, eds. *Nietzsche, Power and Politics:
Rethinking Nietzsche's Legacy for Political Thought.* Berlin: De Gruyter,
2008.

Simmel, Georg. "Nietzsche's Moral." In *Aufsätze und Abhandlungen
1909–1918,* 170–76. Frankfurt: Suhrkamp, 2001.

————. *Philosophie der Mode, die Religion: Kant und Goethe, Schopenhauer und Nietzsche.* Gesamtausgabe Band 10. Frankfurt: Suhrkamp,
1995.

Starobinski, Jean. *Portrait de l'artiste en saltimbanque.* Paris: Flammarion,
1970.

Steeves, Peter. *Animal Others: On Ethics, Ontology and Animal Life.* Ed.
Peter Steeves. New York: State University of New York Press, 1999.

Stegmaier, Werner. "Darwin, Darwinismus, Nietzsche: Zum Problem der
Evolution." *Nietzsche-Studien* 16 (1987): 264–87.

————. "Nietzsches Neubestimmungen der Wahrheit." *Nietzsche-Studien* 14 (1985): 69–95.

Stiegler, Barbara. *Nietzsche et la biologie.* Paris: PUF, 2001.

Strong, Tracy B. *Friedrich Nietzsche and the Politics of Transfiguration.*
Berkeley and Los Angeles: University of California Press, 1975.

Taylor, Quentin P. *The Republic of Genius: A Reconstruction of Nietzsche's
Early Thought.* Rochester, N.Y.: Rochester University Press, 1997.

Tocqueville, Alexis de. *Democracy in America and Two Essays on America.*
London: Penguin Books, 2003.

Tongeren, Paul von. "Nietzsche's Greek Measure." *Journal of Nietzsche
Studies* 24 (2002): 5–24.

Vatter, Miguel. *Between Form and Event: Machiavelli's Theory of Political
Freedom.* Dordrecht: Kluwer Academic Publishers, 2000.

Villa, Dana. "Democratizing the Agon: Nietzsche, Arendt and the Agonistic Tendency in Recent Political Theory." In *Why Nietzsche Still?*
ed. Alan D. Schrift, 224–46. Berkeley and Los Angeles: University of
California Press, 2000.

Weber, Max. *Political Writings.* Cambridge: Cambridge University Press,
1994.

Williams, Bernard. *Truth and Truthfulness: An Essay in Genealogy.* Princeton, N.J.: Princeton University Press, 2002.

Wolfe, Cary, ed. *Zoontologies: The Question of the Animal.* Minneapolis: University of Minnesota Press, 2003.

Wotling, Patrick. *Nietzsche et le problème de la civilisation.* Paris: PUF, 1995.

Zuckert, Catherine. "Nature, History and the Self: Nietzsche's Untimely Considerations." *Nietzsche-Studien* 5 (1976): 55–82.

Zweig, Stefan. *Nietzsche: Le combat avec le démon.* Paris: Editions Stock, 1993.

Index

Abraham (Biblical character), 174n29
absolute truth. *See* truth
abstract thinking, 126, 134–38,
    209n49–10n49
    See also pictorial thinking
abstract world of regulating and imperative
    (linguistic) laws, 117, 119, 120, 121,
    137
Acampora, Christa D., 176n43
Acéphale, 46
Adorno, Theodor W., 172n17
aesthetics of existence, 213n14
aggression, 165n23
agon. *See* competition
all-too-human, 23, 52, 163n13–64n13
alms, 78
alms, giving, 83–84
Also Sprach Zarathustra. See *Thus Spoke
    Zarathustra*
the animal, 1–3, 26, 34–35
    See also animals; humans, animality of
animal forgetfulness
    artistic historians and, 100
    Christian forgiveness and, 62
    culture versus civilization and, 10–11
    dreaming, comparison with, 26
    forgiveness and, 6

gift-giving as, 80, 84
historicity, influence on, 90–91
human memory, relationship to, 7, 87
importance of, 69, 155
intuited metaphors and, 117
memory of the will and, 34, 36
nature of recovery of, 84
redeeming power of, 68–71
under rule of culture, 12
sociability and, 68
of sovereign individuals, 37
suffering and, 68–69
    See also the animal; animals
animality
    barbaric, 52
    becoming-animal, 6, 88
    becoming overhuman and, 4–5, 7
    biopolitics and, 152–156
    Christian morality's denial of, 20
    civilization and, 17–19, 139
    culture, relationship to, 1–2
    denial of, effects of, 18
    greatness of human culture and, 193n18
    of Greek culture, 16–17
    historicity, relationship to, 87
    nature of recovery of, 84
    as otherness, 7

overhuman, relationship to, 4–5
political life and, 5
return to, philosophy and, 112–13
as source of nobility, 193n23
See also culture; humanity; humans,
animality of
animals
a-historicity of, 89–90
able to make promises, 36
animal life, 153, 154, 212n2, 213n15
animal passions, 23
children, comparison with, 89
cruelty of, Greek views of, 16
dream life of, 4
Eastern religions' respect for, 20
exceptional, 35, 36
forgetfulness of, 88–89
(*See also* animal forgetfulness)
forgiveness of, 73
historicity of, 89–91
individuality of, 171n15
language, results of lack of, 115
life forces of, antagonism with humans,
10–11
morality of, 13
over-animals, 21–23
pictorial thinking of, 8
silence of, 8–9
silent truth of, 114–15
taming of, 20
unhistoricity of, 114
vigor of, 148
Anschauungsmetapher. See intuited
metaphors
Ansell-Pearson, Keith, 7, 165n26–66n26,
178n1
antagonism
of culture and civilization, 10–17,
18–19, 35–36, 48
of humans and animal life forces, 10–11
of memory and forgetfulness, 31–32
anthropocentrism, 2
The Antichrist (Nietzsche), 208n41
anticipated future, 43
antiquarian history, 96, 97–98, 169n6
Apollo, 14–15
appearance, 123

Arendt, Hannah
on forgiveness, 64, 65, 70, 73, 186n39
mentioned, 62
on need, freedom from, 179n7
on the past, 70
public action, views on, 182n24
on totalitarian ideologies, 156
aristocratic society, 53, 178n1
aristocraticism, 181n21–82n21
Aristotle, 153
art, 99, 100, 127–28, 147–48
art of dissimulation, 133
artistic historiography, 99–10
artists, 8, 145
ascetic priests, 170n11, 171n14, 211n61
"An Attempt at Self-Criticism"
(Nietzsche), 102–5, 108–10, 144
attempters, philosophers of the future as,
123
authors, 106, 109

bad memory, 194n26
Balke, Friedrich, 212n7–13n7, 213n10
Bataille, Georges, 56, 174n34,
180n15–81n15
Beasts of Modern Imagination (Norris), 1–2
becoming
as artistic phenomenon, 148
becoming-animal, 6, 88
becoming what one is, 107–8
of culture, 59
forgetfulness and, 93–94
humans as, 7, 23
incompleteness of, 53–54
innocence of, 66, 67
of life forms, 3
overhuman as, 23
begging, 83–84
beginnings, 24, 94, 96, 104
Begriffsdenken. See conceptual thinking
being, 121
See also humans
being with the habit of ordering in
dreaming. *See* whole organic world
beings. *See* humans
bending bows (weapons), as metaphor, 103
Beyond Good and Evil (Nietzsche), 55, 58,
103, 127
Bilderdenken. See pictorial thinking

biologism, 2
biopolitics, 152–56
The Birth of Tragedy (Nietzsche)
  circumstances of writing of, 144
  crossing of Dionysus and Apollo in,
    14–15
  Nietzsche on, 103–4, 108
  Nietzsche's rereading of, 109
  open questions of, 110
Blondel, Eric, 161n2
body, trust in, 212n65
books, 45, 105–6, 109–10
Bornedal, Peter, 200n8, 202n19, 205n31,
  206n32
breeding. *See* taming and breeding
Brobjer, Thomas H., 191n4
The Brothers Karamazov (Dostoevsky),
  Grand Inquisitor in, 170n11
Brown, Wendy, 175n40

Canning, Peter, 176n44
care of the self, 154
Cavell, Stanley, 169n1
Centaur (Chiron), 27
chaos. *See Urgrund* (world as chaos)
children, 89
Chiron (Centaur), 27
Christian forgiveness, 62–69
Christian love, 77–78
Christian morality, 19–21, 62, 67
Christianity, 19–21
  See also forgiving and forgiveness
churches, 168n43, 171n14
Circe, 24, 25
civilisation (Fr.), 161n2
civilization, 10–29
  in age of democratization, 57
  the animal as enemy of, 34–35
  animality and, 52, 155
  as Apollonian, 14–15
  Christianity and, 19–21
  critique of, truth and, 138–43
  culture
    antagonism of, 10–17, 18–19,
      35–36, 48, 154
    dependence on, 18–19, 60
    distinction from, 4, 10–11
    priority of, 60

  economy of, 5
  education under, 58
  effects of, 36
  forgetfulness of, 17–19, 71, 125, 135,
    164n16
  highpoints of, alternation with culture,
    11–12
  incompleteness, as locus for, 53
  intellect under, 147–48
  memory of the will and, 12, 32–33
  moral discipline of, 50
  morality as false overcoming and, 19–23
  narratives of creation, 19
  nature's use of, 55
  necessity as problem of, 51
  politics of, 48–49, 154–55
  process of, 4, 50–51
  promise of, 31–36
  purpose of, 11, 32
  Romans as exemplar of, 17
  rule of, memory of the will and, 139
  sickness of, 18
  slavery as aspect of, 49
  stupidity of, 55, 164n18
  "truth" and, 139
  Umgekehrten's subversion of values of,
    28–29
  value of, 35–36
  waking life, comparability with, 26
  See also culture; morality
Clark, Maudemarie, 203n25–4n25,
  207n38–8n38
columbaria, Roman, 136, 137, 140
comedy, 104–5
common good, 127
communication, 141–42
competition (agon), 104, 176n43
  See also antagonism
completeness, 53
  See also overcoming
Conant, James, 162n3
concept formation, 135
concepts, metaphors, and schemes,
  117–19, 137
conceptual language, 120–22
  abstract thought and, 134–37
  Roman columbaria, comparison with,
    136, 137, 140
  vulgarity of, 203n24

conceptual thinking (*Begriffsdenken*),
116–19, 125, 126–27
See also abstract thinking
conscience, 38
conscious virtues, 210n53
consciousness
analysis of, in *The Gay Science*, 141–42
emergence with foundation of society,
141
as group function, 142
humans' reliance on, 208n41
illusory, 209n42
nature of, 132
truth and, 142–143
utility of, 170n8
continuity, of life, 2–3
Conway, Daniel W., 162n3,
164n19–65n19, 178n3–79n3
correct sense perception, and truth,
123–25
correctness, 201n11
corruption, of great moments of culture,
58
counterbecomings, 3
"Counterfeit Money" (Derrida), 187n46
counterhistory, 94–99
countermemory, 103
courage, 74
creation, 25
See also becoming
creation narratives, 19
creativity, 153–54
criminals, 35
critical history, 96, 98–99
critical thinking (freedom of thought), 134
cruelty, 16, 34, 37
See also violence
cultivation, 12–13
culture, 10–29
aim of, 11, 13, 55
animality, relationship to, 1–2, 52, 155,
193n18
biocentric approach to, 1–2
civilization
antagonism of, 10–17, 18–19,
35–36, 48, 154
countermemory on, 12
dependence on, 18–19, 60

distinction from, 4, 10–11
priority over, 60
completeness, as locus for, 53
decline of, 60
differing approaches to, 2
Dionysian versus Socratic, 129–30
economy of, 5–6
education under, 58
forgetfulness of, 167n39
freedom of, 59–60
greatness of, 102
Greek, 16–17, 19, 87, 102, 128
higher culture, 52, 58–60
highpoints of, alternation with
civilization, 11–12
historical, origins of, 197n55
importance of, 37
intellect under, 148
liberating task of, 24
luxury cultivation of, 58–59
memory of, 23–28
modern, problem of, 102
nature, relationship to, 24
nature of
as cultivation, 12–13
as Dionysian, 14–15
as distinguishing feature of humans, 1
as freedom from slavery, 51
incompleteness of, 54
as life supportive, 4, 160n18
as memory of the animal, 26–27
as otherness, exposure to, 162n2
as return to nature, 18
politics of, 48–49, 154
promise of, 36–39
public space of, 58–59
reading and, 106
rule of, 59, 149
scientific (Socratic), 99, 129–30
singularity, privileging of, 55
slavery, response to, 49
subversions of, 28–29
understanding of, 197n60–98n60
See also animality; civilization; genius of
culture; higher culture; memory
culture (Fr.), 161n2
cycle of life, 156

Darwin, Charles, 166n26
the dead, life of, 44
death, 46, 90, 193n24–194n24
debt. *See* slavery
decadence, response to, 198n63
deception, 211n57
degeneration, 211n61
Deleuze, Gilles, 176n44
democracy, 175n40, 181n21–82n21
democratic movements, 57
Derrida, Jacques
  on Christian forgiveness, 63–64
  on "Counterfeit Money," 187n46
  on distributive justice, 75
  on forgiveness, 71, 72–73, 184n13,
    186n39
  on gift-giving, 80, 84, 184n6
  on giving, 187n47–88n47, 188n48
  on hospitality, 162n2
  mentioned, 62
  on Nietzsche's self-identities, 107
  on responsibility, 45
  on the signature, 176n45–77n45
  on truth, 207n36
Dialect of Enlightenment (Adorno and
  Horkheimer), 206n35–7n35
dialectic of enlightenment, 172n17
the Dionysian, open question of, 110
Dionysian laughter, 105
Dionysian pessimism, 163n9
Dionysus, 14–15
dissimulations, 124, 131–34, 148–49
  See also illusions
distance, gift-giving virtue and, 80–85
distributive justice, 75
domestic animals, 23
domination and exploitation
  conscience in contrast to, 38
  culture's role against, 11, 60
  democratic movements as, 57
  discourses of, 19
  higher culture's incompatibility with, 6
  memory of the will as, 31, 32
  political life and, 5, 48, 49
  promise of the sovereign individual and,
    31, 37–38
  taming and breeding, 12–13, 34,
    164n19–65n19

Dostoevsky, Fyodor, 170n11
dreams and dreaming, 4, 25–26, 116, 119,
  167n33–34
  See also illusions
drives
  drive for truth, 138–40, 143
  primordial, 116
duels, 104

Ecce Homo (Nietzsche), 106–9, 196n54,
  198n68–99n68, 199n71
Eckhart von Hochheim (Meister Eckhart),
  91
economy, 5–6, 49, 54–57
  of goodness, 180n14
  of life, 49, 54–57, 180n13
education, 58, 101
enemies, 190n63
enlightenment, 172n17, 197n57
enslavement. *See* slavery
equalities, 31, 42–43, 135
Esposito, Roberto, 150
ethics of conviction, 171n11
Europe, democratization of, 57
events, gifts and, 84
evil, 28, 67
evolution, 14, 166n26
  See also becoming
exceptional human beings. *See* great
  human beings; overhumans
exploitation. *See* domination and
  exploitation
eyes, pictorial thinking and, 116

faith, 174n29
falsity
  of judgments, 136
  of sensation, Bornedal on, 202n19
fear of wild animals, 169n2
final redemption, 91
Fink, Eugene, 199n3
first metaphors, 120, 202n19
forgetfulness
  animal unhistoricity and, 114
  Apollonian versus Dionysian, 15
  of civilization, 13, 17–19
  civilization and, 10–11, 71
  control of, 99–100

of culture, 167n39
Derrida on, 71
effects of, 26
as essential, 192n13
happiness and, 90
humans' need for, 91–94
importance of, 155
as life force, 31, 92
locus of, 2
memory, relationship to, 87, 94–95
of memory of the will, 33–34
of monumental history, 97
morality and, 196n49
past, redemption of, 69
promise as, 39
under rule of culture, 12
"truth," as prerequisite for, 140–141
See also animal forgetfulness; memory
forgiving and forgiveness
Arendt on, 64
Derrida on, 71–72, 184n13
Derrida on Arendt's views on, 186n39
between friends, 72
gift-giving and, 6, 62, 188n48
political friendship and, 71–75
promise versus, 70
punishment and, 64
silence and, 72–73
See also Christian forgiveness; friendship;
giving
Foucault, Michel
aesthetics of existence, 213n14
biopolitics of, 152–56
on counterhistory, 194n31
on dreams, 167n33
on human beings, origins of, 109
on totalitarian ideologies, 156
fragmentation, 52, 107
Franco-German War, 144
freedom
of animals and of the spirit, 12
of culture, 59–60
free societies, 51
free will, 66–67
as freedom from need, 179n7
memory of the will and, 36
nature of, 41–42, 178n49
as responsibility, 5, 40–41
responsibility and, 177n47

of thought (critical thinking), 134
true, nature of, 174n29
Freud, Sigmund, 4, 26, 166n31, 203n23
friendship
Arendt on, 73
forgiving and, 72
love for one's neighbor, comparison
with, 81
nature of, 82–83
political friendship, 6, 71–75, 82
silence and, 72–73
solitude and, 189n51
source of, 62
See also forgiving and forgiveness; giving
future
anticipated future, 43
becoming overhuman and, 23
future life, 119
higher aristocracy of, 48, 56–57
human life as prefiguring, 161n26
past future, 176n44
present, relationship to, 43–46

The Gay Science (Nietzsche)
analysis in, relationship to analysis in
"On Truth and Lies in an Extra-
Moral Sense," 141
analysis of consciousness in, 141–42
on animality as source of nobility,
193n23
on consciousness, 132
on dreaming, 166n31
on equality and preservation of life,
209n48
on pure and honest drive for truth, 146
on virtues, conscious versus
unconscious, 210n53
Gedächtnis des Willens. See memory of the
will
genius, 173n26, 182n27–83n27
Genius (Roman mythology), 27
genius of culture, 15–16, 27–28, 41, 55,
194n24
genocide, 156
Gerhardt, Volker, 182n27
German nationalism, 150
gift-giving
Derrida on, 71, 187n47–88n47
events and, 84

giving alms, comparison with, 83–84
logic of, 187n47
nature of, 81, 183n4, 184n6
thankfulness in, 188n48
gift-giving virtue, 74–85
    as all-inclusive love, 77
    as animal forgetfulness, 80
    distance and, 80–85
    forgetfulness and, 80, 155
    Gooding-Williams on, 188n49
    human animality and, 74
    justice as, 74
    nature of, 62
    nonprofitability of, 76–77
    other-directedness and, 77–80
    as overflowing of the self, 78
    overview of, 6, 61–62
    political nature of, 61–62
    as power, 83
    recognition of, 84
    as relationship between self and other,
        80
    singularity and, 75–77
giving, 72, 78, 84, 85
    See also forgiving and forgiveness;
        friendship; gift-giving
God, 67
going under, 46, 77, 84
gold, metaphor of, 74, 80, 174n33
Gooding-Williams, Robert, 187n41,
        188n49, 188n50–89n50
goodness, 34, 67, 180n14
gratefulness, 188n48, 189n57
the great Hazar, 84, 85
great human beings, 34–35, 53, 173n23
    See also overhumans
great politics, 114, 150, 179n3, 211n60,
        213n10
greater health, 150–51
greatness, 104, 163n13–64n13
Greeks
    city-states, 175n39
    culture of, 16–17, 19, 87, 102, 128
    knowledge, use of, 102
    polis, 173n25, 179n5
    political friendship of, 62
    superficial profundity of, 207n36
    unknowability of, 110
guilt, 66

happiness, 89, 90
Hatab, Lawrence, 175n36, 181n21–82n21
haunting, of history, 99–100, 108
Hegel, George Wilhelm Friedrich, 73
Heidegger, Martin, 199n2, 201n11
herd animals, 32, 34
herd morality, 175n42
heroes, 40, 82, 97, 193n24–94n24
    See also great human beings; overhumans
hierarchy, 22–23
higher aristocracy of the future, 48, 56–57
higher culture, 52, 58–60
higher education, 58
historians, 100–101, 103, 104, 108
historical culture, 197n55
historical education, 101
historical sciences, 87–88
historicism, modern, 101
historicity, 86–87, 90–91, 114
historiography, 7–8, 87, 99–10
history
    animals' unhistoricity, 114
    antiquarian history, 96–98, 169n6
    counterhistory, 94–99
    critical history, 96, 98–99
    as fiction, 195n47–96n47
    forms of, 96, 195n37
    haunting of, 99–100, 108
    as life, 96
    measurement of strength and, 197n59
    monumental history, 96–97,
        195nn39–40
    necessity of, 101
    as pure science, 101
    reintroduction of Greek culture into,
        102
    the suprahistorical versus, 92
    the unhistorical, 92–93, 102, 192n16
    See also the past
Hobbes, Thomas, 30
"Homer's Contest" ("Homer on
    Competition," Nietzsche), 19,
    193n18
honest and pure drive for truth, 126, 129,
    145
honesty (Redlichkeit), 113–14

"The Honey Sacrifice" (*Thus Spake Zarathustra*, Nietzsche), 79
horizons, 55
Horkheimer, Max, 172n17
hospitality, 13, 162n2
Human, All Too Human (Nietzsche), 109
humanity, 16, 102
  See also the animal
humans (human beings, human animals)
  activities of, 180n15–81n15
  animal beginnings of, 4
  animal forgetfulness and, 88–89, 91
  animal life forces, antagonism with,
    10–11
  animality of
    biopolitics and, 152–56
    civilization as force against, 11–12, 18
    cultural refinement and, 15
    culture versus civilization on, 12
    Nietzsche on, 14
    promise of the sovereign individual
      and, 31
    return of, 29
    See also the animal; animality; animals
  animals, encounters with, 89–90
  as becoming, 7, 23
  becoming, animality and, 92
  becoming overhuman of, 47
  breeding and taming of, 139–40
  comforting truths, preference for, 145
  communication as basis for
    consciousness of, 141–42
  conceptual thinking of, 116
  consciousness of, 208nn41–42
  culture as distinguishing feature of, 1
  development of, principal feature of, 5,
    30–31
  Dionysian versus Socratic culture of,
    129–30
  as dissimulators, 133
  distinctions from other animals, 24
  forgetfulness, need for, 91–94
  fragility of, 6
  fragmented nature of, 52–53, 180n10
  highest purpose of, 93
  historicity of, 114
  inhumans versus, 16
  intellectual capacity of, 131–32

lack of existence of, 24
as machines, 56
mass political ideologies and, 56
mechanization of, 56, 57
narratives of creation of, 19
noble, 76
perception by, 125
posthumous, 43–44
promises, ability to make, 36
self-understanding of, 14–15
truth, need for, 210n51
types of, 34–35, 50, 53
Umgekehrten (opposite human beings),
  28–29
uniqueness of, 132–33
violence of, 37
See also animals; overhumans; sovereign
  individuals

Ibanez-Noé, Javier A., 204n25, 205n31,
  206n33
identity, 31, 35, 107–8
illusions, 24, 25, 127–28, 129
  See also dissimulations; dreams and
    dreaming; intuited metaphors
illusory consciousness, 209n42
illusory dissimulation (*Verstellung*), 124,
  130, 133
image, 206n35–7n35
imaginary thinking, 211n57
immortality of movement, 106
incompleteness, 53, 54
  See also slavery
individuals. *See* humans; singularity;
  sovereign individuals
inequality of nature, 55
inner beast, 169n2
inner world, 205n32–6n32
innocence of becoming, 66–67
innocence of life, 13
inorganic world, 159nn13–14
instincts, 22–23, 168n44
institutions, 31, 41, 42, 68
intellect
  dissimulations of, 131–34
  free, responsibility of, 149–50
  freedom of, 147–49
  nature of, 99, 131–32, 208n40

quality of, 170n8
in service of life, 130
interpretation, 106
intuited metaphors (*Anschauungsmetapher*)
as basis for critique of metaphysics, 112
concepts, contrast with, 117–18, 137
importance to philosophy, 128
intuition, pictures, and dreams, 116,
119
mentioned, 8
nature of, analogy with Bornedal on
sensation, 202n19
singular truths and, 115–19
singularity of, 116–17, 118
as term, translation of, 200n6
truthfulness of, 202n19
invention, philosophy as, 127
"it was." *See* the past

Jesus, 64, 65
judging others, 64–65
judgments, 136
jumps, image of, 103
justice, 61–62, 65, 74, 81

Kant, Immanuel, 181n16, 185n16,
197n57, 205n29
Kaufmann, Walter, 168n1
Kierkegaard, Søren, 171n16–72n16,
173n24, 174n29
knowledge, 146
Kofman, Sarah, 24, 106, 162n2, 166n26
Kultur, 10, 161n2
See also culture

Lampter, Laurence, 187n41
language (human)
conceptual, "truth" and, 140
forgiveness and, 72–73
metaphorical nature of, 140
nature of, 118
process of, 134–35
sources of, 8–9
truth and, 115
utility of, 170n8
See also conceptual language; silence;
speech
laughter, 105

Lévi-Strauss, Claude, 191n3
liberalism, 181n18
liberation, 11, 13–14, 154, 213n15
See also freedom
life
animal life, 153, 154, 212n2, 213n15
as continuum, 2–3
cycle of, 156
as dream, 4, 25–26, 119
dreams and, 167n33
economy of, 54–57
forgetfulness's importance to, 92
future, intuited metaphors and, 119
as a gift, 76
historical nature of, 2, 3, 92
history and, 96, 99, 101
innocence of, 13
memory as threat to, 92
nature of, 175n35
philosophy, relationship with, 144
pluralization of, 3–4, 40–41
suffering as source of, 91
truth, relationship to, 207n38–8n38
untruth as condition of, 136
as will to power, 158n5
See also culture
the light, as essential, 192n13
lived truth, 146
logic, 29
Loraux, Nicole, 173n25
loss, 56
love, 77–78, 81, 190n60
Luther, Martin, 193n20
lying, 139
See also dissimulations

Machiavelli, Niccolo, 170n11, 171n12,
196n50
macro-politics, 178n3–79n3
Manu, 165n19
Marathon Messenger, myth of, 44, 46
Mason, André, 46
mass political ideologies, 56, 57
Mauss, Marcel, 184n6
me-ontology, 111
Meister Eckhart, 91
memory
as artistic force, 7–8, 87

artistic memory, 100
bad memory, 194n26
conscious versus unconscious, 132
control of, 99–100
countermemory, 103
of culture, 23–28
culture as, 11
forgetfulness, relationship to, 87, 94–95
for the Greeks, 102
as life force, 31
locus of, 2
necessity for, 91
process of, 134–35, 209n46
seeing and, 135
the signature, 176n45–77n45
sleep and, 167n37
source of, 191n3
as threat to life, 92
types of, 176n44
as weakness, 32
See also forgetfulness
memory of the will (Gedächtnis des Willens)
animal forgetfulness and, 36
breeding of socialized beings and, 68
civilization and, 12, 32–33, 139
forgetfulness of, 33–34
great human beings and, 35
promise of the sovereign individual and,
30, 31–32, 41
violence of making of, 33
metaphoric dissimulation, 124
metaphors
characteristics of, 8
first metaphors, 120, 202n19
of gold, 74, 80, 174n33
of Nietzsche's self-identity, 107
second metaphor, 120
See also concepts, metaphors, and
schemes; intuited metaphors; pictorial
thinking
metaphysics
ground for, 129
Kantian critique of, 123–24
laughter and, 105
metaphysical truth, 120–23
Western tradition of, Nietzsche's
conceptual break with, 4, 115
See also philosophy

micro-politics, 178n3–79n3
midges (insects), 131
the miraculous, 45, 53
modern culture, 102
modern states, 63
monumental history, 96–97, 195nn39–40
moral beings, 13
moral discipline of civilization, 50
moral perfectionism, 162n3–63n3
morality
Christian morality, 19–21, 62, 67
effects of, 163n8
as false overcoming, 19–23
forgetfulness and, 196n49
herd morality, 175n42
moral improvement, link with
civilization, 34
moral responsibility, 38
moral sensibilities, 139–40
noble morality, 68, 90
slave morality, 68, 90
of taming, versus of breeding,
164n19–65n19
movement, 77
See also going under

Nachlass (Nietzsche), 56, 132, 209n45
narrations, 29, 34
nationalism, German, 150
natural history, 29
natural sciences, 87–88
nature
Ansell-Pearson on, 166n26
becoming overhuman and, 24
civilization, use of, 55
culture, relationship to, 24
economy of, 54–55
human life, use of, 3
as inaccessible and indefinable, 123
inequality of, 55
interpretation of, 106
return to, culture as, 18
See also animality
necessity, 51
need, 58, 179n7
negative biopolitics, 154
Nietzsche, Friedrich
biopolitics and, 152–56

Christianity, basis of rejection of, 61
culture and civilization,
    misrepresentation of views on, 10
Darwin, differences from, 166n26
Freud, similarities to, 4
metaphysics, overcoming of,
    210n56–11n56
multiple identities of, 104–5, 107
own past, rewriting of, 8
perfectionist interpretation of, 162n3
pessimism of, 14
philosophical style of, 110
philosophy of (*See* animality; animals;
    civilization; culture; forgetfulness;
    humans; life; memory; spirit; truth)
philosophy of culture, differing
    approaches to, 2
as political thinker, 5
self-identification, 106–7
slavery, use of term, 49
views on dreams, Shapiro's analysis of,
    167n34
Western tradition of metaphysics,
    conceptual break from, 4, 115
writings, new prefaces for, 102–10, 144,
    210n56
See also titles of individual writings
Nietzsche et la scène philosophique
    (Kofman), 24
nobility, 193n23
noble morality, 68, 90
Norris, Margot, 1–2, 160n18,
    198n68–99n68, 199n71
now (present time), 43–46, 90, 114

On the Genealogy of Morals (Nietzsche)
    analysis in, relationship to analysis in
        "On Truth and Lies in an Extra-
        Moral Sense," 139
    on animals able to make promises, 36
    on antagonism of memory and
        forgetfulness, 31–32
    on consciousness, 208n41
    on humans, taming and breeding of,
        139
    on memory, 32
    on socialized beings, breeding of, 68
"On Truth and Lies in an Extra-Moral
    Sense" (Nietzsche)

on abstract thinking, 136
analysis in, relationship to analysis in
    The Gay Science, 141
analysis in, relationship to analysis in *On
    the Genealogy of Morals*, 139
Clark on, 203n25
on consciousness, 208n42–9n42
content of, 129
on forgetfulness, 99
On the Genealogy of Morals, relationship
    to, 139
on the intellect, 131, 132, 147, 149
on intuited metaphors and pictorial
    thinking, 115–16
on investigation of intellect, 130–31
mentioned, 8
on metaphysical truth, critique of,
    123–24
reception of, 112
Schrift's defense of originality of, 200n8
on truth, 99
on "truth," 138, 139, 146
"On the Use and Disadvantage of History
    for Life" (Nietzsche)
    on animals, 7, 26, 88, 114–16
    artistic versus scientific in, 99
    commentary on animality and animal
        forgetfulness in, 86–87
    on forgetfulness and memory, 91
    on horizons, 55
    as response to Kant, 197n57
opposite human beings (*Umgekehrten*),
    28–29
optimism, 163n9
order, hierarchy versus, 22–23
organic life, 3, 159nn13–14, 209n45
origins. *See* beginnings
the other
    animal forgetfulness and relationship
        with, 62
    freedom and, 41
    friendship and, 82
    gift-giving virtue and, 77–81
    nature of relationship with, 186n30
    pluralization of life and, 41
    under the rule of culture, 149
    Sartre's versus Nietzsche's conception of,
        177n47

self, asymmetrical relationship with, 61–62
See also the animal
over- (as prefix), 21
over-animals, 21–23
overcoming (completion), 21, 45, 147
See also self-overcoming
overhumans
  aggression in, 165n23
  becoming, 4–5, 7, 54
  as becoming, 23
  conscious breeding of, 182n25
  description of, 24
  forces competing within, 22–23
  genius of culture, affinity with, 15–16
  Norris on, 160n21
  over-animal, distinction from, 21–23
  promise of, 30
  as response to mechanization of humans, 56
  Zarathustra's adoption of idea of, 166n28
  See also great human beings
ownership, 81

pain, 206n34
parting (of individuals), 190n61
passions, animal, 23
the past
  antiquarian history and, 96, 98
  Arendt on, 70
  artistic historians and, 100–101
  counterhistorical view of, 95–96
  critical history and, 96, 98–99
  forgetfulness and, 69–70, 94–95
  Greek's use of, 102
  knowledge of, 194n30
  meaning of, 69–70
  monumental history and, 96, 97
  present, influence on, 90
  reconstruction of, 108
  redemption of, 192n11
  understanding of, 196n51
  See also history
past future, 176n44
pastoral politics, 213n10
perceptions, 123–25, 203n25–4n25
perfection, 162n3

perspectives, horizontal versus vertical, 21–22
perspectivism, 205n32–6n32
pessimism, 14, 163n9
philia politiké (political friendship), 71–75, 82
philosophers
  of the future, 123, 127
  hatred of, 144–45
  life of, 143–51
  as physicians, 150–51
  pictorial thinking by, 126–27
  pure and honest drive to truth and, 144
  truth as a woman and, 207n36
  on validity of truth over "truth," 147
philosophy
  goals of, 110, 151
  life, relationship with, 144
  metaphysical truth versus singular truth, 151
  nature of, 126, 127–28
  philosophical intuition, 126
  (*See also* intuited metaphors)
  philosophical life, truth and, 143–51
  under scientific culture, 128
  self-overcoming of, 112–13
  tragic philosophy, 128–29
  truth in, 123
  See also metaphysics
Philosophy in the Tragic Age of the Greeks (Nietzsche), 89, 126
physicians, 83, 151
pictorial thinking (*Bilderdenken*), 112, 116–20, 125–27
  of animals, 8
  See also abstract thinking
plastic power, 197n58
Plato, 150
plurality
  animality and, 156
  of life, 3–4, 40–41
  of the other, 41
  of the self, 41
  of singular truths, 117
politics, 30–47
  agonistic politics of responsibility, 41–43
  animality and political life, 5

of civilization, versus politics of culture, 48–49
culture, false identification with, 48
of domination and exploitation, 48
freedom from, 173n26
great politics, 114, 150, 179n3, 211n60, 213n10
hypocrisy of, 33
Nietzsche's perspective on, 30
perspectives for studying, 30
political friendship, 6, 71–75, 82
political ideologies, 42, 56, 57
political institutions, 31, 41, 42
political power, 33, 37, 140, 170n10
political rule, 140
positive biopolitics, 9
promise of the sovereign individual against the power of, 40
See also promise
the posthumous, 43–46
power
forgiveness as, 63
gift-giving virtue as, 83
political, 33, 37
of the sovereign individual, 40
of the tragic hero, 40
will to accumulate, 51
prefaces, new, to Nietzsche's works, 102–10
of "An Attempt at Self-Criticism," 102–5, 108–10
of *Ecce Homo*, 106–9
function of, 104
life-philosophy link and, 144
multiple meanings and, 109–10
nature of, 103
purpose of, 110
present (now), 43–46, 90, 114
priests, 21, 170n11, 171n14, 211n61
primordial drives, 116
Prince (Machiavellian), 170n11
progress, 180n12
promise, 30–47
of civilization, 31–36
of culture, 36–39
forgiveness versus, 70
of freedom, posthumous nature of, 43–46

freedom as responsibility, 41–43
Greek polis and, 173n25
locus of, 2
nature of, 38–39
overview of, 30–31
of sovereign individuals, 31–32, 39–41
types of, 39
public space of culture, 58–59
punishment, 64, 65
pure and honest drive to truth
emergence of, 146
intuited metaphors and philosophy as, 112
and metaphysical truth, denial of, 121–22
origins of, 143
philosophers as representative of, 144
philosophy and illusions and, 127
social and political significance of, 134
society and, 145–46
as tragic pursuit, 128
as weakest form of knowledge, 146

racism, 155
rational thought. *See* abstract thinking
reading, 104–6
reality, 127–28
rebeginnings, 69, 96
rechtschaffendes Gastgeschenk (righteous guest gift), 74
redemption, 91, 192n11
Redlichkeit (honesty), 113–14
regulating and imperative (linguistic) laws, 138
See also abstract world of regulating and imperative (linguistic) laws
remembering. *See* forgetfulness; memory
republics, Machiavelli on, 171n12
resentment, 171n16–72n16
resistance, freedom and, 42
responsibility, 38, 40–46, 192n12
Sartre's versus Nietzsche's conception of, 177n47
Sartre's view on, 44–45
return to nature, 18
revenge, 62, 65, 68–70, 189n57
risk-taking, 46
Romans, 16–17, 171n12

Rorty, Richard, 132, 204n25, 206n32
rule, 176n43
rule of higher culture, 58–60
ruminants, 192n17–93n17

saint (in *Zarathustra*), 77–78
sameness, 203n21
Sartre, Jean-Paul, 43–46, 177n47–78n47
schemes. *See* concepts, metaphors, and
    schemes
scholars, nature of, 98, 196n52, 197n57
"Schopenhauer as Educator" (Nietzsche),
    52, 54, 144–45, 197n57
Schrift, Alan D., 173n28–74n28, 178n53,
    183n4, 200n8
science
    function of, 122
    historical sciences, 87–88
    nature of, 87–88, 196n48
    problem of, 196n54
    scientific (Socratic) culture, 99, 129–30
    scientific historians, 100–101
    scientific knowledge, 121, 122
    scientists, 98, 126–27
second metaphor, 120
second natures, 99
seeing, memory and, 135
seeing as equal (*Gleichsehen*) and taking as
    equal (*Gleichnehmen*), 135–36,
    209n48
self, 41, 61–62, 77–80, 107–8, 110
self-determination, 168n44
self-healing physicians, 83
self-overcoming
    animal forgetfulness and, 37
    conscience and, 38
    friendship and, 83
    of philosophers, 107
    possibility of infinite numbers of, 23
    as promise of the overhuman, 30
    writing as, 189n58
    See also overhumans
self-preservation, 51, 52, 60
self-responsibility, 37, 42, 49
self-sacrifice, 79
self-sufficiency, 78
selfishness, 80
selflessness, 79–80

sensation, 202n19
sense perception, correct, 123–25,
    202n19, 206n33
Shapiro, Gary, 167n34, 183n4, 187n41
Siemens, Herman W., 182n27
sign, image, separation from,
    206n35–7n35
the signature, 176n45–77n45
silence, 72, 73, 114–15
similarity, sameness versus, 203n21
singularity
    civilization and socialization and, 135
    cultivation of, as redemption of nature,
        54–55
    gift-giving virtue and, 75–77
    of intuited metaphors, 116–17, 118
    intuitive philosophers and, 126–27
    silence and, 118
    singular individuals, 31, 35, 58–59,
        134, 155–56
    (*See also* sovereign individuals)
    singular (lived) truth, 112, 117, 145–47
    of translations in intuited metaphors,
        125
slavery, 50–54
    democratic movements and, 57
    economy of civilization and, 49
    in Greek culture, 179n5
    life in society as, 50–51
    nature of, 179n8
    new type of, 50
    Nietzsche's uses of term, 49
    slave morality, 68, 90
sleep, 167n37
small men of virtue, 83
sociability, 62, 68
social contracts, 33
socialists, 51
socialization, 135
society
    dissimulation as preserver of, 134
    emergence of consciousness with, 141
    free societies, 51
    incompleteness as goal of, 53
    life in, as slavery, 49
    nature of, 33–34
    pure and honest drive to truth and,
        145–46

requirements for life in, 139
See also civilization; states
Socrates, 128, 150
solitude, 189n51
sounds, imitation of pictures by, 120, 125
sovereign individuals, 5, 37, 38, 39–41
See also singular individuals *under* singularity
sovereignty, 38, 39, 40
species life, animal life versus, 153
speech, 72–73, 203n24
See also language (human)
spirals, 198n63
spirit, 2
squandering, 79–80
stability, 94
states, 33, 63, 171n12, 171n14, 175n40
See also society
Stendhal (Henri-Marie Beyle), 104
Stiegler, Barbara, 158n5, 159n11
strength, 197n59
Strong, Tracy, 201n10, 205n32–6n32
struggle, 22, 42
struggle for existence. *See* self-preservation
stupidity, 55, 164n18, 181n16
subversions, 28–29, 168n43
suffering, 68–69, 89–91
the suprahistorical, 92

taking as equal. *See* seeing as equal
taming and breeding, 12–13, 34, 164n19–65n19
Taylor, Quentin P., 162n2, 163n13–64n13
temporality. *See* anticipated future; future; time
thankfulness, 188n48
thing in-itself, 120, 124, 203n25–4n25
See also truth
thinking
abstract thinking, 126, 134–38, 209n49–10n49
conceptual versus pictorial, 116–19, 125, 126–27
critical thinking, 134
imaginary, 211n57
See also pictorial thinking
Thus Spoke Zarathustra (Nietzsche)

the animal in the human, example of, 15
on animals, 90
on chance encounter with animality, 84
on forgetfulness and revenge, 69
on friendship, 81
on gift-giving, 61, 74, 77–80
gold as metaphor in, 74
on inspiring others, 83
time, 43, 46, 91, 94
See also future; past; present
totalitarianism, 156
tragedy, 104–5, 128–29
tragic (Dionysian) culture, 129–30
tragic heroes, 40, 155
tragic philosophy, 128–29
transcendent perspectivism, 206n32
tricks, humans' love of, 211n57
truth, 111–51
abstract thought and, 135–38, 209n49–10n49
biopolitical treatment of, 113–14, 150–51
comforting, humans' preference for, 145
conceptual language and, 134–37
consciousness and, 142–43
correct sense perception and, 123–25
as correctness, Heidegger on, 201n11
creation of, 194n25
Heidegger on Nietzsche's views of, 199n2
humans' need for, 210n51
and intellect, dissimulations of, 131–34
intuited metaphors and singular truths, 115–19
life, relationship to, 207n38–8n38
life-preserving nature of, 136
lived truth, 146
as metaphor, 8, 122
metaphysical, 120–23, 151, 203n25–4n25
nature of, 99
perception of Nietzsche's views on, 111
philosophical intuition and, 125–28
philosophical life and, 143–51
practical versus theoretical treatments of, 113
pure and honest drive to, 112, 121–22
as seduction, 24

as set of regulating and imperative (linguistic) laws, 138
silent animal truth, 114–15
singular (lived) truth, 145–47
tragic philosophy and, 128–29
"truth," comparison with, 138
truthful representation (*Vorstellung*), 124, 130
truthfulness (*Wahrhaftigkeit*), 113–14, 202n19, 210n56
Western metaphysical tradition of, 115
as will to power, 204n27–5n27
as a woman, 207n36
"truth" (sociopolitical treatment of institutionalized "truth"), 138–43, 145
Twilight of the Idols (Nietzsche), 21, 209n44

Umgekehrten (opposite human beings), 28–29
unconscious virtues, 210n53
unconsciousness, 132
the unhistorical, 92–93, 102, 192n16
unhistoricity of animals, 114
untimeliness, 46, 95
Untimely Meditations (*Untimely Considerations,* Nietzsche), 24
untruth, 136
Urgrund (world as chaos), 202n19, 205n31
utilitarianism, 61

value, 76
veritas aeterna (absolute truth). *See* truth
Verstellung (illusory dissimulation), 124, 130, 132–33
vigor of animals, 148
violence, 21, 33, 37, 170n11–71n11
   See also cruelty
virtù, 196n50
virtue (the virtuous), 75, 77, 83, 84, 210n53
   See also gift-giving virtue
voice. *See* language; silence; speech
Vorstellung (truthful representation), 124, 130

Wagner, Richard, 145
Wahrhaftigkeit (truthfulness), 113–14, 202n19, 210n56
waking life, 25–26
war, 144
Weber, Max, 170n11–71n11
Western metaphysics, Nietzsche's conceptual break from, 4, 115
Western philosophy, 209n44
What is Enlightenment? (Kant), 181n16, 197n57
"what there is," 111
whole organic world, 25
wholeness, 67
will
   free will, 66–67
   will to power, 2, 204n27–205n27
   will to truth, 113–14
   See also memory of the will
wisdom, 126
woman, truth as, 207n36
worlds. *See* abstract world of regulating and imperative (linguistic) laws; whole organic world
Wotling, Patrick, 161n2
writers, 44–46
writing, 44, 189n58
writings, 103
   Nietzsche's (*See individual titles*)

Zarathustra (fictional character)
   descent of, 188n50–89n50
   disciples of, 83
   distance and, 82
   on forgetfulness, 80
   on gift-giving, recognition of, 84
   gift-giving of, 74
   on gift-giving virtue, 79
   on giving, 84–85
   on the great *Hazar,* 85
   on love, 77–78
   overhuman, adoption of idea of, 166n28
   on sacrifice, 79
   on self-sufficiency, 78
   on the sun, 77
Zivilization, 161n2
   See also civilization
Zweig, Stefan, 177n47–78n47

Perspectives in Continental Philosophy Series
John D. Caputo, series editor

John D. Caputo, ed., *Deconstruction in a Nutshell: A Conversation with Jacques Derrida.*

Michael Strawser, *Both/And: Reading Kierkegaard—From Irony to Edification.*

Michael D. Barber, *Ethical Hermeneutics: Rationality in Enrique Dussel's Philosophy of Liberation.*

James H. Olthuis, ed., *Knowing Other-wise: Philosophy at the Threshold of Spirituality.*

James Swindal, *Reflection Revisited: Jürgen Habermas's Discursive Theory of Truth.*

Richard Kearney, *Poetics of Imagining: Modern and Postmodern.* Second edition.

Thomas W. Busch, *Circulating Being: From Embodiment to Incorporation—Essays on Late Existentialism.*

Edith Wyschogrod, *Emmanuel Levinas: The Problem of Ethical Metaphysics.* Second edition.

Francis J. Ambrosio, ed., *The Question of Christian Philosophy Today.*

Jeffrey Bloechl, ed., *The Face of the Other and the Trace of God: Essays on the Philosophy of Emmanuel Levinas.*

Ilse N. Bulhof and Laurens ten Kate, eds., *Flight of the Gods: Philosophical Perspectives on Negative Theology.*

Trish Glazebrook, *Heidegger's Philosophy of Science.*

Kevin Hart, *The Trespass of the Sign: Deconstruction, Theology, and Philosophy.*

Mark C. Taylor, *Journeys to Selfhood: Hegel and Kierkegaard.* Second edition.

Dominique Janicaud, Jean-François Courtine, Jean-Louis Chrétien, Michel Henry, Jean-Luc Marion, and Paul Ricœur, *Phenomenology and the "Theological Turn": The French Debate.*

Karl Jaspers, *The Question of German Guilt.* Introduction by Joseph W. Koterski, S.J.

Jean-Luc Marion, *The Idol and Distance: Five Studies.* Translated with an introduction by Thomas A. Carlson.

Jeffrey Dudiak, *The Intrigue of Ethics: A Reading of the Idea of Discourse in the Thought of Emmanuel Levinas.*

Robyn Horner, *Rethinking God as Gift: Marion, Derrida, and the Limits of Phenomenology.*

Mark Dooley, *The Politics of Exodus: Søren Keirkegaard's Ethics of Responsibility.*

Merold Westphal, *Overcoming Onto-Theology: Toward a Postmodern Christian Faith.*

Edith Wyschogrod, Jean-Joseph Goux and Eric Boynton, eds., *The Enigma of Gift and Sacrifice.*

Stanislas Breton, *The Word and the Cross.* Translated with an introduction by Jacquelyn Porter.

Jean-Luc Marion, *Prolegomena to Charity.* Translated by Stephen E. Lewis.

Peter H. Spader, *Scheler's Ethical Personalism: Its Logic, Development, and Promise.*

Jean-Louis Chrétien, *The Unforgettable and the Unhoped For.* Translated by Jeffrey Bloechl.

Don Cupitt, *Is Nothing Sacred? The Non-Realist Philosophy of Religion: Selected Essays.*

Jean-Luc Marion, *In Excess: Studies of Saturated Phenomena.* Translated by Robyn Horner and Vincent Berraud.

Phillip Goodchild, *Rethinking Philosophy of Religion: Approaches from Continental Philosophy.*

William J. Richardson, S.J., *Heidegger: Through Phenomenology to Thought.*

Jeffrey Andrew Barash, *Martin Heidegger and the Problem of Historical Meaning.*

Jean-Louis Chrétien, *Hand to Hand: Listening to the Work of Art.* Translated by Stephen E. Lewis.

Jean-Louis Chrétien, *The Call and the Response.* Translated with an introduction by Anne Davenport.

D. C. Schindler, *Han Urs von Balthasar and the Dramatic Structure of Truth: A Philosophical Investigation.*

Julian Wolfreys, ed., *Thinking Difference: Critics in Conversation.*

Allen Scult, *Being Jewish/Reading Heidegger: An Ontological Encounter.*

Richard Kearney, *Debates in Continental Philosophy: Conversations with Contemporary Thinkers.*

Jennifer Anna Gosetti-Ferencei, *Heidegger, Hölderlin, and the Subject of Poetic Language: Towards a New Poetics of Dasein.*

Jolita Pons, *Stealing a Gift: Kirkegaard's Pseudonyms and the Bible.*

Jean-Yves Lacoste, *Experience and the Absolute: Disputed Questions on the Humanity of Man.* Translated by Mark Raftery-Skehan.

Charles P. Bigger, *Between Chora and the Good: Metaphor's Metaphysical Neighborhood.*

Dominique Janicaud, *Phenomenology "Wide Open": After the French Debate.* Translated by Charles N. Cabral.

Ian Leask and Eoin Cassidy, eds., *Givenness and God: Questions of Jean-Luc Marion.*

Jacques Derrida, *Sovereignties in Question: The Poetics of Paul Celan.* Edited by Thomas Dutoit and Outi Pasanen.

William Desmond, *Is There a Sabbath for Thought? Between Religion and Philosophy.*

Bruce Ellis Benson and Norman Wirzba, eds. *The Phenomoenology of Prayer.*

S. Clark Buckner and Matthew Statler, eds. *Styles of Piety: Practicing Philosophy after the Death of God.*

Kevin Hart and Barbara Wall, eds. *The Experience of God: A Postmodern Response.*

John Panteleimon Manoussakis, *After God: Richard Kearney and the Religious Turn in Continental Philosophy.*

John Martis, *Philippe Lacoue-Labarthe: Representation and the Loss of the Subject.*

Jean-Luc Nancy, *The Ground of the Image.*

Edith Wyschogrod, *Crossover Queries: Dwelling with Negatives, Embodying Philosophy's Others.*

Gerald Bruns, *On the Anarchy of Poetry and Philosophy: A Guide for the Unruly.*

Brian Treanor, *Aspects of Alterity: Levinas, Marcel, and the Contemporary Debate.*

Simon Morgan Wortham, *Counter-Institutions: Jacques Derrida and the Question of the University.*

Leonard Lawlor, *The Implications of Immanence: Toward a New Concept of Life.*

Clayton Crockett, *Interstices of the Sublime: Theology and Psychoanalytic Theory.*

Bettina Bergo, Joseph Cohen, and Raphael Zagury-Orly, eds., *Judeities: Questions for Jacques Derrida.* Translated by Bettina Bergo, and Michael B. Smith.

Jean-Luc Marion, *On the Ego and on God: Further Cartesian Questions.* Translated by Christina M. Gschwandtner.

Jean-Luc Nancy, *Philosophical Chronicles.* Translated by Franson Manjali.

Jean-Luc Nancy, *Dis-Enclosure: The Deconstruction of Christianity.* Translated by Bettina Bergo, Gabriel Malenfant, and Michael B. Smith.

Andrea Hurst, *Derrida Vis-à-vis Lacan: Interweaving Deconstruction and Psychoanalysis.*

Jean-Luc Nancy, *Noli me tangere: On the Raising of the Body.* Translated by Sarah Clift, Pascale-Anne Brault, and Michael Naas.

Jacques Derrida, *The Animal That Therefore I Am.* Edited by Marie-Louise Mallet, translated by David Wills.

Jean-Luc Marion, *The Visible and the Revealed.* Translated by Christina M. Gschwandtner and others.

Michel Henry, *Material Phenomenology.* Translated by Scott Davidson.

Jean-Luc Nancy, *Corpus.* Translated by Richard A. Rand.

Joshua Kates, *Fielding Derrida.*

Michael Naas, *Derrida From Now On.*

Shannon Sullivan and Dennis J. Schmidt, eds., *Difficulties of Ethical Life.*

Catherine Malabou, *What Should We Do with Our Brain?* translated by Sebastian Rand, Introduction by Marc Jeannerod.

Claude Romano, *Event and World.* Translated by Shane Mackinlay.